The
Salt
Solution™
COOKBOOK

MORE THAN 200 DELICIOUS MEALS
to Cut Salt, Boost Flavor, and Drop Pounds

HEATHER K. JONES, RD,
WITH THE EDITORS OF **Prevention**.

RODALE

Library of Congress Cataloging-in-Publication Data

Jones, Heather K.
    The salt solution cookbook : more than 200 delicious meals to cut salt, boost flavor, and drop pounds / Heather K. Jones with the editors of Prevention.
        p.   cm.
    Includes index.
    ISBN 978-1-60961-014-2   hardcover
    1. Salt-free diet—Recipes.   I. Title.
    RM237.8.J655   2011
    641.5'6323—dc22   2010045876

2   4   6   8   10   9   7   5   3   1   hardcover

RODALE
LIVE YOUR WHOLE LIFE™

We inspire and enable people to improve their lives and the world around them

For more of our products visit **prevention.com** or call 800-848-4735

Acknowledgments

A special thank-you to Kate Mueller, MPH, RD, for all her hard work on this book! Thank you to all of the Salt Solution chefs—David Bonom, Paul Piccuto, and Sarah Reynolds. And to everyone at Rodale including Carol Angstadt, Hope Clarke, Anne Egan, Andrea Au Levitt, Mitch Mandel, Myatt Murphy, and Marielle Messing. Thanks to all of the men and women who participated in the Salt Solution test panel, and to my agent, Janis Donnaud.

Contents

Introduction

PESTICIDES. PLASTICS. PCBs. IT seems like every time we turn on the TV these days, we hear about a scary new chemical that's poisoning our food supply. But one of the most damaging ingredients in our food supply is actually a natural flavoring humans have been eating since antiquity—salt. Having worked at the Center for Science in the Public Interest (a health advocacy group who has been ringing alarms about the amount of sodium, or salt, in our diet for decades) for 7 years, I was well aware of the health dangers of excess salt. But when *Prevention* asked me to put together the Salt Solution program, even I was astonished to learn how widespread the problem is.

You probably know that too much salt is linked to high blood pressure, which in turn can cause heart attacks, strokes, and kidney disease. But a high-sodium diet has also been linked to dementia, diabetes, metabolic syndrome, osteoporosis, and cancer.[1,2,3] As if those diseases aren't frightening enough, recent research has also shown that salt can make you pack on the pounds. Researchers call this sodium obesity, and with most Americans eating nearly double the recommended amount of salt, it's no wonder that sodium obesity has been getting more attention in recent years.

How is salt making us fat? Briefly, elevated levels of salt in the American diet come from calorie-packed, nutrient-poor, processed foods, like those found on fast food and restaurant menus, as well as packaged food in supermarkets. And when you eat a lot of salt, it increases your thirst (especially for calorie-packed sodas) and your hunger (for more of those salty, high-calorie foods), and, as I am sure you've experienced, it causes uncomfortable bloating. Overall, our high-salt diets mean we eat more calories, and this translates into higher numbers on the scale.

But don't worry—by picking up this book, you're already taking the first step to improving your health by learning how to lower your sodium intake.

Those of you who have already lost weight, lowered your blood pressure, and improved your energy using the Salt Solution know how deadly sodium can be for your health—and how easy it can be to go low-salt. *The Salt Solution Cookbook* builds on the information you learned in *The Salt Solution*, and provides more than 200 recipes to keep you on the low-sodium path. Making homemade meals is a habit that many of us have lost as our lives have become increasingly hectic, but it's one of the simplest ways to limit the salt (and salty processed foods) in your diet. When you choose the recipes and ingredients, you are controlling how much salt you consume. In fact, getting back to cooking basics is one of the best things you can do for your health *and* your waistline.

If you haven't read *The Salt Solution*, no problem—this book contains all of the background you need to understand the science behind slashing the salt. We'll teach you how to fight sodium obesity, improve health, and increase energy. First, you'll begin with the 2-Week Salt Solution Cleanse, a set menu designed to purify your system and adjust your taste buds. Then you'll move on to the 4-Week Shake the Salt Meal Plan, an eating plan that allows you to mix and match your meals. Both phases include lots of nutrient-dense fruits and veggies, whole grains, lean protein, and lots of filling fiber. The diet also features the Salt Solution Stars, powerful foods packed with potassium, magnesium, and calcium—the Miracle Minerals that counteract sodium's ill effects.[4]

The goal throughout the plan is to keep your sodium level at 1,500 milligrams per day—the amount recommended for optimum health and to reduce chronic disease risk—and the entire eating plan is designed to cater to your tastes as you can mix and match the recipes and meals.

Throughout the diet, you'll notice your taste buds reset. They'll be adapting to the lower levels of salt—the healthy levels that health experts recommend. You'll also eat fewer processed and chemically enhanced foods on this diet, which will prepare you for a lifetime of healthy habits. We tested the Salt Solution plan with amazing results—test panelists not only overcame their dangerous addiction to salt, but they also lost pounds and inches (up to 18 pounds and 11½ inches!), increased energy, and gained confidence.

Because regular exercise helps banish sodium-induced bloat, reduces stress, and combats disease, we also provide you with a walking and exercise plan to burn more calories. This exercise program isn't a must, but doing it will turn your body into a more efficient calorie- and fat-burning machine—meaning that you'll lose even more weight!

With more than 200 delicious, simple, low-salt recipes, sticking to the Salt Solution eating plan will be a snap. This isn't about deprivation—it's about eating the food you love, while slashing salt. You'll be changing the way you eat, over the course of the plan (and beyond!), to stay slim and healthy.

Let's start living the Salt Solution way!

★ **BEET GREENS** ★

Packed with potassium, magnesium, and calcium

Beyond Bloat

Sodium is essential to life. This vital mineral is needed to maintain fluid balance, control nerve impulses, and manage muscle contractions in the body. But, unfortunately, most of us are seriously overdoing it on sodium. The U.S. Dietary Guidelines recently recommended that the general population eat no more than 1,500 milligrams of sodium a day (about $2/3$ teaspoon of table salt)—especially people with high blood pressure, all African Americans, and everyone over 40. Instead, Americans on average consume 3,436 milligrams of sodium daily![1]

Most of us know that a high sodium intake raises blood pressure, but did you know overdoing it on salt could also lead to a host of other health issues, including weight gain? It's true. In fact, reducing sodium intake can help you lose weight; dodge stroke, diabetes, and heart and kidney disease; and boost bone health. Let's take a look at the salty facts.

Sodium and Weight Gain

MORE THAN TWO-THIRDS OF AMERICAN ADULTS are currently overweight or obese, and it's not just calories, fat, and carbs that are to blame—salt is also responsible for our expanding waistlines.[2] How can this calorie-free flavor booster, which we sprinkle on popcorn and shake into soup, cause us to pack on the pounds? Salt (sodium chloride) can bring about weight gain in three different ways: by increasing hunger, by increasing thirst, and by increasing bloat. The Salt Solution plan combats all three by not only lowering the amount of salt you eat, but also by including specific foods and nutrients designed to help you stay satisfied and slim down easily and quickly.

The Salt Solution Defuses Hunger

Excessive salt intake causes weight gain by increasing eating. It's a vicious cycle—salt enhances the flavor of foods and promotes overeating. And many of these high-sodium foods that you overeat are high in calories—like potato chips, salted nuts, and hot dogs.

But why do we overeat these foods? Why can't we stop at a few potato chips, and instead eat the entire bag? Some foods can actually change our brain chemistry. These foods—which scientists call highly palatable—are often high in fat, sugar, and yes, sodium. Researchers studying brain scans of people eating high-sodium foods have found that as these foods are consumed, the brain releases dopamine, the neurotransmitter associated with the brain's pleasure center. This means that these high-salt foods can become as addictive as nicotine or cocaine. So your craving for chips may not be a signal that you're hungry; it's your brain wanting to get high on dopamine. This may explain why you sometimes find that you've eaten the entire bag of potato chips without noticing it—and why you've gained weight. Blame the addictive properties of salt.

Keep in mind that while we're using "salt" and "sodium" interchangeably, there is a difference. Table salt is actually sodium chloride, a compound made from 40 percent sodium and 60 percent chloride. And salt is not the only source of sodium in our diet; you'll also find it in additives that contain sodium—such as sodium bicarbonate, sodium citrate, sodium chloride, and sodium nitrate/nitrite—and in flavor boosters such as monosodium glutamate (MSG). In fact, something doesn't need to taste salty in order to be loaded with sodium.

Also blame our hectic, fast-paced lives! Calorie-packed, nutrient-poor, processed foods (think fast foods, take-out and restaurant foods, and convenience foods in supermarkets) tend to be loaded with sodium, and as our lives have become increasingly busy, salty processed and fast foods have become staples.

Our brains may be wired to appreciate and seek out sodium from an evolutionary perspective, as well. Our ancestors ate primarily vegetarian diets that contained little salt. Therefore, the human body evolved to conserve sodium, and taste buds evolved to enjoy salty flavors. For good reason—without any salt, we'd die. But in our current sodium-rich environment, this evolutionary preference is doing us more harm than good. Studies have been conducted in isolated, indigenous populations who consume very little added salt. After being exposed to modern diets rich in sodium, researchers say these populations can become addicted to salty foods.[3]

The Salt Solution eating plan will break your salt addiction so you can enjoy real foods the way nature intended. Think juicy peaches, sweet potatoes, crusty whole grain rolls, and wild salmon instead of chips, soda, cookies, and fish sticks. The satisfying recipes you'll find in this book are bursting with flavor and are packed with fiber, so you'll never be hungry. And you'll learn how to make your healthy Salt Solution changes last—for life!

The Salt Solution Quenches Thirst

As you've no doubt noticed, when you eat salty foods, you get thirsty. And when you slake your thirst with high-calorie sodas, juices, or sugary coffee drinks (as many Americans do), you gain weight. Not to mention, caffeine acts as a diuretic, so drinks such as coffee and soda actually cause you to *lose* water by increasing your urine output, and increasing (rather than slaking) your thirst.

In the past few decades, salt intake in the United States has increased dramatically, and it continues to increase despite public health campaigns against the dangers of doing so. The average daily sodium intake for Americans over the age of 2 years was estimated at 3,436 milligrams per day in 2005–2006, which was increased from 3,329 milligrams per day just 4 or 5 years earlier.[4] Consumption of calorie-packed drinks has increased as well. Between 1965 and 2002, calories from sweetened beverages increased by 222 calories per person per day. This translates to just under a half a pound of weight gained per week—or 23 pounds of weight gained per year![5] Indeed, a close link has been found between the sales of salt and carbonated beverages in the United States.

Conversely, cutting sodium intake in half could reduce total fluid intake by about 350 milliliters per day—the equivalent of a 12-ounce, 140-calorie can of cola.[6] Making just this one simple change can help you lose more than a pound per month! Of course, you don't want to stop drinking fluids altogether. In general, you should drink 8 or 9 cups of fluids per day, and most of your fluids should come from calorie- and sodium-free water.

Bottom line: Reduce your salt intake by eating the Salt Solution way, and you'll reduce your intake of high-calorie drinks and lose weight. The fresh fruits and vegetables in the Salt Solution eating plan also add healthy fluids to your diet because they tend to be naturally high in water content (hence all the juicy goodness!), so you won't feel thirsty.

The Salt Solution Decreases Bloat

You've probably experienced the third way too much salt can cause weight gain: bloating. Too much sodium in your diet causes your body to retain water in order to dilute the amount of salt in your bloodstream. You can add up to 2 pounds of water weight just from eating too much salt! And sure, this water weight isn't "fat" caused by eating too many calories, but it can make you feel sluggish, puffy, and uncomfortable. And we know it's never fun to find that your favorite pair of jeans won't button.

Also, as we've seen, we tend to drink more sweetened beverages when we binge on salty foods. In addition to the empty calories that sugary sodas add to our waistlines, the carbonation leads to bloat, as does the caffeine in tea and coffee and the acidity in fruit juices.

The best news about bloating: By following the Salt Solution eating plan, you'll drop the water weight in no time. Not only will you be cutting out the sodium that causes bloat, but you'll be eating more foods high in potassium, a mineral known to combat the puffiness. You'll also be eating lots of hydrating fruits and veggies (water flushes out the system), getting lots of fiber (helps keep you regular), having smaller but more frequent meals, and consuming an all-around healthy diet. All of this promotes good digestion and decreases bloat. You'll immediately notice your clothes fitting differently and will likely feel more comfortable and energized.

Sodium and Health

NOT ONLY CAN TOO MUCH SALT make you fat, but a high-sodium diet can be harmful to your health. The evidence linking salt to a number of serious health issues is mounting. Cutting the sodium with the Salt Solution plan is not only good for your waistline, it's good for your health.

The Salt Solution Helps Your Heart

Sodium is linked to many conditions that affect your heart. With too much salt, your heart has to work harder and your arteries become damaged. Studies have shown a strong link between sodium and heart disease. An analysis of more than 177,000 people showed that higher salt intake was associated with a greater risk of heart disease.[7]

- **High blood pressure.** Too much salt increases your blood pressure. When you eat too much salt, your body is unable to excrete it all. The excess sodium remains in your bloodstream, and your body retains water to dilute your salty blood. This increases the total volume of your blood, which means your heart has to work harder to pump, therefore increasing your blood pressure. High blood pressure, or hypertension, increases your risk of dying of a heart attack or stroke more than any other risk factor—including smoking, high cholesterol, and obesity. Over their lifetimes, 90 percent of all American adults will develop hypertension.[8]

- **Atherosclerosis and aneurysms.** When you eat too much salt, your blood pressure increases, which damages your arteries. When artery walls are damaged, they become stiff, a process known as arteriosclerosis.[9] When fats enter your bloodstream and stick to the damaged artery cells and walls, blood flow can become blocked. This condition, called atherosclerosis, can happen in your heart, arms, legs, kidneys, and brain. An aneurysm is a bulge in the wall of an artery caused by high blood pressure, and it can also occur anywhere in your body. When aneurysms rupture, they cause massive internal bleeding, and they can be life-threatening.

- **Heart disease.** Too much salt damages your heart by increasing blood pressure, and making your heart work harder to pump blood. Like when you lift weights at the gym, the heart muscle gets bigger when it works harder. But an enlarged heart muscle is not a good thing—an enlarged heart muscle increases your risk of heart failure, heart attack, and sudden death.

DON'T PASS THE SALT

The vast majority—almost 80 percent—of the sodium we eat comes from processed food. Why exactly do food manufacturers need so much sodium? Salt not only acts as a preservative so products can stay on the shelves longer, it also helps to bind foods together, increases the speed of fermentation, and improves foods' color and texture. The best way to decrease your sodium intake? Simply replace salty processed foods with fresh foods you prepare yourself, using the delicious recipes in this book!

Increased blood pressure accounts for 49 percent of coronary heart disease.[10] By lowering your sodium intake and therefore your blood pressure, the Salt Solution plan can help prevent and combat these heart conditions. The Miracle Minerals (potassium, magnesium, and calcium) you'll be adding to your diet increase sodium loss, enabling you to slash the salt even more quickly. And many of the other Salt Solution foods (fresh vegetables and fruit, whole grains, fish, nuts, soy products) can help improve your heart health.

The Salt Solution Feeds Your Brain

How can salt affect your brain? Simple—just as too much sodium damages your heart's arteries, it also damages arteries in your brain.

- **Stroke.** Your brain is fed by blood through arteries—and just like any other artery in your body, the brain's can become damaged by high blood pressure. A stroke is a disruption of blood flow to your brain, which causes brain cells to die from lack of oxygen and nutrients. More than 60 percent of strokes are caused by high blood pressure.[11]

- **Dementia.** High blood pressure caused by too much salt can affect your thinking. Dementia can be caused by a narrowing or blockage of the brain's blood vessels from hypertension. Studies have shown that people with high blood pressure are up to 600 times more likely to develop stroke-related dementia.[12] And treating hypertension has been shown to reduce dementia due to Alzheimer's disease by half.[13]

High blood pressure stresses the arteries that feed your brain. Slash your sodium intake with the Salt Solution plan and you relieve the pressure, dodge the largest contributor to stroke risk, and improve your brain health. Many Salt Solution foods may have especially protective effects on your brain, including dark-skinned fruits and vegetables (blueberries, kale, beets), fish rich in omega-3 fatty acids (halibut, salmon, tuna), and some nuts (almonds, pecans, and walnuts).

The Salt Solution Balances Blood Sugar

Salt and sugar—they may seem like opposites, but too much salt can affect your blood sugar, or blood glucose levels. And similar to not wanting sodium levels that are too high, you also don't want blood sugar levels that are too high, or serious health complications can occur.

- **Diabetes.** A person with diabetes already has a higher risk for developing hypertension and heart disease—and a high salt intake will only make that risk greater. Controlling blood pressure in people with diabetes is particularly critical, because hypertension is an important risk factor for the development and worsening of many complications of diabetes, including diabetic eye disease and kidney disease. A higher salt intake has also been associated with an increased risk of diabetes.[14]

- **Metabolic syndrome.** Metabolic syndrome is a group of symptoms, including elevated blood sugars, abdominal fat, high blood pressure, and high cholesterol. People with metabolic syndrome may benefit more than others from a low-sodium diet to reduce blood pressure. In one study, reducing salt intake decreased the blood pressure of those with metabolic syndrome by 9/1 mmHg more, on average, than the subjects without metabolic syndrome.[15]

Controlling your blood sugar is the first step in preventing diabetes and metabolic syndrome. The Salt Solution plan will help keep your blood sugar levels in the safe range by including foods that may help control blood sugar, like oatmeal and other whole grains; non-starchy vegetables like kale, spinach, and broccoli; and lean proteins like chicken breast, halibut, and salmon.

The Salt Solution Does a Body Good

You probably weren't surprised to learn that decreasing your salt intake can decrease your blood pressure and hence your risk of heart disease, stroke, and diabetes. What is surprising is just how many other dangerous health conditions sodium is linked to.

- **Cancer.** Yet another reason to reduce your salt intake: Researchers have found that salted foods may increase cancer risk, and high salt intake has been associated with deaths from stomach cancer in some studies.[16]

- **Kidney disease.** Both high blood pressure and high salt intake have been shown to cause scarring to the kidneys, called renal fibrosis.[17,18] When scar tissue builds up, your kidneys can't work properly, and they start to fail. End-stage renal disease (ESRD) is complete (or almost-complete) kidney failure. Researchers estimate that one-quarter of the cases of ESRD in the United States are due to high blood pressure.[19]

TOP 20 SALT SOURCES

Here are the top 20 sources of salt in the American diet, based on the 2003–2004 National Health and Nutrition Examination Survey (NHANES). These are not the foods with the highest amounts of salt per serving, but are the food sources that contribute the most to Americans' overall salt intakes. How frequently do you eat these items?

1. Meat pizza	11. Salty snacks/corn chips
2. White bread	12. Whole milk
3. Processed cheese	13. Cheese pizza
4. Hot dogs	14. Noodle soups
5. Spaghetti with sauce	15. Eggs (whole, fried, or scrambled)
6. Ham	16. Macaroni and cheese
7. Ketchup	17. 2% milk
8. Cooked rice	18. French fries
9. White rolls	19. Creamy salad dressings
10. Flour tortillas	20. Potato chips

- **Osteoporosis.** Osteoporosis develops when your bones lose calcium. When sodium intake increases, calcium excretion increases. Researchers think that your body leeches calcium from your bones to replace the calcium lost and keep your blood calcium levels stable. High-salt diets have been shown to increase calcium loss by an average of 20 to 60 milligrams of calcium lost for every 2,300 milligrams of sodium ingested.[20]

- **Sleep apnea.** Cut the salt to improve your sleep. Sleep apnea, or blocked breathing when you sleep, occurs more often in people with high blood pressure. People with sleep apnea may have two to three times the risk of having high blood pressure than people without sleep apnea. And new research shows that hypertension may actually trigger sleep apnea.

- **Erectile dysfunction.** Too much salt can affect your sex life? Yes—the vessels bringing blood to your sexual organs can also be damaged by high blood pressure. Researchers have found that among men with high blood pressure, almost 70 percent are likely to have some form of erectile dysfunction. Another reason to avoid developing hypertension: Erectile dysfunction is a common side effect of medications used to treat high blood pressure.

Clearly, reducing your sodium intake with the Salt Solution plan can help all aspects of your health—from your brain, to your heart, to your bones, to your sex life. Now can you think of any good reason not to start living the Salt Solution way? Didn't think so.

Your Solution for Lasting Weight Loss and Good Health

OKAY, SO NOW YOU KNOW HOW much havoc too much salt can wreak on your body. But you're pretty savvy about how to identify healthy foods, and you're careful not to add too much salt when cooking. So do you really need to worry?

It's estimated that about one-quarter of Americans with normal blood pressure levels, and about 58 percent of those with hypertension, are salt-sensitive.[21] These individuals retain sodium more easily and are more likely to suffer the ill effects of sodium even if their salt intake is relatively low. Older people, African Americans, and people with a family history of high blood pressure are most likely to be salt-sensitive, but unfortunately there's no reliable predictor or test of salt sensitivity. So it's best for everyone to watch salt intake. Our test panelists certainly found this to be true. Even those who didn't think they had a salt problem saw improvements in their weight, overall health, and energy.

In the next chapter we'll show you just how easy it is to shake the salt with the Salt Solution plan. You'll learn how to reset your taste buds and clean out your diet, and we'll introduce the powerful Salt Solution Stars—foods that are especially rich in potassium, magnesium, and calcium, the Miracle Minerals that counteract the negative effects of sodium.

See if you can spot where the salt is hiding in your life. Which of these has the highest salt content?

1. BREAKSTONE'S FAT FREE COTTAGE CHEESE VS. SARGENTO LIGHT RICOTTA CHEESE

2. KRAFT GARLIC RANCH SALAD DRESSING VS. KRAFT LIGHT RANCH SALAD DRESSING

3. QUAKER INSTANT OATMEAL CINNAMON & SPICE FLAVOR VS. QUAKER INSTANT OATMEAL ORIGINAL FLAVOR

4. PREGO HEART SMART TRADITIONAL ITALIAN SAUCE VS. PREGO TRADITIONAL ITALIAN SAUCE

5. PILGRIM'S PRIDE BONELESS SKINLESS SPLIT CHICKEN BREAST VS. FOSTER FARMS BONELESS SKINLESS CHICKEN BREAST FILLETS

6. MRS. DASH LEMON PEPPER SEASONING BLEND VS. McCORMICK PERFECT PINCH LEMON & PEPPER SEASONING

7. KELLOGG'S RAISIN BRAN CEREAL VS. POST SHREDDED WHEAT SPOON SIZE CEREAL

8. DUNKIN' DONUTS MULTIGRAIN BAGEL VS. LENDER'S WHOLE GRAIN MULTI GRAIN BAGEL

9. V8 V-FUSION CRANBERRY BLACKBERRY JUICE VS. V8 100% VEGETABLE JUICE

10. KRAFT SINGLES AMERICAN CHEESE VS. ALPINE LACE REDUCED-FAT YELLOW AMERICAN CHEESE

(See page 12 for the answers.)

BEYOND BLOAT

11

ANSWERS:

1. The Sargento Light Ricotta is a better bet. Per ¹/₂ cup, the ricotta cheese has 120 calories and 105 milligrams (mg) sodium. The same amount of Breakstone's cottage cheese has 80 calories and 450 mg sodium. If you want cottage cheese, look for versions without added salt.

2. The Kraft Light Ranch (80 calories and 440 mg sodium per 2 tablespoons) has more sodium than the Kraft Garlic Ranch (120 calories and 360 mg sodium per 2 tablespoons). However, both of these prepared salad dressings are too high in sodium! Make your own low-salt salad dressing with a splash of olive oil, balsamic vinegar, and fresh or dried herbs.

3. The Cinnamon & Spice flavor oatmeal has way more salt (160 calories and 210 mg sodium per packet) than the Original flavor (100 calories and 75 mg sodium per packet). Stick with the original, and add your own (salt-free!) shakes of cinnamon and brown sugar.

4. Prego's Heart Smart Traditional Italian sauce is indeed better for your heart, with less sodium than Prego's Traditional Italian sauce (70 calories and 360 mg sodium versus 70 calories and 480 mg sodium per ¹/₂-cup serving). A better bet than either of these? Make your own tomato sauce with a can of no-salt-added crushed tomatoes and a few shakes of oregano and red-pepper flakes.

5. This is an example of "plumping" or "enriching"—producers add salt water to chicken parts to make them look bigger. The Pilgrim's Pride Boneless Skinless Split Chicken Breast (110 calories and 330 mg sodium per 4 ounces) is "plumped," while the Foster Farms Boneless Skinless Chicken Breast Fillets (120 calories and 75 mg sodium per 4 ounces) aren't. How can you tell the difference? Look at the sodium content on the Nutrition Facts label, or look for small print on the label saying, "contains up to 15 percent salt water."

6. Mrs. Dash is salt-free (0 calories and 0 mg sodium per ¹/₄ teaspoon), so shake away! McCormick Perfect Pinch Lemon & Pepper Seasoning has lots of added salt (0 calories and 210 mg sodium per $\frac{1}{4}$ teaspoon).

7. Pick the Post Shredded Wheat Spoon Size cereal. One cup has 170 calories and 0 mg sodium, compared to 190 calories and 250 mg sodium per cup of Kellogg's Raisin Bran cereal.

8. The Dunkin' Donuts multigrain bagel (390 calories and 560 mg sodium) has more sodium than the Lender's Whole Grain Multi Grain Bagel (250 calories, 490 mg sodium), but they both have too much. Instead, look for low-sodium bagels (they may be hard to find, but ask your grocery store if they can special-order them) or switch to a multigrain or whole wheat English muffin, which will generally have much less sodium (check the label first, though!).

9. V8 100% Vegetable Juice is chock-full of salt (50 calories and 420 mg sodium per 8 fluid ounces), while V8 V-Fusion Cranberry Blackberry Juice has much less (110 calories and 70 mg sodium per 8 fluid ounces). A better choice: Eat whole fruits and vegetables for low-sodium, fiber-packed nutrition.

10. A slice of Kraft Singles American Cheese (60 calories and 250 mg sodium) has much less sodium than an ounce of Alpine Lace Reduced-Fat yellow American cheese (90 calories and 380 mg sodium). But these still contain tons of salt, especially for something that's just going to be one component of your sandwich! Instead, choose Alpine Lace 25% Reduced Sodium Muenster Cheese, which has 90 calories and 110 mg sodium per slice.

Bottom line—It's hard to determine sodium-friendly picks just by their names. Always inspect labels before buying.

★ **HALIBUT** ★

Full of magnesium
and potassium

Salt
SOLUTION
Principles

It sounds simple, and it is—shake the salt, and you'll lose the weight and improve your health. You'll not only feel better, you'll look better too! The Salt Solution plan contains the perfect combination of vitamins, minerals, protein, fiber, carbs, and fat. And while you fill your diet with healthful and clean ingredients, you'll shake out the damaging foods and chemicals that can drag you down.

Shake Out . . .

H ERE, WE'LL TELL YOU all about the four things you'll shake out of your life on the Salt Solution plan—excess sodium, excess calories, bad fats, and salty packaged and processed foods—as well as why you want to shake them and how we'll help you do it.

Excess Sodium

In Chapter 1 you learned all about the dangerous effects of too much salt and its main consequences—weight gain and disease. But did you know that reducing sodium intake has the potential to save millions of lives—and billions of dollars? Researchers recently calculated that 8.5 million deaths could be prevented over a 10-year period with only a 15 percent decrease in salt intake.[1] And researchers at the University of California, San Francisco; Stanford University; and Columbia University calculated that if Americans reduced their sodium intake by 1,200 milligrams per day, or ½ teaspoon table salt—described by researchers as "hardly detectable" in terms of the taste of food—it would result in savings in health-care costs worth $24 billion.[2]

So how can you shake the salt without condemning yourself to bland food or hours in front of the stove? Easy—the Salt Solution plan isn't about deprivation. You'll be eating tons of delicious, healthy, easy-to-prepare food; the only thing missing will be the salt. By preparing meals with fresh, minimally processed, and naturally delicious ingredients—like whole grains, fruits, veggies, herbs, and lean meats—you won't need excess amounts of salt in order to make your food taste good. And as your taste buds adjust to less salt, fresh flavors will come alive and your overall food satisfaction will increase. Bonus: You'll lose the bloat (an instant weight loss of 1 to 2 pounds!); you'll lose the craving for salty, processed foods, and eventually you'll lose those extra pounds you've been carrying around for far too long!

Extra Calories

Weight loss is a simple math equation: If you eat fewer calories than you burn, you'll lose weight. A pound of fat equals 3,500 calories, so this means that you have to burn 3,500 extra calories to lose a pound. Divided over a week, this translates to 500 calories per day. But this doesn't mean you have to run 5 miles or swim for 2 hours every day to burn these calories. (Although it certainly wouldn't hurt.) Just eat 500 fewer calories per day, and you'll lose a pound per week. You've heard of the term "metabolism"—this refers to the number of calories your body burns for all of your physiological functions, including breathing, digestion, and involuntary muscle movements. Metabolism varies from person to person (which is why people complain about having a "slower" metabolism than others) and depends on sex, age, and weight. But on average, a 40-year-old woman who's 5 foot 6 inches and weighs 140 pounds burns 1,800 calories per day for everyday physiologic functions. If she eats fewer than 1,800 calories, she'll lose weight.

On the Salt Solution plan, you'll be eating 1,200 calories per day in the 2-Week Salt Solution Cleanse, and 1,500 calories per day in the 4-Week Shake the Salt Meal Plan. Don't worry about the increase in calories in the second phase in fact, this small increase can help you lose more weight. It sounds counterintuitive, but if you stay on a very low calorie diet for too long, your metabolism slows down. The extra 300 calories once you enter the 4-Week Shake the Salt Meal Plan will maintain your metabolism to keep you losing weight.

Bad Fats

Everyone needs to eat some fat to survive. The problem starts when we eat too much of it, especially when it's saturated or trans fat.

Of all the fat you eat, saturated fats are most responsible for high cholesterol. Saturated fat is mostly found in fats from animals, including beef, pork, chicken, and dairy products

LABEL LINGO: NATURAL

In the United States, the term "natural" isn't regulated by the government, unlike the term "organic," which has a specific legal definition. Something that's "all-natural" might contain high fructose corn syrup, food colorings, and other artificial ingredients. You can't rely on the term "natural" to indicate a healthy, low-sodium food. In fact, chicken meat can be labeled "all-natural" even after it's been injected with salty water to plump it up!

Organic foods are produced without synthetic fertilizers, conventional pesticides, genetic engineering, irradiation, or sewage sludge. Organic animal products, such as meat and dairy, come from animals given no antibiotics or growth hormones.[3] While organic products are good for the environment, they aren't necessarily good for you. Organic doesn't automatically equal low-sodium (or low-sugar, low-fat, or low-calorie for that matter), as many organic foods, especially processed and packaged ones, are high in salt. So be sure to read food labels of all products carefully, even organic ones, to confirm they're low in sodium.

made from whole and 2% milk. Some plant-based fats are saturated, including coconut and coconut oil, palm oil, and cocoa butter. The American Heart Association recommends that saturated fats make up no more than 7 percent of your total daily calories.[4]

The term "trans" in trans fats refers to how atoms are positioned in the fat molecule. Trans fats are found naturally in small amounts in animal products (like beef, pork, and lamb), but they're made in much larger and more dangerous quantities through the process of hydrogenation. Hydrogenation is used to produce margarine, shortening, and foods containing these fats, like packaged cookies and crackers. Trans fats raise LDL cholesterol (the "bad" kind of cholesterol) and lower HDL cholesterol (the "good" kind), and can thus increase your risk for heart disease. Also important, the foods high in trans fats, like fried items and packaged snacks, are likely to be very salty!

The American Heart Association recommends limiting trans fat intake to no more than 1 percent of your total daily calories.[5] How can you tell if an item has trans fats? Check the Nutrition Facts label for partially hydrogenated oils in the ingredients list or trans fats in the main panel.

In general, plant-based fats—like the fat from olive oil, nuts, and avocados—are healthier than meat-based fats. Also, meat-based fats are often present in very salty foods—including hot dogs, bacon, and cheeseburgers. Double the reason to avoid these items!

The foods included in the Salt Solution plan will be full of the healthy fats your body needs, in just the right amounts, and will naturally slash your intake of unhealthy saturated and trans fats.

Salty Packaged and Processed Foods

On the Salt Solution plan, you'll be eating lots of "whole" foods (including whole grains and tons of fresh fruits and vegetables), low-fat or fat-free dairy, healthy fats, and lean meats, poultry, and fish. This doesn't mean that you'll be eating an expensive all-organic diet, though (see "Label Lingo: Organic"). It just means that you'll be cutting out unhealthy packaged and processed foods. Since about 80 percent of the salt we consume comes from packaged and prepared foods, cutting these is a surefire way to shake the salt.

Convenience foods that are commercially produced for the ease of consumption are not necessarily bad for you—processing includes pasteurizing fat-free milk and freezing fresh vegetables. But many packaged foods (think hot dogs, deli meats, canned soups, and crackers) are incredibly high in sodium. The Salt Solution plan teaches you which prepared, packaged, and processed (we use these words pretty much interchangeably) foods to avoid, and which to enjoy.

Take In . . .

You won't even miss your old way of eating. With the Salt Solution plan, you'll be shaking out the harmful stuff while you consume more of all the good stuff—like essential minerals, lean protein, fruits and vegetables, low-fat dairy, whole grains, and healthy fats.

The Miracle Minerals: Potassium, Calcium, and Magnesium

Potassium, calcium, and magnesium are all very important minerals—ones that we're not getting enough of. Why do we want more of these? One reason is that increasing your intake of these minerals increases your body's excretion of sodium, and helps you to achieve the optimum balance of minerals.[6] In addition, each of these minerals counteracts hypertension and other negative effects of excess sodium.

Potassium, for instance, is essential for nerve function, muscle control, and blood pressure. Just as sodium can increase blood pressure, potassium can lower blood pressure. It may also protect against stroke and other cardiovascular disease, including the development of atherosclerosis (plaque deposits in your arteries). It's likely that you're getting only about half of the potassium you should be.

Calcium is essential for bone health, and, like potassium, it increases sodium excretion and lowers blood pressure. Calcium intake prevents osteoporosis, but also helps speed weight loss and prevent weight gain! You're probably getting only about 35 to 40 percent of the calcium you need.

Magnesium is the most abundant mineral in the human body—in fact, more than 300 biochemical processes in your body depend on magnesium, including muscle and nerve function and blood sugar regulation. Increased magnesium increases sodium excretion and may lower blood pressure. Chances are, if you're like most Americans, you're getting about half as much magnesium as you should.

The Salt Solution plan contains high levels of these three minerals—which will help you shake the salt even more. The plan, and the delicious recipes in this book, feature the Salt Solution Stars (see below), foods that are not only bursting with flavor but also provide your body with the minerals you need!

THE SALT SOLUTION STARS

The Salt Solution plan features the following Salt Solution Stars. They're all excellent sources of either calcium, potassium, or magnesium (the Miracle Minerals that counteract the negative effects of sodium)—and many are great sources of all three!

★ BANANAS: Packed with potassium, bananas are Salt Solution staples. More good banana news: They're also chockful of vitamin B$_6$, filling fiber, and vitamin C. **CHEF'S TIP:** Buy overripe bananas for use in sweet dishes and slightly underripe for savory.

★ BEET GREENS: These root-vegetable greens are full of potassium, magnesium, and calcium! A true Salt Solution superfood, beet greens are also loaded with vitamin K and beta-carotene. **CHEF'S TIP:** Buy beet greens that are crisp and without bruises.

★ HALIBUT: This high-quality protein source is brimming with magnesium and potassium. It's also low in heart-harming saturated fats and high in heart-healthy omega-3 fats, making this fish a Salt Solution win-win.

CHEF'S TIP: When buying halibut, ask for fillets that are from the thicker center portion of the fish. Halibut's mild flavor pairs well with many sauces, chutneys, salsas, etc.; just be sure to use small amounts so as not to overwhelm the fish.

★ KALE: Full of not only calcium and potassium, but also beta-carotene, vitamin C, and iron—including this nutrient-dense leafy green in your diet is a surefire way to boost your health.

CHEF'S TIP: Look for crisp leaves when buying kale. If your kale becomes limp, trim the stems and soak in a bowl of cool water for 15 minutes to help it perk up.

★ MILK: Milk really does do a body good! It's a convenient source of calcium, and it's loaded with protein and is forti- fied with vitamins D and A. Just be sure to choose low-fat or fat-free versions to reduce the bad-for-you fat found in whole milk.

CHEF'S TIP: Fat-free (skim) milk and 1% milk are best used as a drink, over cereal, or in dishes that have another fat source to provide creaminess (like maca- roni and cheese).

★ SARDINES: These tiny fish pack a powerful potassium and calcium punch and are loaded with omega-3 fatty acids and protein. While fresh sardines are a delicious choice, canned no-salt-added sardines are an affordable option and a tasty Salt Solution pantry staple.

CHEF'S TIP: Buy canned sardines that are packed in water to help reduce fat. When using canned sardines, drain well and pat dry before adding to your dish.

★ SOYBEANS: Rich in calcium, potas- sium, and magnesium, soybeans are nutritional powerhouses. Whether fresh, roasted, or dried, this "wonder veggie" is also rich in iron, zinc, and lots of B vitamins.

CHEF'S TIP: Fresh or frozen green soybeans (also known as edamame) should only be briefly blanched in boiling water for best flavor. They will be bright green with a slightly firm texture. Roasted soybeans are very versatile and are great sprinkled into a salad, added to snack mixes, or stirred into grain dishes.

★ SOYMILK: Soymilk is rich in potassium and magnesium, and if you use a calcium-fortified brand like Silk, you'll be getting as much of this important mineral as you would from cow's milk.
CHEF'S TIP: When purchasing soymilk, be sure to read the label. Flavored soymilk is usually sweetened, which will add unwanted calories to your dishes.

★ SPINACH: Popeye was no fool. Crammed with potassium, magnesium, and calcium, as well as beta-carotene, vitamin C, and folate, spinach is a nutrient-packed Salt Solution superfood.
CHEF'S TIP: To save time in the kitchen, purchase bags of prewashed spinach. Because of its high water content, spinach shrivels or "wilts" quickly, so make sure your skillet is hot before adding it and cook briefly.

★ SWEET POTATOES: Like bananas, these root veggies are an excellent source of potassium. They're also a rich source of antioxidants including vitamin C and beta-carotene. Eat the skin and you'll also get a hefty dose of fill-you-up fiber.
CHEF'S TIP: When buying sweet potatoes, look for firm ones that feel heavy in your hand with wrinkle- and blemish-free skins. Store them in a cool, dry location for best shelf life.

★ WHITE BEANS: These legumes are packed not only with protein, fiber, and iron, but also potassium, magnesium, and calcium. They're a three-in-one Salt Solution must-have.
CHEF'S TIP: Save time by quick-soaking dried beans: Add them to a pot with enough water to cover by 3 inches, bring to a boil, cook for 2 minutes, turn off, and let stand 1 hour. Drain the beans and cook as you would normally.

★ YOGURT: Most know this dairy snack is loaded with calcium, but did you know it's also a good source of potassium and magnesium? Yup, it's true. Just be sure to stick with low-fat or fat-free varieties to limit bad-for-your-heart saturated fat.
CHEF'S TIP: If adding yogurt to a hot dish, be sure to add it after the dish has been removed from the heat so the yogurt won't separate.

Loads of Lean Protein

Lean proteins include chicken breast, pork tenderloin, turkey, and seafood. Why are these so great? Protein is essential for building and repairing muscle, and it takes longer to digest than simple carbohydrates, so you'll feel fuller longer. Eating protein can even boost your metabolism—it takes three times as much energy to digest protein as it does to digest carbs or fats.

So why can't you just eat lots of protein? First, carbohydrates and fats are essential. And just like anything, too much protein will make you fat. When you eat more protein than you need (just about 8 grams of protein for every 20 pounds of body weight), it's not packed on to your muscles—it's stored as fat.

Why is lean protein so important? Fatty meats, like high-fat ground beef, bacon, or hot dogs, contain not only protein, but also unhealthy saturated fats. Lean meats, like those featured in the Salt Solution menus, give you all the benefits of protein without all of the harmful saturated fat.

LABEL LINGO: FREE-RANGE

It sounds ideal—free-range eggs are laid by chickens who have acres of land to themselves, right? Unfortunately, this may not be the case. The term "free range" indicates only that the animals have access to the outdoors for an undetermined time period each day. This could be hours, or it could be minutes. If this is important to you, look for the products labeled "Certified Humane Raised & Handled." Or talk to the butcher at your supermarket—he or she should know about their meat suppliers' conditions for their animals. Free-range on the label also doesn't indicate if the cluckers are enhanced with sodium. Before you buy, flip the package over and investigate. If sodium is added, the label will say something like (in small print, of course!) "contains up to 15 percent salt water." Or just check the Nutrition Facts—chicken should have no more than 70 milligrams of sodium per 4-ounce serving. Any more, and it's likely sodium-enhanced.

Remember that you'll want to check the labels of the packaged meats you purchase. Some meats are sold as "enhanced," which means they're injected with or soaked in a solution of salt and broth to add moisture and improve flavor. Check the ingredient list for sodium or salt, and check the product label for statements such as "self-basting" or "percent solution" or "broth," all terms that indicate salt may have been added. Meat naturally contains some salt (an ounce of chicken breast contains less than 20 milligrams of natural sodium), but this is nothing compared to the amount in these "enhanced" meats (which can reach up to 100 milligrams of sodium per ounce).

The Salt Solution plan contains the right amount of delicious, lean low-sodium protein to keep you feeling full and energized. Don't eat meat? No problem—the plan is packed with healthy, vegetarian protein sources, like unsalted peanut butter, tofu and other soy products, beans, nuts, and eggs.

FYI ON CSA

CSAs, or Community Supported Agriculture programs, have become more popular in recent years. How do they work? Local farmers offer consumers the opportunity to buy locally grown, seasonal produce directly from the farm. Normally, consumers pay up front for a "share" (i.e., a membership), and every week (or every other week, or every month) they receive a box of super-fresh produce, straight from the farm. CSAs benefit both farmers and consumers— farmers get money before the growing season to invest, and consumers generally receive more produce than their share would pay for at the market. Not to mention all of the nutritional benefits of eating locally grown fresh fruits and vegetables! Another benefit is that you get to experiment with produce you might not pick up at the supermarket.

In addition to fruits and veggies, many farms offer CSA shares for meat, eggs, cheese, and other farm-fresh products. To find a CSA in your area, check out www.localharvest.org.

Plenty of Produce

Fruits and vegetables are critical parts of the Salt Solution plan. They're naturally very low in sodium, and they're packed with essential vitamins, minerals, and fiber, and have almost no saturated fat. And they're delicious!

How should you pick which fruits and vegetables to eat? First, start with the Salt Solution Stars: bananas, beet greens, kale, soybeans, spinach, sweet potatoes, and white beans. These fruits and veggies are loaded with potassium, magnesium, and calcium, the minerals that help counteract the negative effects of sodium.

Next, go for a mix of colors. Bright colors indicate a high level of phytochemicals and antioxidants, which are compounds that may help slow down the aging process and reduce the risk of many diseases, such as cancer, heart disease, stroke, high blood pressure, osteoporosis, urinary tract infections, and cataracts.[7] Aim for several different colors of fruits and vegetables a day—yellow squash, orange carrots, red peppers, green broccoli, blueberries, and purple eggplant.

You'll also want to choose the freshest fruits and vegetables available. Canned fruits and vegetables are often very high in sodium—canned peas, for example, may have almost 400 milligrams of sodium per serving, while fresh have about 60 milligrams per serving. Instead of using canned, take a trip to the local farmers' market (in season) or ask an employee at your grocery store which items are at their peak. And if you can't get fresh produce, frozen fruits and vegetables with no added sodium are a great option.

What about organic produce? If eating an all-organic diet is too much for your wallet, don't despair. The key is to be selective about your purchases. The Environmental Working Group (EWG), an advocacy group for public health and environmental issues, suggests that consumers focus on buying organic alternatives for the 12 fruits and vegetables with the highest pesticide levels; they call these the dirty dozen.[8] So try to go for organics when possible for these foods:

- Celery
- Peaches
- Strawberries
- Apples
- Blueberries
- Nectarines

- Bell peppers
- Spinach
- Cherries
- Kale/collard greens
- Potatoes
- Grapes (imported)

Also, many fruits and vegetables sold at your local farmers' market or farm stand may qualify as organic, but the farmers may not have registered for the designation. Talk to your local farmers about their crops and whether they use pesticides or chemical fertilizers.

Lots of Low-Fat Dairy

Dairy products are high in calcium, which increases sodium excretion. Calcium keeps bones healthy and has been shown to lower blood pressure. But dairy products have another amazing benefit: They can help promote weight loss!

Some studies have found that adults who ate a high-dairy diet lost significantly more weight and fat than those who consumed a low-dairy diet containing the same number of calories.[9] And one study found that people who followed a diet that included 800 milligrams of calcium supplements lost significantly more weight than those who had only about half that calcium in their diets; those who got their calcium through dairy products (three servings a day, or about 1,200 to 1,300 milligrams of calcium) lost even more weight.[10] The exact mechanisms by which dairy products support weight loss are unknown, but researchers think that dietary calcium may increase fat-burning and decrease fat storage.

To get the best benefits from dairy, the Salt Solution plan uses only low-fat and fat-free choices, like fat-free milk, yogurt, and cottage and ricotta cheese, and other types of reduced-fat cheeses. While full-fat milk and cheeses do have the benefits of calcium, they also come with saturated fat and calories. In addition, low-fat and fat-free dairy products usually have *more* calcium than their high-fat relatives! Some dairy products (like processed cheeses) can be high in sodium, so make sure you check the labels for the salt content. There are low-sodium options for all of your favorite dairy products.

Heaps of Whole Grains

Whole grains are products that haven't been refined, so they contain more of the healthy, high-fiber, vitamin- and mineral-packed portion of the grain. Whole grains are complex carbohydrates (the "good" kind of carbs) that keep you fuller longer than refined, simple carbohydrates (the "bad" carbs) because they take longer to digest.

In addition to keeping you fuller longer, whole grains are also healthier—they're a better source of fiber and the Miracle Minerals potassium and magnesium.[11] Diets high in whole grains have been linked with lower risks of heart disease, diabetes, and cancer—as well as a lower risk of weight gain![12, 13]

You'll enjoy many whole grains on the Salt Solution plan. Instead of a white hoagie roll, you'll be eating a slice of whole wheat bread; instead of cornflakes, you'll eat oatmeal; and instead of white rice, you'll eat brown rice. You'll find that the whole grain substitutes are just as delicious as—and much healthier than—refined grain products.

How do you know if you're getting whole grains? Check the labels. Something that says "multigrain" may only have a tiny bit of whole wheat flour, and the rest white, refined flour. If a product doesn't say "100 percent whole grain," skip it. If you see "wheat flour" and "unbleached wheat flour" in the ingredient list, these are not whole grains. Foods can be labeled as "multigrain" and still be packed with refined grains—and lots of salt. You should also look for the grams of fiber—products with at least 3 grams of dietary fiber per serving are your best bet.

Check the sodium content of all products you purchase, and stay away from preflavored rice and grain mixes. These added flavors are generally high in salt. Instead, buy plain brown rice and other whole grains, and add your own fresh and dried herbs for tons of flavor (but not tons of sodium). And of course, you can follow the recipes in the Salt Solution plan for delicious, low-salt, whole grain dishes.

Good-for-You Fats

We've discussed that "bad" fats are trans fats and saturated fats—so what are the "good" fats? Overall, the good fats are plant-based fats. Healthy monounsaturated fats are found in nuts (including peanut butter, walnuts, and pistachios), avocados, canola oil, and olive oil. They've been shown to lower total cholesterol, decrease "bad" (LDL) cholesterol, and increase "good" (HDL) cholesterol—and they also may help lower body fat.

LABEL LINGO: HIGH FIBER

Fiber is a weight-loss and nutritional powerhouse, but it's best to get your fiber from foods that are naturally high in fiber, like fruits, veggies, beans, and whole grains. Artificially added fiber, now found in everything from cereal bars, yogurt, ice cream, and more, and hyped on the label as being "high in fiber," may not have all the health benefits of natural fiber. Maltodextrin, inulin, polydextrose, and oat fiber on food labels and ingredient lists indicate that fiber has been added to a product. Fiber-added products are also likely to have added salt, and they still don't deliver the nutrients of naturally fiber-rich foods.

Polyunsaturated fats, like monounsaturated, can lower total and LDL cholesterol. They're found in seafood, corn oil, and safflower oil. Omega-3 fatty acids, a type of polyunsaturated fat (found in the Salt Solution Stars halibut and sardines), have been shown to decrease risk of abnormal heart beats, decrease triglyceride levels, slow growth of atherosclerotic plaque, and lower blood pressure.

The 2005 Dietary Guidelines for Americans recommend that 20 to 35 percent of our daily calories come from fat, and less than 10 percent of those calories from saturated fat. Stick with unsalted items like unsalted butter; unsalted "natural" peanut and other nut butters; unsalted nuts; and olive and vegetable oils. And these fats as they're found in nature (i.e., an avocado or a whole nut) have no added sodium. You'll find plenty of good fats in the Salt Solution plan.

Putting It All Together

A LL OF THE SALT SOLUTION MEALS (breakfasts, lunches, dinners, snacks, and desserts) are structured the exact same way. Each has one serving each of protein, dairy, produce, grains, and fat. Each has no more than 300 calories and

300 milligrams of sodium per meal. Love a recipe in this book or a Salt Solution meal? You can repeat it. You're also free to have a breakfast meal for dinner or even a lunch meal as a snack, whatever works. This plan is really tailored for you, to fit your taste buds and needs. The more than 200 recipes in this book are packed with flavor, and after your taste buds reset, you'll never miss the salt!

THE SALT SOLUTION BREAKDOWN

The 2-Week Salt Solution Cleanse

In just 2 weeks you can rev up your metabolism, increase your energy, and cleanse your system of excess sodium, bad fats, and other harmful substances. And you can reset your taste buds, an important part of the Salt Solution strategy. The Cleanse includes:

- **Three satisfying 300-calorie low-salt** meals per day, each featuring a Salt Solution Star, designed to jump-start weight loss and eliminate bloating caused by salt.

- **A daily Mineral Boost Juice,** a smoothie pumped with the Miracle Minerals and other nutrients you need to get your body back into balance. Choose from six delicious varieties.

The 4-Week Shake the Salt Meal Plan

At the end of this program you'll be leaner and on your way to a healthier, low-salt lifestyle! Enjoy 4 weeks of delicious nutrient-packed meals and recipes that you can mix and match. The plan consists of:

- **Four filling 300-calorie meals** per day. Choose from the quick-fix Cleanse meals (page 42) or from the more than 200 Salt Solution recipes in the recipe chapters.

- **A daily dose of Mineral Boost Juice.** This tasty concoction, available in six flavors, keeps your health at an optimum level while you drop pounds.

An Optional Exercise Program

You already own the best weight-loss equipment—your feet. The secret is knowing how to use them. The optional Salt Solution Weight-Loss Workout includes a walking program designed to turn your body into a more efficient calorie- and fat-burning machine. And the Salt Solution strength-training routine will help you develop even more muscle, so you can burn even more calories.

SALT SOLUTION STAR

★ **SOYMILK** ★

Rich in potassium,
magnesium, and
(if fortified) calcium

THE 2-WEEK Salt SOLUTION Cleanse

The 2-Week Salt Solution Cleanse is designed to purify your system of excess sodium, saturated and trans fats, and unnecessary chemicals and substances, including food dyes, artificial sweeteners, and alcohol. It will also boost metabolism, increase energy, and jump-start weight loss! But this is not some crazy "detox" diet. Nope, you'll be filling your body with natural, real food, like fruits, vegetables, whole grains, herbs, chicken, fish, and more. And by cutting out processed items and eating clean, whole foods, you'll not only cleanse your body, you'll also get your taste buds back!

Over time our taste buds can get accustomed to aggressively flavored and highly salted processed foods that are designed to taste like the real thing (think fruit-flavored candy, cheese puffs, and orange soda). When your taste buds get used to these types of intense flavors and seasonings, food in its natural form can taste bland in comparison. But in just a few weeks you can turn things around.

Most of us have around 10,000 taste buds, and each taste bud is made up of between 50 to 150 receptor cells. Receptor cells live for only 1 to 2 weeks and then are replaced by new receptors. So, after eating a clean diet for a week or two, your taste buds will adjust and you will begin to taste the subtle flavors in real foods, the way Mother Nature intended!

The Cleanse will also reduce bloating. You know that water loves sodium, and the more sodium in your bloodstream, the more water, which leads to extra water weight and a sluggish feeling. Lose the salt and you'll lose the bloat. But losing the salt is only half the battle. For optimum mineral levels and good health, it's important that you not only decrease sodium, but also increase potassium, calcium, and magnesium. The Cleanse meals and the Mineral Boost Juices featured in the 2-Week Salt Solution Cleanse are packed with the Salt Solution Stars, foods high in these important minerals (see page 19), and will bring your body back into balance. During the next 2 weeks you will:

- **Balance meals.** During the Cleanse you will eat three 300-calorie meals per day, each featuring a nutrient-packed Salt Solution Star (see page 20). You will also have a daily 300-calorie Mineral Boost Juice (see page 36). Be sure to have the meals and/or Mineral Boost Juice approximately every 4 to 5 hours to manage hunger. You may repeat meals that you find most enjoyable if you wish, but variety is encouraged. For accuracy, it's best that you measure all of your food. Without measuring it's very easy to accumulate extra calories. It only takes an extra minute to measure food. For this reason, we recommend that you continue to measure your food throughout the 4-Week Shake the Salt Meal Plan, as well.

- **Control beverages.** It's best, while you are doing the Cleanse, to stick with plain water and unsweetened hot or cold brewed green, red, white, black, or herbal tea. Alcohol is completely forbidden, and coffee consumption should be limited to no more than 1 cup a day. (Black coffee doesn't add calories in and of itself, but can irritate your intestinal tract, and of course, any milk or sugar adds calories.)

- **Limit eating out.** For the duration of the 2 weeks it's best to eat the Cleanse meals as often as possible. This will yield not only the best weight-loss results, but also ensure that you reduce your sodium intake enough to reset your taste buds. Restaurant meals tend to be loaded in sodium, as well as fat and calories. However, if you absolutely need to dine out during the Cleanse, be sure to plan ahead and to select your choices carefully.

- **Track your intake.** Documenting why you eat, when you eat, and how much you eat will keep you from deviating from the plan. We've created *The Salt Solution Journal*, available at www.prevention.com/shop or 800-848-4735, which will help keep you honest and uncover hidden diet foes; but you can also create your own journal. Or, if you'd prefer to track electronically, try My Health Trackers at www.prevention.com/healthtracker.

- **Pump up exercise.** While exercise on the Salt Solution plan is optional, we certainly encourage you to get moving! Most experts recommend a minimum of about $2\frac{1}{2}$ hours of exercise per week—or 30 minutes of exercise 5 days a week—but you also can break it into smaller amounts (such as three 10-minute mini workouts over the course of a day). The Salt Solution Weight-Loss Workout in Appendix A has been specifically designed to help you lose weight while you cut the salt and clean out your diet.

The 2-Week Salt Solution Cleanse will be challenging—you'll be changing your diet, eliminating alcohol, and limiting dining out as much as possible—but it'll be worth it! At the end of the 14 days you'll be slimmer and healthier, and your salt addiction will be a thing of the past. In fact, some of our test panelists lost up to $10\frac{1}{2}$ pounds and 5 inches in just 2 weeks! And all of the participants were astonished at how painless (and helpful!) it was to break their salt habits.

The 2-Week Cleanse Basics

Mix & Match Cleanse Meals: Have Three per Day

Twenty different Cleanse meals to choose from are provided beginning on page 42. Each meal features one or more of the Salt Solution Stars—foods that provide significant amounts of all three of our key beneficial minerals (potassium, magnesium, and calcium)—and each is loaded with fiber to help you feel full.

All of the Cleanse meals provide around 300 calories, so you can move them around or swap them out at will. For example, a breakfast meal can be eaten for dinner; a snack can be eaten as breakfast, and a lunch meal as a snack. These meals are carefully designed to give you balanced nutrition, so you should not swap out ingredients in a meal. (However, if you have an allergy, do not hesitate to swap a similar ingredient within the same food group—such as tomatoes for red peppers or turkey for chicken.)

You may repeat meals that you find most enjoyable if you wish, but variety is strongly encouraged. Also, dessert and snack meals should be limited to no more than one per day, as they don't provide the same balanced nutrition as the other meals. Though you should eat the meals exactly as is, you can add herbs, spices, and other seasonings as desired (see "The Salt Solution Seasoning Guide" on page 38). Just steer clear of sauces or dressings that may contain added oil, sugar, salt, and calories. If you find you are still hungry, you can also add any of the foods from "The Salt Solution Freebies" list. These "free" foods are nutrient-dense, low-calorie foods you can use to add "bulk" to your meals without adding many calories.

Mineral Boost Juice: Have One per Day

A hallmark of this plan is the daily Mineral Boost Juice—a smoothie pumped with calcium, magnesium, and potassium, the minerals that counteract the negative effects of excess sodium. Drinking a Mineral Boost Juice every day in addition to your three Cleanse meals will not only replenish your body with what it needs, but also serve as a reminder that you are working hard to decrease your sodium, increase your nutrients, and improve your life. It will keep you focused on the weight-loss task ahead. There are six versions of the Mineral

Boost Juice to choose from (pages 40–41). (If you're already familiar with *The Salt Solution*, you'll find your favorites here; we've just added a few more varieties for you to try!) Test them out and choose the varieties that taste best to you. You can stick with just one flavor, or you can mix them up—the choice is yours. Like the Cleanse meals, all of the Mineral Boost Juices provide around 300 calories.

When you finish the 2-Week Salt Solution Cleanse, you'll be slimmer, more energized, and motivated to move on to the next phase of the Salt Solution, the 4-Week Shake the Salt Meal Plan. Your taste buds will be reset, your mineral levels will be restored, and you'll be primed to lose the salt and the weight—forever!

THE SALT SOLUTION FREEBIES

Add any of these vegetables to meals as desired. Because they're very low in calories, it's impossible to eat too much. Choose fresh or frozen vegetables, not canned. And be sure not to cook them in a lot of oils or sauces with lots of added calories and/or salt. Preferred cooking methods are steaming, microwaving, roasting, and boiling.

Artichoke hearts	Carrots	Mushrooms
Asparagus	Cauliflower	Onion
*Beet greens	Celery	Radishes
Beets	Collard greens	*Spinach
Bell peppers	Cucumbers	String/green beans
Broccoli	Eggplant	Tomatoes
Brussels sprouts	*Kale	Water chestnuts
Cabbage	Lettuce	Zucchini/summer squash

*(include this Salt Solution Star as often as possible)

THE SALT SOLUTION SEASONING GUIDE

Who needs salt when you have fresh herbs and spices? These seasonings can take a dish from just okay to fabulous! They boost flavor without adding sodium, calories, or fat. Use these no-calorie, no-sodium suggestions to add flavor to your Salt Solution meals and/or recipes. When a seasoning pairs especially well with a Salt Solution Star, we've listed that food in bold, but feel free to experiment for yourself with these herbs and spices.

BASIL: Great in salsas, tomato sauce, and pesto. Use as a flavor boost in salads, sandwiches, and soups (especially tomato, **white bean**, and minestrone). Great with green vegetables like **beet greens, kale, spinach,** broccoli, and peas.

MINT: Refreshing and versatile. Use on lamb and in grain salads, or infuse into hot or iced tea and lemonade. Great when added to fruit salad.

ROSEMARY: The herb of romance pairs wonderfully with meats, poultry, and fish (like **halibut**), especially when roasting. Also excellent in savory baked items such as bread and pizza. Use in marinades, or simply rub on roasts before cooking. But use sparingly as it can overwhelm.

OREGANO: A staple of both Greek and Italian cooking, oregano can be used in marinara and other tomato-based sauces, on pizza, or mixed with lemon juice and olive oil to serve over grilled or roasted fish fillets (like **halibut**). It adds depth to soups, especially white bean and vegetable soups.

THYME: A great addition to marinades for fish (like **halibut**), poultry, and meat. Thyme has a strong flavor, so be sure to add it at the beginning of cooking to help mellow it. A must for soups, stews, chili, and roasts.

CILANTRO: A key component of Latin American, Middle Eastern, and Southeast Asian cuisine, this pungent herb is the perfect finish to salsas and bean salads, and pairs beautifully with citrus. Cilantro is great with poultry and seafood dishes, or as a sprinkle to brighten up flavor.

PARSLEY: Often relegated to garnish duty, this overlooked herb is key to soups and stocks. A sprinkle on salads or over grilled fish (like **halibut**) adds a light, fresh taste. It is an essential component of tabbouleh and is great with grains, corn, and peas.

CHIVES: Chives have a slight onion flavor and are good to add to beef and potato dishes. They should be added close to the end of cooking to get the best flavor.

DILL: Great paired with smoked and fresh fish (like **halibut** and **sardines**), in salads, and with cabbage, green beans, beets, and **beet greens**. Dill can be added to potatoes, meat dishes, and stews.

SAGE: Excellent in stuffing, on poultry, and with veal. Sage is also delicious with pastas and in starchy bean dishes, like those made with **white beans**.

TARRAGON: The licorice flavor found in tarragon melds nicely with fish (like **halibut**) and chicken, as well as in salad dressings, veal, and egg dishes. It's also good with green vegetables like **kale, spinach,** asparagus, broccoli, green beans, and peas.

NUTMEG (AND OTHER SPICES LIKE ALLSPICE, GINGER, AND CLOVES): These sweet-spicy seasonings go very well with sweet potatoes and all forms of winter squash. **Spinach,** carrots, asparagus, and green beans also pair well with nutmeg.

PEPPER: Try pepper on everything! Freshly ground is the most flavorful.

CURRY POWDER: Curry powder is a blend of up to 20 different herbs and spices, including cardamom, cinnamon, coriander, nutmeg, and pepper. Use to flavor soups and stews, or to add a kick to the following Salt Solution Stars: **halibut, sardines, soybeans, spinach, kale,** and

beet greens. Mix with yogurt for a quick marinade or as a topper for Asian dishes.

CINNAMON: You know that cinnamon is delicious in baked goods, but you can also use it in savory dishes too. Try cinnamon on sweet potatoes and winter squashes or in chicken soups and stews.

CHILI POWDER: Add chili powder to chili, of course, but also to any Mexican or Tex-Mex dish for a rich and spicy flavor.

PAPRIKA: Paprika has a sweet and smoky flavor that's perfect for many dishes, including barbecue and chili, and the cuisines of India, Morocco, Europe, and the Middle East.

ALLSPICE: Allspice is used in Jamaican jerk seasonings and many soups, stews, and curries. It's pungent and fragrant and used in both savory and sweet foods. Try it in a **white bean** stew, with sweet potatoes, or in baked goods.

GINGER: Ginger provides a sweet and spicy note to many foods. Fresh ginger looks like a knobby root—peel and grate it into your recipes. Dried ginger is usually ground. Whatever type you use, ginger is perfect in Asian, North African, Indian, and Caribbean cuisines.

GARLIC: Like pepper, you can add garlic to everything for a salt-free flavor punch.

MINERAL BOOST JUICE OPTIONS

Your daily Mineral Boost Juice will help get you closer to your daily requirements for the Miracle Minerals—calcium, potassium, and magnesium. Depending on age and sex, adults need between 1,000 and 1,300 mg of calcium per day, 4,700 mg of potassium, and 310 to 420 mg of magnesium. Please note that each of these recipes makes 1 serving.

Almond, Blueberry, and Banana Smoothie

Combine 1½ cups plain unsweetened almond milk, ¾ of a medium frozen banana, 1 cup frozen or fresh blueberries, 1 cup chopped kale, 5 unsalted whole almonds, and 2 teaspoons honey in a blender. Puree until smooth, 1 to 2 minutes.

Calories: 323
Saturated Fat: 0 g
Fiber: 11 g
Sodium: 300 mg
Potassium: 957 mg
Calcium: 413 mg
Magnesium: 89 mg

Banana-Spinach Smoothie

Combine 1 medium frozen banana, 1 cup fresh spinach, 1 cup unsweetened plain soymilk, 2½ teaspoons unsalted almond butter, and 1 teaspoon honey in a blender. Puree until smooth, 1 to 2 minutes.

Calories: 319
Saturated Fat: 1 g
Fiber: 5 g
Sodium: 174 mg
Potassium: 805 mg
Calcium: 359 mg
Magnesium: 72 mg

Berry-Mango Smoothie

Combine 1 cup chopped kale, ¾ cup frozen mixed berries, ¾ cup fat-free milk, ½ medium frozen banana, ½ cup fresh or frozen mango cubes, and 2 teaspoons honey in a blender. Puree until smooth, 1 to 2 minutes.

Calories: 321
Saturated Fat: 1 g
Fiber: 4 g
Sodium: 191 mg
Potassium: 934 mg
Calcium: 526 mg
Magnesium: 88 mg

Mango-Avocado Smoothie

Combine ½ fresh mango, 1 cup fresh spinach, 1 cup chilled low-fat vanilla soymilk, ¼ Hass avocado, and 5 teaspoons agave nectar in a blender. Puree until smooth, 1 to 2 minutes.

Calories: 304
Saturated Fat: 1 g
Fiber: 6 g
Sodium: 145 mg
Potassium: 786 mg
Calcium: 343 mg
Magnesium: 79 mg

Orange-Banana Cream Smoothie

Combine 1 medium frozen banana, ¾ cup calcium-fortified orange juice, ½ cup fat-free milk, and 1 tablespoon honey in a blender. Puree until smooth, 1 to 2 minutes.

Calories: 293
Saturated Fat: 0 g
Fiber: 3 g
Sodium: 65 mg
Potassium: 947 mg
Calcium: 385 mg
Magnesium: 72 mg

Peanut Butter Smoothie

Combine ¾ medium banana, ½ cup fat-free vanilla yogurt, ½ cup fat-free milk, and 1 tablespoon unsalted natural creamy peanut butter in a blender. Puree until smooth, about 1 minute.

Calories: 325
Saturated Fat: 2 g
Fiber: 3 g
Sodium: 210 mg
Potassium: 891 mg
Calcium: 382 mg
Magnesium: 83 mg

THE 2-WEEK SALT SOLUTION CLEANSE MENUS

During the 2-Week Salt Solution Cleanse, we ask you to stick with the meals we provide here. We've organized 1 week's worth of meals into sample daily menus, with assigned time slots so you can see how you can space your meals and when to have your Mineral Boost Juice. You can even see how to squeeze in some desserts and snacks!

Keep in mind that the time slots in these menus are just suggestions. Your meal times will vary according to your schedule, but try to space your meals about 4 to 5 hours apart. Feel free to mix and match the meals in the menus in any order that works for you; and you can repeat the ones you like. Just don't have more than one dessert or snack each day. For instance, you could have Eggplant Parmesan for both lunch and dinner, with Chocolate Fondue as a dessert, but don't have Chocolate Fondue for both breakfast and a snack, or White Bean Hummus for a snack and Chocolate Fondue for dessert because that will leave you with only one "real" meal that day. To put together your own week's worth of menus, use the full list of options in "The 2-Week Salt Solution Cleanse Mix & Match Meals" (page 42).

Also, while you'll get the best results if you can stick to just these meals, if you are really strapped for time, substitute with one of the foods listed in "4-Week Ready-Made Meal Ideas" on page 66. These will be a better option than either starving yourself or cheating and scarfing down some fast food. But don't resort to these meals more than once a week.

THE 2-WEEK SALT SOLUTION CLEANSE MIX & MATCH MEALS

Breakfasts

Yogurt Parfait with Berries (page 43)

Cranberries-on-a-Banana (page 44)

Spinach Scramble (page 45)

Hot Couscous Bowl (page 47)

Soy Oatmeal (page 48)

Lunches and Dinners

Cinnamon Sweet Potato (page 47)

Sardine Salad (page 43)

Fish Taco (page 44)

Edamame Salad (page 46)

Tarragon Chicken Salad (page 45)

Steamed Salmon with Creamy Dill Sauce (page 46)

Eggplant Parmesan (page 42)

Pork and Beans (page 42)

Greens and Couscous Salad (page 48)

Mini Pizza (page 43)

Desserts and Snacks (limit the following desserts and snacks to no more than one per day)

Berry Kebabs (page 46)

Chocolate Fondue (page 45)

PB&J Graham (page 42)

Orange-Yogurt Pops (page 48)

White Bean Hummus (page 44)

WHAT ABOUT SALT SUBSTITUTES?

These products replace some or all of the sodium chloride (ordinary salt) with potassium chloride and/or lysine, and are fine to use (though you should consult your doctor if you have diabetes, a heart condition, high blood pressure, or kidney disease). But between the freshness of the ingredients and the combination of herbs and spices, you'll find that the Salt Solution meals are bursting with so much flavor that you won't need a salt substitute.

DAY
1

MINERAL BOOST JUICE (8:30 A.M.)

Almond, Blueberry, and Banana Smoothie (page 40)

Per serving: 323 calories, 300 mg sodium

MEAL 1: LUNCH (12:30 P.M.)

Eggplant Parmesan

Place 2 cups cubed eggplant in a baking dish, top with 2 ounces low-sodium mozzarella cheese, 1 medium tomato, chopped, and ½ teaspoon dried oregano. Bake at 375°F for 20 minutes or until tender. Serve with 1 cup beet greens (or spinach) sautéed in cooking spray with 1 clove minced garlic, until greens are wilted. Enjoy with 1 medium orange.

Per serving: 290 calories, 11 g fat, 6 g saturated fat, 20 g protein, 33 g carbohydrates, 12 g fiber, 104 mg sodium

MEAL 2: DINNER (5:30 P.M.)

Pork and Beans

Cook 2 ounces boneless pork loin. Top with 1 small tomato, chopped, 1 teaspoon chopped fresh parsley, and 1 teaspoon fresh lemon juice. Sprinkle with ¼ cup roasted unsalted soybeans. Serve with 1 cup steamed green beans sprinkled with 2 tablespoons slivered almonds.

Per serving: 285 calories, 14 g fat, 2 g saturated fat, 24 g protein, 18 g carbohydrates, 9 g fiber, 199 mg sodium

MEAL 3: DESSERT* (8:30 P.M.)

PB&J Graham

Spread 1 tablespoon unsalted peanut butter and 1 tablespoon all-fruit spread onto 1 graham cracker sheet. Serve with 1 cup fat-free milk.

Per serving: 283 calories, 10 g fat, 2 g saturated fat, 14 g protein, 35 g carbohydrates, 2 g fiber, 195 mg sodium

Do not have more than one dessert per day.

THE 2-WEEK SALT SOLUTION CLEANSE

43

DAY
2

MEAL 1: BREAKFAST (7:30 A.M.)
Yogurt Parfait with Berries

Layer 1 cup fat-free plain yogurt with 1 cup sliced strawberries and/or raspberries and 2 tablespoons walnuts.

Per serving: 282 calories, 9 g fat, 1 g saturated fat, 17 g protein, 33 g carbohydrates, 4 g fiber, 191 mg sodium

MINERAL BOOST JUICE (11:00 A.M.)
Banana-Spinach Smoothie (page 40)

Per serving: 319 calories, 174 mg sodium

MEAL 2: LUNCH (2:30 P.M.)
Sardine Salad

Add 1 teaspoon chopped fresh parsley, 1 teaspoon fresh lemon juice, and 1 small tomato, chopped, to 1 ounce cooked sardines (low-sodium canned sardines are okay). Serve on top of 2 cups spinach leaves. Dress salad with 1 tablespoon olive oil and $1\frac{1}{2}$ tablespoons toasted pine nuts.

Per serving: 293 calories, 26 g fat, 3 g saturated fat, 11 g protein, 7 g carbohydrates, 4 g fiber, 196 mg sodium

MEAL 3: DINNER (7:00 P.M.)
Mini Pizza

Top $\frac{1}{2}$ of a whole wheat English muffin with $\frac{1}{2}$ cup chopped tomatoes and 1 ounce low-sodium mozzarella cheese; toast until the cheese melts. Serve with a salad made from 2 cups spinach and 1 small carrot, chopped. Dress the salad with 1 teaspoon olive oil and 2 teaspoons fresh lemon juice. Enjoy with 1 medium orange.

Per serving: 286 calories, 10 g fat, 4 g saturated fat, 15 g protein, 39 g carbohydrates, 9 g fiber, 228 mg sodium

DAY
3

MEAL 1: BREAKFAST (8:00 A.M.)

Cranberries-on-a-Banana

Spread 1 tablespoon unsalted natural peanut butter on a medium peeled banana. Sprinkle with 2 tablespoons dried cranberries.

Per serving: 289 calories, 13 g fat, 3 g saturated fat, 7 g protein, 43 g carbohydrates, 5 g fiber, 6 mg sodium

MEAL 2: LUNCH (12:00 P.M.)

Fish Taco

Cook 3 ounces halibut in a nonstick pan. Just before the fish is cooked through, add 1 cup cooked corn kernels and 1 cup quartered cherry tomatoes. Serve with 1 corn tortilla (6" diameter) and 1 cup sliced jicama.

Per serving: 309 calories, 4 g fat, 1 g saturated fat, 24 g protein, 51 g carbohydrates, 13 g fiber, 110 mg sodium

MEAL 3: SNACK* (4:30 P.M.)

White Bean Hummus

Mash together $1/2$ cup cooked (or no-salt-added canned) white beans with 1 tablespoon olive oil, 2 teaspoons fresh lemon juice, and $1/2$ teaspoon ground cumin. Serve with $1/2$ of a whole wheat pita and 5 baby carrots for dipping.

Per serving: 298 calories, 14 g fat, 2 g saturated fat, 10 g protein, 34 g carbohydrates, 8 g fiber, 317 mg sodium

*Do not have more than one snack per day.

MINERAL BOOST JUICE (7:30 P.M.)

Mango-Avocado Smoothie (page 40)

Per serving: 304 calories, 145 mg sodium

MEAL 1: BREAKFAST (8:30 A.M.)

Spinach Scramble

Heat 2 cups spinach leaves in a nonstick skillet coated with cooking spray until wilted. Scramble with 1 egg. Serve on top of 1 slice toasted whole wheat bread. Enjoy with Broiled Brown Sugar Grapefruit (halve a grapefruit and sprinkle each half with 1 teaspoon brown sugar; broil until the sugar bubbles).

Per serving: 280 calories, 6 g fat, 2 g saturated fat, 13 g protein, 45 g carbohydrates, 6 g fiber, 257 mg sodium

MEAL 2: LUNCH (12:30 P.M.)

Tarragon Chicken Salad

Cube 2 ounces cooked chicken breast. Toss with 1 teaspoon chopped fresh tarragon, 1 tablespoon chopped pecans, 1 teaspoon fresh lemon juice, and 1 teaspoon olive oil. Serve over 2 cups spinach leaves. Enjoy with 1 cup mango slices.

Per serving: 296 calories, 12 g fat, 2 g saturated fat, 20 g protein, 31 g carbohydrates, 5 g fiber, 273 mg sodium

MINERAL BOOST JUICE (5:00 P.M.)

Orange-Banana Cream Smoothie
(page 41)

Per serving: 293 calories, 65 mg sodium

MEAL 3: DESSERT* (8:30 P.M.)

Chocolate Fondue

Dip 1 small banana (or $\frac{1}{2}$ of a large banana), sliced, $\frac{1}{2}$ cup cubed honeydew melon, and $\frac{1}{2}$ cup cubed cantaloupe into 1 ounce melted dark chocolate.

Per serving: 295 calories, 10 g fat, 6 g saturated fat, 3 g protein, 55 g carbohydrates, 6 g fiber, 36 mg sodium

Do not have more than one dessert per day.

DAY
5

MINERAL BOOST JUICE (7:30 A.M.)

Berry-Mango Smoothie (page 40)

Per serving: 321 calories, 191 mg sodium

MEAL 1: LUNCH (11:30 A.M.)

Edamame Salad

Combine $1/2$ cup cooked edamame with
$1/2$ cup cubed tofu, 1 small tomato, chopped,
2 teaspoons chopped fresh cilantro, and
2 teaspoons fresh lemon juice. Drizzle with
1 teaspoon peanut oil.

Per serving: 283 calories, 17 g fat, 3 g
saturated fat, 24 g protein, 15 g carbohydrates, 7 g fiber, 223 mg sodium

MEAL 2: SNACK* (4:00 P.M.)

Berry Kebabs

Arrange the following on wooden skewers: 1
cup cubed strawberries, 1 cup raspberries,
and 1 cup blackberries. Dip into a sauce made
from $3/4$ cup low-fat plain yogurt, 1 teaspoon
chopped fresh mint, 1 teaspoon brown sugar,
and 1 drop of vanilla extract.

Per serving: 305 calories, 5 g fat, 2 g saturated fat, 14 g protein, 57 g carbohydrates,
19 g fiber, 134 mg sodium

*Do not have more than one snack per day.

MEAL 3: DINNER (8:00 P.M.)

Steamed Salmon
with Creamy Dill Sauce

Steam 3 ounces salmon. Top with a sauce
made from $1/2$ cup fat-free plain yogurt,
1 teaspoon fresh dill, and 2 teaspoons fresh
lemon juice. Serve on top of 2 cups steamed
spinach. Sprinkle with 1 teaspoon sesame
seeds. Enjoy with 1 cup honeydew melon
cubes.

Per serving: 286 calories, 7 g fat, 2 g saturated fat, 29 g protein, 28 g carbohydrates,
3 g fiber, 213 mg sodium

DAY 6

MEAL 1: BREAKFAST (8:00 A.M.)

Hot Couscous Bowl

Combine ½ cup fat-free milk with ¾ cup cooked whole wheat couscous. Heat for a minute in the microwave. Top with 1 cup blueberries and 1 tablespoon chopped pecans.

Per serving: 304 calories, 6 g fat, 1 g saturated fat, 10 g protein, 56 g carbohydrates, 6 g fiber, 276 mg sodium

MEAL 2: LUNCH (12:00 P.M.)

1 Kind Nut Delight bar (page 66)

And 1 medium banana.

Per serving: 305 calories, 16 mg sodium

Note: *While the low-sodium bars and frozen meals on page 66 are okay in a pinch, you should limit these meals as much as possible during the Cleanse as they're not as nutritious as the Salt Solution Cleanse meals.*

MEAL 3: DINNER (5:00 P.M.)

Cinnamon Sweet Potato

Sprinkle 1 small baked sweet potato with ¼ cup dried cranberries, ½ teaspoon ground cinnamon, ¼ teaspoon cayenne pepper (optional), and ¼ cup plain fat-free yogurt. Serve with 1 cup steamed broccoli florets and 1 large apple.

Per serving: 307 calories, 1 g fat, 0 g saturated fat, 7 g protein, 74 g carbohydrates, 11 g fiber, 289 mg sodium

MINERAL BOOST JUICE (8:30 P.M.)

Peanut Butter Smoothie (page 41)

Per serving: 325 calories, 210 mg sodium

DAY

7

MEAL 1: BREAKFAST (7:30 A.M.)

Soy Oatmeal

Cook $1/2$ cup old-fashioned rolled oats according to package directions, using $3/4$ cup soymilk instead of milk or water. Top with $1/2$ small banana, sliced, and 1 teaspoon brown sugar.

Per serving: 299 calories, 6 g fat, 1 g saturated fat, 11 g protein, 53 g carbohydrates, 6 g fiber, 92 mg sodium

MINERAL BOOST JUICE (11:30 A.M.)

Banana-Spinach Smoothie (page 40)

Per serving: 319 calories, 174 mg sodium

MEAL 2: DINNER (5:30 P.M.)

Greens and Couscous Salad

In a nonstick pan, cook 2 cups spinach (or beet greens) with 2 cloves minced garlic until the greens are wilted. Combine the cooked greens with $3/4$ cup cooked whole wheat couscous. Top with a sauce made from $1/4$ cup fat-free plain yogurt, $1/2$ teaspoon ground cumin, and 1 teaspoon fresh lemon juice. Sprinkle with 2 tablespoons pine nuts.

Per serving: 301 calories, 12 g fat, 1 g saturated fat, 12 g protein, 38 g carbohydrates, 4 g fiber, 319 mg sodium

MEAL 3: DESSERT* (8:30 P.M.)

Orange-Yogurt Pops

Mix $1/2$ cup orange juice with $1/2$ cup fat-free vanilla yogurt. Add a drop of vanilla extract. Freeze in a freezer-pop mold. Enjoy with 25 almonds.

Per serving: 293 calories, 15 g fat, 1 g saturated fat, 14 g protein, 28 g carbohydrates, 4 g fiber, 97 mg sodium

*Do not have more than one dessert per day.

★ **SPINACH** ★

Chockful of calcium,
potassium, and magnesium

THE 4-WEEK SHAKE THE Salt Meal Plan

With your taste buds in check and your body in balance, you're ready to start the 4-Week Shake the Salt Meal Plan. By eating only 1,200 calories a day for 2 weeks with the Salt Solution Cleanse, you jump-start weight loss. Then by switching to 1,500 calories for the 4-Week Shake the Salt Meal Plan, you keep your metabolism on track and set yourself up for consistent weight loss. And you can keep repeating the 4-Week Meal Plan for months, or even a year, until you reach your final goal.

How to Shake the Salt

URING THIS PHASE YOU GET TONS of additional meals and recipes to choose from, loads of flexibility, and you get to eat more food! Here's a breakdown of how you'll be eating and living during this phase.

Increase Your Calories

One of the best ways to sabotage weight loss is by eating too little. At first this seems counter-intuitive—you want to lose weight, so you eat less, right? But once you start eating too little (the exact calorie amount varies from person to person), your body goes into "starvation mode" and starts conserving calories that it needs to perform your basic body functions. The reason the Cleanse lasts just 2 weeks is that your metabolism will slow down (as will your weight loss) if you stay on such a low-calorie diet for a prolonged period of time. That's why during the 4-Week Shake the Salt Meal Plan, you will eat *four* 300-calorie meals per day (300 more calories per day than the Cleanse) and have a daily Mineral Boost Juice. So don't be tempted to skip meals in order to save calories! You'll just make it harder to lose weight.

If you find you're hungry, check out "The Salt Solution Freebies" list (page 37). It includes nutrient-dense, low-calorie foods you can use to add "bulk" to your meals without adding significant calories. But before you do, be sure your appetite is "real" hunger (hunger of the body), as opposed to "phony" hunger (hunger in the mind). Phony hunger tends to come on fast and accompanies a gnawing feeling of urgency as well as a craving for something specific—like brownies or cheese puffs. Real hunger, on the other hand, comes on slowly, accompanies a growling stomach, and can be satisfied with a variety of foods.

Add Variety

You get more food during this phase, and more flexibility! While we asked you not to swap out ingredients in a meal during the 2-Week Salt Solution Cleanse, during this phase, you can swap out foods within a meal as long as you substitute like foods for like foods within the building blocks. Swap lean protein (chicken) for lean protein (fish, turkey, etc.); a fruit for a fruit; a grain for a grain (one slice of bread for $\frac{1}{2}$ cup rice); almonds for walnuts, etc.

And if you find a few favorite meals you really like, by all means feel free to repeat them as many times as you like. For the best balance in nutrition, though (and to stave off boredom), we do encourage you to choose a variety of meals with different foods.

Also, during the 4-Week Shake the Salt Meal Plan, if you want to add some other beverages for variety, feel free to do so. Just be careful to account for the added calories. You'll lose weight and inches faster if you stick with the calorie- and carbonation-free choices you've been drinking on the Cleanse: plain water and unsweetened hot or cold brewed green, red, white, black, or herbal tea.

SALT SOLUTION PANTRY STAPLES

Clear out the salty processed foods and restock with these Salt Solution pantry must-haves:

- Dried herbs and spices (see "The Salt Solution Seasoning Guide" on page 38)
- Low-sodium seasonings like Mrs. Dash and Spice Hunter
- Vinegars like sherry vinegar, red wine vinegar, champagne vinegar, and rice vinegar
- Olive oil
- Canned fruit (packed in its own juice or water, not heavy syrup)
- Low-sodium or no-salt-added canned vegetables, including tomato products
- Low-sodium or no-salt-added canned or dehydrated soups, broth, and bouillon
- Whole grain and low-sodium bread
- Whole grain pasta
- Brown rice
- Unsalted seeds and nuts, such as almonds and walnuts
- Dried peas, beans, and lentils (including Salt Solution Stars such as white beans)
- No-salt-added or low-sodium canned peas, beans, and lentils (including Salt Solution Stars such as white beans)
- Roasted soybeans (a Salt Solution Star)
- Low-sodium canned fish (including Salt Solution Stars such as sardines)
- Low-sodium ready-to-eat cereals and oatmeal
- Unsalted popcorn and pretzels

SALT SOLUTION FRIDGE STAPLES

Clear out the salty processed foods and restock with these Salt Solution fridge must-haves:

- ☑ Fresh herbs (see "The Salt Solution Seasoning Guide" on page 38)
- ☑ Onions
- ☑ Fruits (including Salt Solution Stars such as bananas)
- ☑ Vegetables (including Salt Solution Stars such as beet greens, kale, spinach, and sweet potatoes)
- ☑ Low-fat or fat-free milk and yogurt (both are Salt Solution Stars)
- ☑ Soymilk (a Salt Solution Star)
- ☑ Low-fat, fat-free, or reduced-fat cheeses with low sodium, such as ricotta, mozzarella, and Swiss
- ☑ Fresh lean meats, poultry, and fish that haven't been seasoned or breaded
- ☑ Lemons
- ☑ Limes
- ☑ Eggs and egg substitutes
- ☑ Low-sodium salsas and other low-sodium condiments
- ☑ Unsalted margarine or butter
- ☑ Water

SALT SOLUTION FREEZER STAPLES

Clear out the salty processed foods and restock with these Salt Solution freezer must-haves:

- ☑ Frozen fruit (unsweetened varieties)
- ☑ Frozen vegetables—varieties without added butter, sauces, or seasoning (including Salt Solution Stars such as spinach and edamame)
- ☑ Frozen lean cuts of meat, poultry, and fish that haven't been seasoned or breaded

Track Your Progress

Weekly (not daily!) weigh-ins provide a better gauge of where you are in the pounds department. Just be sure to weigh yourself at the same time (preferably in the morning), on the same day of the week, using the same scale. And for best results, weigh yourself in the buff. Be aware that the scale is not the only way to measure progress: Take body measurements with a tape measure, compare personal photos over time, and assess the fit of your clothing to monitor your improvements.

You should lose about 1 to 2 pounds a week on the Shake the Salt Meal Plan. If you are carefully following the plan and still not dropping pounds, you can try a few things:

- **Exercise.** If you are already working out, pick it up a notch. If you have yet to lace up those sneakers and get moving, start now. The Salt Solution Weight-Loss Workout (page 346) has been specifically designed to help you lose weight while you reduce sodium.

- **Go back to the Cleanse.** If you have completed the 4-Week Meal Plan, then go back to the Salt Solution Cleanse for a week or two. The Cleanse is a good go-to plan that you can use again and again to either jump-start weight loss, or to detox after a decadent vacation. However, as mentioned above, the Cleanse is too low in calories to follow for long-term weight loss, and should be used no more than twice in a 4-month period.

Be a Sodium Sleuth

Since you've made a commitment to cook the Salt Solution way, you're already a step ahead of everyone else in living a low-salt lifestyle. But you still need to be careful not to sabotage your good work by picking up packages in the grocery aisles that might be full of sodium. The good news is that more and more low-sodium products are becoming available. In 2003, the United Kingdom introduced a voluntary strategy to decrease the sodium content of processed and packaged food, which has resulted in reductions of 20 to 30 percent in most processed food sold in stores. Meanwhile, New York City's health department has called on restaurant chains and food producers to lower the amount of salt in their products by 25 percent over the next 5 years, spurring even more food companies, like Starbucks and H.J. Heinz Co., to jump aboard the low-sodium train.[1, 2]

In April 2010, a report released by the Institute of Medicine recommended a new, coordinated approach to gradually reduce sodium content in food, one requiring new government standards for acceptable levels.[3] Some of the ways food manufacturers are trying to reduce the amount of sodium in products are space-age: PepsiCo Inc. is actually developing a new shape for salt crystals that will reduce the amount of sodium sprinkled onto chips without affecting taste.

But there's no need to wait for new products to appear before you start making changes. Follow these guidelines to find the lowest-sodium options available now.

- **Look at labels.** In general, you'll want to choose foods with no more than 300 milligrams of sodium per serving. A good rule of thumb is that a serving of food should not contain more milligrams of sodium than it does calories. Or, just stick to the meals in the Salt Solution plan—they all contain about 300 milligrams of sodium.

- **Compare and contrast.** It seems wrong that one brand of whole wheat bread might have much less sodium per slice than another brand. But this happens all the time. Check out the labels on foods you buy frequently. Once you know which brands offer the lowest sodium, stick with them.

- **Plan ahead.** If you are going out to eat, doing a bit of research ahead of time can ensure that you'll already know your low-sodium options in advance and what questions you need to ask. This can help you make the best possible low-sodium choices, as well as avoid a last-minute meal decision that will lead to soaring sodium levels. Many restaurants and fast-food chains have their menus available online, or you can ask for a nutrition fact sheet once you get there. Also, if you know ahead of time that you will be eating out later, go extra light on the sodium throughout the day so you can cheat a little more at night. The bad news is that we can't always rely on our taste buds to indicate high-sodium meals—salt is often hidden where we least expect it.

4-Week Shake the Salt Meal Plan Basics

Mix & Match Meals and Recipes: Have Four per Day

The 4-Week Shake the Salt Meal Plan is a mix and match meal plan. You will eat four 300-calorie meals per day; each meal will have approximately 300 milligrams of sodium. Again, be sure to eat every 4 to 5 hours. Your body needs frequent refueling, just like a car, and eating regularly helps prevent extreme hunger (and the overeating that often goes with it).

During this phase you can choose any recipes in this book (or *The Salt Solution* book), or any of the meals from the 2-Week Salt Solution Cleanse, to provide you with your four daily meals—they all have the right number of calories and sodium. You can move them around or swap them out at will. For example, a breakfast meal can be eaten for dinner; a snack can be eaten as breakfast, and a lunch meal as a snack. Again, you may repeat meals that you find most enjoyable if you wish, but variety is strongly encouraged. Desserts and sweet snacks should be limited to no more than one per day as they're not as nutritious as the savory snacks or the breakfast, lunch, and dinner meals. (Also, in a pinch, you can select from the "4-Week Ready-Made Meal Ideas" on page 66, but try to limit them to once or twice a week as they are higher in sodium and lower in nutrients than the Salt Solution meals and recipes.)

Mineral Boost Juice: Have One per Day

As in the 2-Week Salt Solution Cleanse, you will continue to have one daily Mineral Boost Juice—a smoothie pumped with calcium, magnesium, and potassium, the minerals depleted by excess sodium. Again, you can choose from the six versions of the Mineral Boost Juice. Mix and match them any way you please. See page 40 for recipes.

How to Build Your Own
Salt Solution Meals

FOR THE DURATION OF the 4-Week Shake the Salt Meal Plan, it's probably best to stick with meals and recipes you'll find in this book or *The Salt Solution*, which have been carefully designed to give you the right balance of nutrients. The meals and recipes in this plan are low in sodium; high in calcium, magnesium, and potassium; and have just the right balance of protein, carbs, and fats—not to mention they're tasty!

Once you've become accustomed to eating the Salt Solution way, we encourage you to experiment and make your own meals. It's easy! Just follow the structure of a Salt Solution meal, which is designed to have:

- One serving of Protein
- One serving of Dairy
- One serving of Produce
- One serving of Grains
- One serving of Fat

If you use the serving sizes listed in "The Salt Solution Meal Building Blocks" (below), you won't even have to count calories.

Just remember your target number is 300—no more than 300 calories or 300 milligrams of sodium per meal. You'll also want to keep the filling fiber in your meals high (at least 5 grams) and the heart-harming bad fats in your diet low (no more than 3 grams). Stick with the building-block foods listed below and you'll be all set. And be sure to include the Salt Solution Stars as often as possible.

Keep in mind it's best to try this only after you've carefully followed the 2-Week Salt Solution Cleanse and the 4-Week Shake the Salt Meal Plan for a few weeks. Those meals and recipes will teach you about portion size and meal components, making it that much easier for you to create your own Salt Solution meals.

The Salt Solution Meal Building Blocks

- **Protein** (a serving is about 75 calories)
  1 to 3 ounces cooked lean meat, poultry, or fish; $\frac{1}{3}$ cup tofu; $\frac{1}{3}$ cup cooked beans or lentils; 1 egg; $\frac{1}{3}$ cup 1% or 2% low-sodium cottage cheese; $1\frac{1}{2}$ ounces reduced-fat hard or semi-hard cheese; 1 ounce regular cheese*; 1 tablespoon unsalted natural peanut butter or nut butter*
  *If you have this higher-fat choice, then you have used up a fat serving, too.

- **Dairy** (a serving is around 50 calories)
  $\frac{1}{2}$ cup fat-free milk or 1% milk or $\frac{1}{4}$ cup low-fat or fat-free plain yogurt; $\frac{1}{2}$ cup calcium-enriched soymilk; 1 ounce reduced-fat hard or semi-hard cheese; $\frac{1}{2}$ ounce regular cheese*
  *If you have this higher-fat choice, then you have used up a fat serving, too.

- **Produce** (a serving is about 50 calories; have two fruit and three vegetable servings daily)
  Fruit: a medium-size fruit or 1 cup chopped fruit or berries; $\frac{1}{2}$ cup grapes; 2 tablespoons dried fruit; $\frac{1}{2}$ cup fruit juice. You can choose any fruit, but be sure to include apples,

Calories: around 300
Saturated fat: no more than 3 grams

Fiber: at least 5 grams
Sodium: no more than 300 milligrams

apricots, bananas, dates, grapefruit, grapefruit juice, grapes, oranges, mangoes, melons, peaches, pineapples, raisins, strawberries, and tangerines.

OR

Vegetables: 2 cups raw leafy vegetables; 1 cup chopped nonleafy vegetables; 1 cup cooked vegetables. You can choose any, but be sure to include beet greens, broccoli, carrots, collards, cucumbers, green beans, green peas, kale, lima beans, potatoes, spinach, squash, sweet potatoes, and tomatoes.

- **Grains** (a serving is about 75 calories)

$\frac{1}{2}$ cup cooked brown rice, whole wheat pasta, or hot whole grain cereal; about 1 cup cold whole grain cereal; 1 slice whole grain bread; 1 tortilla (6"); $\frac{1}{2}$ medium bagel or English muffin

- **Fat** (a serving is about 50 calories)

1 teaspoon olive or canola oil; 3 tablespoons chopped avocado; 1 tablespoon unsalted nuts; 1 tablespoon ground flaxseeds; 2 teaspoons unsalted natural peanut or nut butter or tahini; 8 olives

SAMPLE 1

Spread 1 tablespoon peanut butter on 1 slice whole grain bread, top with 1 medium banana, sliced. Serve with $\frac{1}{2}$ cup calcium-enriched soymilk.

SAMPLE 2

Stir together 1 chopped hard-boiled egg, ½ cup chopped carrots, ½ cup chopped cucumber, and 3 tablespoons chopped avocado. Spread on 1 whole grain tortilla (6"). Serve with 1 ounce reduced-fat mozzarella string cheese.

SAMPLE 3

Sauté ½ cup chopped tomatoes and 1 cup spinach leaves in a skillet coated with cooking spray. Serve the sauce on ½ cup cooked whole wheat pasta; top with 3 ounces grilled chicken breast. Grate 1 ounce Parmesan cheese on top.

Five Secrets to Salt Solution Success

CHANGING YOUR HABITS, LIFESTYLE, and diet takes time and patience, and we understand it can seem a bit overwhelming, but just take it one day at a time and soon you'll be slimmer, healthier, and happier! Here are our five favorite secrets (recommended by our test panelists!) to success that will help you live the Salt Solution way.

1 **Change for life.** The Salt Solution isn't a diet that you go on or go off—think of it as a lifestyle change. This means that you should be in it for the long haul, and if you make a mistake one day and eat a high-sodium fast-food sandwich, don't beat yourself up. Living low-salt is a learning process, and it will take time to get fully comfortable with the program.

Instead of thinking that you have to be 100 percent perfect right off the bat, celebrate small victories at first. Did you go a whole week following the Salt Solution plan? Celebrate—walk with a friend, see a movie, try on clothes (you'll probably notice them fitting better!). Once you've met some short-term goals, making the long-term lifestyle changes will seem a lot less daunting.

2 **Seek out sodium swaps.** *The Salt Solution* book is a great source for low-sodium foods, but you are also going to have to be your own sodium detective. Before you go to a restaurant, look for nutrition information online so you'll know what the best low-salt

choices are. At the supermarket, read labels—you'll be shocked at how the same types of food can have vastly different sodium contents. Once you find brands you love, stock up so you're never without your favorite low-salt products.

3 **Keep a journal.** Studies have shown that people stick with diet programs longer if they write down their progress. Get a journal, or keep a spreadsheet on your computer, and record what you eat, how you feel when you're eating (i.e., hungry, sad, happy, etc.), and when you exercise. Over time you'll be able to see patterns, like if you always tend to crave salty foods at certain times of the month, or if you tend to overeat if you're feeling down. Once you recognize these patterns, you'll be better able to change them. We've created *The Salt Solution Journal* (available at www.prevention.com/shop or 800-848-4735) to help you do this, but you can also make your own. Or, if you prefer to track electronically, try the free My Health Trackers at www.prevention.com/healthtracker.

4 **Manage hunger.** Don't let yourself get too hungry, because extreme hunger leads to overeating. Small, frequent meals help manage hunger and prevent binges. Eating nutrient- and fiber-packed foods, like those you'll be eating with the Salt Solution plan, also helps keep hunger at bay.

To ensure that you never get too hungry, plan ahead. Bring your favorite low-salt, healthy snacks to the office. Stash them in your kitchen, in your car, and in your gym bag. If you always have something low-sodium and healthy to eat, you won't be tempted by salty snacks.

5 **Pass on perfection.** We'll say it again: We don't expect you to be 100 percent perfect. We know there will be some times when you'll get off track—you're stuck in a meeting without low-sodium snacks, you're on vacation, or you're at your in-laws' for a holiday meal. And everyone needs to indulge once in a while! What's important is that you don't let one salty slipup start a downward spiral. Skip the guilt and negative self-talk and recommit to the program. And if you have a few weeks or even months off the Salt Solution plan, consider restarting the 2-Week Salt Solution Cleanse. This will get you back on track with the plan in no time.

Before you toss that soup, entrée, or pizza into your shopping cart, turn that package over and investigate. Swapping one brand and flavor of packaged food for another can save you hundreds of milligrams in sodium per serving.

Frozen Dinners (per serving)

HIGH-SODIUM FOOD	LOW-SODIUM FOOD	SODIUM SAVINGS
Stouffer's White Meat Turkey Pot Pie (1,200 mg sodium)	Kashi Mayan Harvest Bake (380 mg sodium)	820 mg
El Monterey XX Large Bean & Cheese Burrito (740 mg sodium)	Amy's Light in Sodium Bean & Cheese Burrito (290 mg sodium)	450 mg
Stouffer's Chicken Enchiladas with Cheese Sauce & Rice (720 mg sodium)	Amy's Light in Sodium Black Bean Enchilada (380 mg sodium)	340 mg
Stouffer's Chicken & Broccoli Pasta Bake (990 mg sodium)	Celentano Vegetarian Penne with Roasted Vegetables (290 mg sodium)	700 mg
Wanchai Ferry Kung Pao Chicken (1,260 mg sodium)	Ethnic Gourmet Lemongrass & Basil Chicken (310 mg sodium)	950 mg
Hungry Man Sweet & Sour Chicken (1,400 mg sodium)	Kashi Sweet & Sour Chicken (380 mg sodium)	1,020 mg
Stouffer's Five Cheese Lasagna (960 mg sodium)	Amy's Light in Sodium Vegetable Lasagna (340 mg sodium)	620 mg
Banquet Meatloaf (1,000 mg sodium)	Amy's Light in Sodium Veggie Loaf Whole Meal (340 mg sodium)	660 mg
Michelina's Budget Gourmet Stir Fry Rice & Vegetables (530 mg sodium)	Amy's Light in Sodium Brown Rice & Vegetables Bowl (270 mg sodium)	260 mg
Celentano Eggplant Parmigiana (730 mg sodium)	Celentano Vegetarian Vegan Eggplant Parmigiana (460 mg sodium)	270 mg

Soup, Chili, and Broth (per cup)

HIGH-SODIUM FOOD	LOW-SODIUM FOOD	SODIUM SAVINGS
Progresso Lentil Soup (810 mg sodium)	**Amy's Light in Sodium Organic Lentil Soup** (290 mg sodium)	520 mg
Pacific Organic Butternut Squash Soup (550 mg sodium)	**Pacific Organic Light Sodium Butternut Squash Soup** (280 mg sodium)	270 mg
Campbell's Chunky Fully Loaded Beef and Bean Chili (880 mg sodium)	**Amy's Light In Sodium Chili** (340 mg sodium)	540 mg
Progresso Homestyle Minestrone (690 mg sodium)	**Healthy Choice Minestrone** (360 mg sodium)	330 mg
Progresso Rich & Hearty Steak and Roasted Russet Potatoes (690 mg sodium)	**Healthy Choice Steak and Noodle** (340 mg sodium)	350 mg
Progresso Hearty Black Bean (690 mg sodium)	**Health Valley No Salt Added Organic Black Bean Soup** (25 mg sodium)	665 mg
Campbell's Chicken Broccoli Cheese and Potato Soup (880 mg sodium)	**Imagine Light in Sodium Organic Creamy Red Bliss Potato & Roasted Garlic Soup** (220 mg sodium)	660 mg
Progresso Hearty Tomato (690 mg sodium)	**Imagine Light in Sodium Organic Creamy Garden Tomato Soup** (300 mg sodium)	390 mg
Campbell's Chunky Chicken Noodle Soup (790 mg sodium)	**Campbell's Low Sodium Chicken with Noodles Soup** (140 mg sodium)	650 mg
Campbell's Cream of Mushroom Soup (870 mg sodium)	**Campbell's Low Sodium Cream of Mushroom Soup** (60 mg sodium)	810 mg

Beans and Veggies (per serving)

HIGH-SODIUM FOOD	LOW-SODIUM FOOD	SODIUM SAVINGS
Ortega Refried Beans (570 mg sodium)	Amy's Light in Sodium Refried Beans (220 mg sodium)	350 mg
Goya Black Beans (460 mg sodium)	Goya Low Sodium Black Beans (125 mg sodium)	335 mg
Progresso Chick Peas (280 mg sodium)	Eden Organic Garbanzo Beans (30 mg sodium)	250 mg
Green Giant Regular Cut Green Beans (400 mg sodium)	Green Giant Cut Green Beans 50 Percent Less Sodium (200 mg sodium)	200 mg
Del Monte Sweet Peas (390 mg sodium)	Del Monte Fresh Cut No Salt Added Sweet Peas (10 mg sodium)	380 mg
Goya Cannellini Beans (390 mg sodium)	Eden Organic Cannellini Beans (40 mg sodium)	350 mg
Goya Green Lima Beans (330 mg sodium)	Eden Organic Baby Lima Beans (35 mg sodium)	295 mg
S&W Whole Kernel Corn (360 mg sodium)	Green Giant Whole Kernel Sweet Corn 50 Percent Less Sodium (180 mg sodium)	180 mg
S&W Asparagus Spears (365 mg sodium)	Green Giant Cut Asparagus Spears 50 Percent Less Sodium (210 mg sodium)	155 mg
Del Monte Fresh Cut Green Beans (390 mg sodium)	Del Monte Fresh Cut No Salt Added Green Beans (10 mg sodium)	380 mg

Dairy and Cheese (per serving)

HIGH-SODIUM FOOD	LOW-SODIUM FOOD	SODIUM SAVINGS
Friendship 1% Lowfat Cottage Cheese (360 mg sodium)	**Friendship 1% Lowfat No Salt Added Cottage Cheese** (60 mg sodium)	300 mg
Sargento String Cheese (210 mg sodium)	**Sargento Reduced Sodium String Cheese** (110 mg sodium)	100 mg
Tillamook Sliced Colby Jack (190 mg sodium)	**Sargento Reduced Sodium Colby-Jack Cheese** (90 mg sodium)	100 mg
Land O Lakes Muenster Cheese (180 mg sodium)	**Alpine Lace Reduced Sodium Muenster Cheese** (135 mg sodium)	45 mg
Land O Lakes Salted Butter (95 mg sodium)	**Land O Lakes Unsalted Butter** (0 mg sodium)	95 mg
Kraft Natural Shredded Fat-Free Mozzarella (280 mg sodium)	**Sargento Shredded Reduced Sodium Mozzarella Cheese** (140 mg sodium)	140 mg
Kraft Cheddar Classic Melts Four Cheese Shredded (380 mg sodium)	**Sargento Shredded Reduced Sodium Mild Cheddar Cheese** (135 mg sodium)	245 mg
Sargento Deli Style Sliced Provolone Cheese (190 mg sodium)	**Sargento Reduced Sodium Provolone Cheese** (100 mg sodium)	90 mg
Alpine Lace Swiss Cheese (115 mg sodium)	**Finlandia Sandwich Naturals Imported Swiss Cheese** (62 mg sodium)	53 mg
Kraft Deli Deluxe American Cheese Slices (310 mg sodium)	**Organic Valley Sliced Cheddar Cheese** (130 mg sodium)	180 mg

While the following are good in a pinch, you should limit these meals to no more than once or twice a week; they're not as nutritious as the Salt Solution meals.

Bars

Look for bars with no more than 250 calories, 300 milligrams of sodium, or 3 grams of saturated fat, and with at least 3 grams of fiber. Have a piece of fruit or a serving of vegetables with each bar to make it a Salt Solution meal.

BAR (PER BAR)	CALORIES	SODIUM (MILLIGRAMS)	SATURATED FAT (GRAMS)	FIBER (GRAMS)
CLIF Apricot	230	125	0.5	5
CLIF Black Cherry Almond	250	110	1.5	5
CLIF Chocolate Brownie	240	150	1.5	5
CLIF Crunchy Peanut Butter	250	230	1	5
KIND Fruit & Nut Delight	170	25	1.5	4
KIND Nut Delight	200	15	2	4
KIND Walnut & Date	150	40	1	3
Lärabar Apple Pie	190	10	1	5
Lärabar Banana Bread	230	0	1	5
Lärabar Chocolate Coconut	240	0	2.5	5
Lärabar Ginger Snap	240	0	1	6
LUNA Chai Tea	190	95	2.5	3
LUNA Lemon Zest	180	115	2	3
LUNA Nutz Over Chocolate	180	190	2	4
LUNA S'mores	180	140	2	3

Frozen Meals

Look for meals with around 300 calories, no more than 400 milligrams of sodium or 3 grams of saturated fat, and with at least 3 grams of fiber.

FROZEN MEAL (PER MEAL)	CALORIES	SODIUM (MILLIGRAMS)	SATURATED FAT (GRAMS)	FIBER (GRAMS)
Amy's Light in Sodium Bean & Cheese Burrito	330	290	2.5	7
Amy's Light in Sodium Bean & Rice Burrito	320	290	1	8
Amy's Light in Sodium Black Bean Enchilada	320	380	1	3
Amy's Light in Sodium Brown Rice & Vegetables Bowl	260	270	1	5
Amy's Light in Sodium Indian Mattar Paneer	320	390	1.5	6
Amy's Light in Sodium Veggie Loaf Whole Meal	290	340	1	10
Celentano Vegetarian Penne with Roasted Vegetables	300	290	1	8
Kashi Black Bean Mango	340	380	1	7
Kashi Mayan Harvest Bake	340	380	1	8
Kashi Sweet & Sour Chicken	320	380	0.5	6

Soups

Look for soups with no more than 200 calories, 300 milligrams of sodium, or 3 grams of saturated fat, and with at least 2 grams of fiber. Double the serving if the soup is 100 calories or less, and have a piece of fruit or a serving of vegetables with each soup to make it a Salt Solution meal.

SOUP (PER CUP)	CALORIES	SODIUM (MILLIGRAMS)	SATURATED FAT (GRAMS)	FIBER (GRAMS)
Amy's Light in Sodium Organic Butternut Squash Soup	100	290	0	2
Amy's Light in Sodium Organic Lentil Soup	180	290	1	6
Campbell's Low Sodium Chicken with Noodles Soup	160	140	2	2
Health Valley No Salt Added Organic Black Bean Soup	130	25	0	5
Health Valley No Salt Added Organic Potato Leek Soup	100	290	0	3
Imagine Light in Sodium Organic Creamy Garden Tomato Soup	80	300	0	2
Imagine Light in Sodium Organic Creamy Red Bliss Potato & Roasted Garlic Soup	100	220	0	2
Progresso Reduced Sodium Chicken Gumbo Soup	70	35	0.5	2

No matter your motivation or situation, if you're hoping to lose weight, improve health, or break your salt addiction, the Salt Solution will work for you. We tested it on 16 real men and women (just like you!) with exceptional results.

In just 2 weeks, you can lose up to $10\frac{1}{2}$ pounds and 5 inches while you reset your taste buds, like panelists Shannon Ferry, a 35-year-old teacher who lost 10.6 pounds and 5 inches, and Robin Scholtz, a 45-year-old order-entry assistant who shed 10.4 pounds and $4\frac{3}{4}$ inches. "By sticking to the initial 2-Week Cleanse, I was able to break my salt habit and clear my system of all the toxins, including sodium," says Robin. "This made sticking to the plan and changing my lifestyle so much easier!"

During the next phase, the 4-Week Shake the Salt Meal Plan, you'll keep on losing—altogether, over 6 weeks, women can lose up to 18 pounds and $11\frac{1}{2}$ inches, and men can expect to lose even more. Shannon's final weight loss was 18.4 pounds and $11\frac{1}{2}$ inches; Robin lost a total of 14.8 pounds and

$12\frac{1}{4}$ inches. And one panelist—Mark Fatzinger, a 39-year-old teacher—lost an impressive 34.8 pounds and $8\frac{3}{4}$ inches!

But the Salt Solution is not just about dropping pounds and inches. Our 16 panelists also improved many aspects of their health. Most significantly decreased their blood pressure, and many dramatically improved their blood sugar numbers, as well their cholesterol and triglyceride numbers. In fact, Mark's blood sugar numbers improved so much that he no longer needs insulin. All of the panelists reported increased energy, better moods, and improved self-esteem! Says Michael Tonno, a 52-year-old saleman who dropped a total of 19.8 pounds, "Sometimes I find myself going for a jog at 10 p.m. I never had the energy to do that before!"

Like our panelists, by the time you are done with this 6-week program, you'll be slimmer, have better health, be more energetic, and will be well on your way to living the Salt Solution way for life.

YOGURT

Loaded with calcium,
potassium, and magnesium

Breakfast

Mexican-Style Scrambled Eggs

Silken tofu has a soft, creamy texture that melds perfectly with scrambled eggs, and, like all tofu, it is a wealth of nutrients and soy protein.

Prep time: 20 minutes ⊳ **Cook time:** 10 minutes ⊳ **Total time:** 30 minutes ⊳ MAKES 4 SERVINGS

6 ounces lite silken tofu

2 large eggs

3 large egg whites

2 tablespoons olive oil

3 scallions, finely chopped

1/8 teaspoon turmeric

2 plum tomatoes, seeded and chopped

1 jalapeño chile pepper, seeded and minced (wear plastic gloves when handling)

1/3 cup shredded reduced-fat Cheddar cheese

1 ounce baked tortilla chips (about 1 cup), broken into large pieces

3/4 cup fresh cilantro, chopped

1 cantaloupe, cut into 4 wedges

1. Place the tofu on paper towels and let stand for 5 minutes so the paper towels absorb some of the excess water. Beat the whole eggs and egg whites in a small bowl until blended.

2. Heat the oil in a medium nonstick skillet over medium-high heat. Cook the tofu for 1 minute, stirring to break it up, or until the texture of scrambled eggs. Stir in the scallions and turmeric. Cook for 3 minutes, stirring, or until the scallions soften. Reduce the heat to medium-low and add the egg mixture, tomatoes, and jalapeño.

3. Cook for 2 minutes, stirring, or until the eggs are softly scrambled but still moist and creamy. Add the cheese and cook for 1 minute, or until the cheese melts. Stir in the tortilla chips and cilantro. Serve the eggs with the cantaloupe.

Per serving: 247 calories, 13 g fat, 2 g saturated fat, 13 g protein, 21 g carbohydrates, 2 g fiber, 280 mg sodium

Easy Veggie Omelet

For added convenience use prewashed spinach, presliced mushrooms, and prechopped onion and garlic.

Prep time: 10 minutes ⁑ **Cook time:** 10 minutes ⁑ **Total time:** 20 minutes ⁑ MAKES 1 SERVING

¼ cup blueberries

¼ cup quartered strawberries

¼ cup raspberries

1 teaspoon canola oil

½ cup chopped fresh spinach

¼ cup chopped onion

¼ cup sliced mushrooms

1 clove garlic, minced

3 large egg whites, lightly beaten

¼ cup shredded reduced-fat, low-sodium Cheddar cheese

1 slice multigrain bread, toasted

1. Combine the blueberries, strawberries, and raspberries in a small bowl. Set aside.

2. Heat the oil in a small nonstick skillet over medium-high heat. Cook the spinach, onion, mushrooms, and garlic for 3 minutes, stirring occasionally, or until the vegetables start to soften.

3. Add the egg whites and cook for 4 minutes, turning once, or until set. Sprinkle with the cheese and cook for 1 minute, or until melted. Transfer to a plate and serve with the fruit and toast.

Per serving: 261 calories, 8 g fat, 2 g saturated fat, 22 g protein, 29 g carbohydrates, 8 g fiber, 303 mg sodium

Eggs Benedict

This recipe is perfect for entertaining. Make the sauce a day ahead of time and reheat it in the microwave.

Prep time: 15 minutes ⇒ **Cook time:** 15 minutes ⇒ **Total time:** 30 minutes ⇒ MAKES 4 SERVINGS

1 tablespoon unsalted butter or margarine

1 tablespoon unbleached all-purpose flour

$1/2$ cup low-fat (1%) milk

$1/2$ teaspoon grated lemon zest

1 tablespoon fresh lemon juice

$1/8$ teaspoon ground black pepper

2 tablespoons olive oil

1 ounce slice low-sodium ham, cut into 4 pieces

1 bag (6 ounces) baby spinach

4 large eggs

2 light multigrain English muffins, split and toasted

1. Fill a large, deep skillet with water and bring to a simmer.

2. Melt the butter in a small saucepan over low heat. Stir in the flour and cook for 1 minute. Whisk in the milk. Cook, stirring, until the sauce comes to a simmer and thickens. Simmer, stirring, for 4 minutes. Remove the pan from the heat; stir in the lemon zest, lemon juice, and pepper. Cover to keep warm.

3. Heat the oil in a large skillet over medium-high heat. Cook the ham for 1 minute, turning, or until hot and lightly browned. Remove to a plate. Add the spinach and cook for 3 minutes, stirring, or until wilted. Set aside.

4. Crack the eggs, one at a time, into the simmering water. Cook for 4 minutes, or until the whites are set but the yolks are still runny.

5. Divide the muffins among 4 plates. Top each muffin half with a piece of ham, one-fourth of the spinach, 1 egg, and 2 tablespoons of the sauce.

Per serving: 253 calories, 16 g fat, 4 g saturated fat, 13 g protein, 20 g carbohydrates, 6 g fiber, 300 mg sodium

Arugula Omelet

For a change of pace, vary the vegetables—using tomato or zucchini—and try shredded mozzarella cheese instead of goat cheese.

Prep time: 10 minutes ⁑ **Cook time:** 10 minutes ⁑ **Total time:** 20 minutes ⁑ MAKES 1 SERVING

  2 tablespoons chopped onion
  2 tablespoons chopped red bell pepper
  2 tablespoons chopped mushroom
  1 cup fresh arugula
  2 large eggs, lightly beaten
  1 ounce goat cheese

1. Heat a medium nonstick skillet coated with cooking spray over medium heat. Cook the onion for 2 minutes, or until softened. Stir in the bell pepper and mushroom; cook for 2 minutes, or until tender. Add the arugula, cover, and cook for 2 minutes, or until wilted. Transfer the vegetables to a plate; cover with a lid to keep warm.

2. Pour the eggs into the same skillet coated with cooking spray. Cook for 3 minutes, or until the eggs are just set in the center, tilting the skillet and gently lifting the edges of the eggs from the sides of the skillet to let the uncooked portion flow underneath. Sprinkle the cheese and the vegetables over half of the omelet. Fold the omelet over the filling and transfer to a plate.

Per serving: 274 calories, 19 g fat, 1 g saturated fat, 20 g protein, 8 g carbohydrates, 2 g fiber, 327 mg sodium

Skinny Sweet Potato Frittata

Packed with potassium, vitamin C, and beta-carotene, the sweet potato is a Salt Solution Star and a nutritional superhero. This tasty and easy frittata is a delicious way to get your fill.

Prep time: 15 minutes ⁑ **Cook time:** 35 minutes ⁑ **Total time:** 50 minutes ⁑ MAKES 4 SERVINGS

2 medium sweet potatoes (about 1 pound)

2 tablespoons olive oil

1 small red onion, halved and thinly sliced

4 frozen fully cooked chicken and apple breakfast sausages, thawed and sliced

3 large eggs

4 large egg whites

$\frac{1}{8}$ teaspoon ground black pepper

1. Prick the sweet potatoes with the tip of a paring knife. Place on a microwaveable plate. Microwave on high power for 8 minutes, turning once, or until cooked but still slightly firm. Halve lengthwise and let stand until cool enough to handle. Peel the potatoes and cut into 1" chunks.

2. Heat 1 tablespoon of the oil in a large nonstick skillet over medium heat. Add the onion and cook for 3 minutes, stirring, or until softened. Add the sweet potatoes, spread out to cover the pan, and cook for 5 minutes, turning occasionally with a spatula, or until lightly browned. Stir in the sausages and cook for 4 minutes, turning occasionally, or until hot.

3. Beat the whole eggs, egg whites, and pepper in a small bowl. Drizzle the remaining 1 tablespoon oil over the mixture in the skillet and pour in the egg mixture. Cook for 5 minutes, gently lifting the edges of the eggs from the sides of the skillet to let the uncooked portion flow underneath, or until the eggs are set on the bottom.

4. Remove the skillet from the heat. Place a heatproof plate over the skillet and with potholders invert the skillet onto the plate. Slide the frittata back into the skillet. Cook for 3 minutes, or until the eggs are cooked on the bottom. Slide the frittata onto a clean plate. Cut into 4 wedges to serve.

Per serving: 268 calories, 14 g fat, 3 g saturated fat, 14 g protein, 23 g carbohydrates, 4 g fiber, 302 mg sodium

Spinach-Tomato Frittata

Frozen or fresh spinach turns this frittata into a nutrient-packed Salt Solution must. Ready in 15 minutes or less, enjoy this dish any time of day.

Prep time: 5 minutes ⁘ **Cook time:** 10 minutes ⁘ **Total time:** 15 minutes ⁘ MAKES 4 SERVINGS

2 tablespoons olive oil
2 scallions, thinly sliced
10 ounces fresh baby spinach or
    1 package (10 ounces) frozen chopped spinach, thawed and squeezed dry
3 large eggs

5 large egg whites
4 slices (1 ounce each) low-salt mozzarella cheese
1 cup grape or cherry tomatoes
4 slices low-sodium whole grain bread, toasted

1. Heat 1 tablespoon of the oil in a large ovenproof nonstick skillet over medium heat. Cook the scallions for 1 minute, stirring, or until softened.

2. Transfer the scallions to a large bowl. Add the spinach, whole eggs, and egg whites. Beat with a fork until well blended.

3. Preheat the broiler. Heat the remaining 1 tablespoon oil in the skillet over medium heat. Pour the egg mixture into the skillet and scatter the tomatoes on top. Cover the skillet and cook for 4 minutes, or until the eggs are set around the edges.

4. Broil 5" from the heat for 4 minutes, or until the frittata is lightly browned and the center is set. Top with the cheese; cover and let stand for 1 minute to let the cheese melt. Cut into 4 wedges and serve each with 1 slice of toast.

Per serving: 280 calories, 17 g fat, 5 g saturated fat, 22 g protein, 15 g carbohydrates, 4 g fiber, 263 mg sodium

Breakfast Tacos with Tropical Fruit

A simple tropical fruit salad of fresh pineapple, mango, and banana helps to round out this tasty breakfast.

Prep time: 10 minutes ⟫ **Cook time:** 5 minutes ⟫ **Total time:** 15 minutes ⟫ MAKES 4 SERVINGS

4 corn tortillas (6" diameter)
2 medium bananas, sliced
$\frac{1}{2}$ mango, cut into chunks
$\frac{1}{4}$ pineapple, cut into chunks
2 plum tomatoes, seeded and chopped
$\frac{1}{2}$ cup chopped fresh spinach
$\frac{1}{4}$ Hass avocado, cut into $\frac{1}{4}$" pieces
2 teaspoons fresh lime juice

2 teaspoons chopped fresh cilantro
2 large eggs
2 large egg whites
$\frac{1}{8}$ teaspoon salt
1 teaspoon canola oil
$\frac{1}{2}$ cup shredded reduced-fat Cheddar cheese
4 teaspoons fat-free sour cream

1. Wrap the tortillas in paper towels. Set aside.

2. Combine the bananas, mango, and pineapple in a medium bowl. Combine the tomatoes, spinach, avocado, lime juice, and cilantro in another bowl. Lightly beat the whole eggs, egg whites, and salt in a third bowl.

3. Heat the oil in a medium nonstick skillet over medium-high heat. Cook the egg mixture for 4 minutes, stirring occasionally, or until the eggs are set. Remove from the heat.

4. Microwave the tortillas on high power for 30 seconds. Place 1 tortilla on each of 4 plates. Fill each with one-fourth of the egg mixture, one-fourth of the spinach mixture, and 1 teaspoon sour cream. Serve with the fruit mixture alongside.

Per serving: 258 calories, 7 g fat, 2 g saturated fat, 12 g protein, 40 g carbohydrates, 5 g fiber, 243 mg sodium

Breakfast Burritos

Loaded with veggies, eggs, soybeans, and more, these filling burritos are perfect for eating on the go.

Prep time: 15 minutes ⫸ **Cook time:** 10 minutes ⫸ **Total time:** 25 minutes ⫸ MAKES 4 SERVINGS

3 large eggs

3 large egg whites

2 tablespoons olive oil

½ red or green bell pepper, chopped

½ small red onion, chopped

2 whole wheat omega-3 tortillas (8" diameter)

1 plum tomato, chopped

½ teaspoon salt-free garlic-herb seasoning blend

½ cup unsalted black soybeans, rinsed and drained

2 tablespoons fresh cilantro, chopped

¼ cup shredded reduced-fat Cheddar cheese

1. Beat the whole eggs and egg whites in a medium bowl.

2. Heat the oil in a skillet over medium heat. Cook the bell pepper and onion for 5 minutes, stirring, or until softened.

3. Meanwhile, wrap the tortillas in paper towels and microwave on medium power for 30 seconds, or until warm.

4. Add the tomato and seasoning blend to the skillet; cook for 1 minute, stirring, or until the tomato softens. Stir in the soybeans and cilantro. Add the egg mixture and reduce the heat to medium-low. Cook for 2 minutes, stirring, or until the eggs are softly scrambled but still moist and creamy.

5. Place the tortilla on a flat surface. Divide the egg mixture onto the bottom third of each tortilla and sprinkle with the cheese. Roll up tightly and cut in half with a serrated knife. Place one-half on 4 plates.

Per serving: 255 calories, 15 g fat, 3 g saturated fat, 14 g protein, 16 g carbohydrates, 4 g fiber, 322 mg sodium

Salmon and Potato Brunch Skillet

This hearty and tasty dish serves up heart-healthy omega-3s in style!

Prep time: 15 minutes ▷ **Cook time:** 25 minutes ▷ **Total time:** 40 minutes ▷ MAKES 4 SERVINGS

$\frac{1}{3}$ cup fat-free sour cream

1 teaspoon fresh lemon juice

2 tablespoons chopped fresh dill

1 tablespoon olive oil

14 ounces frozen diced potatoes with onions and peppers

8 ounces cooked wild salmon fillet, flaked

3 scallions, chopped

$\frac{1}{4}$ teaspoon ground black pepper

1. Stir together the sour cream, lemon juice, and 1 tablespoon of the dill in a small bowl. Set aside.

2. Heat the oil in a large nonstick skillet over medium heat. Spread the potatoes evenly over the bottom of the pan, cover, and cook for 10 minutes, stirring occasionally, or until heated through. Remove the cover, increase the heat to medium-high, and press the potatoes with a large spatula. Cook for 5 minutes, turning occasionally, or until the potatoes brown and begin to crisp.

3. Stir in the salmon, scallions, pepper, and remaining 1 tablespoon dill. Cook for 2 minutes, turning with a spatula, or until the salmon is heated through. Serve with the dill cream.

Per serving: 241 calories, 9 g fat, 1 g saturated fat, 17 g protein, 21 g carbohydrates, 2 g fiber, 272 mg sodium

Three-Grain Ricotta Pancakes

These pancakes freeze well. Let them cool on a wire rack and then wrap individually in plastic wrap. Place in a resealable food-storage bag and freeze for up to 3 months. To heat, let thaw and toast in a toaster until hot.

Prep time: 15 minutes ⦁ **Cook time:** 20 minutes ⦁ **Total time:** 35 minutes ⦁ MAKES 8 SERVINGS

3 large eggs

1 cup part-skim ricotta cheese

¾ cup unsweetened plain soymilk

1 container (6 ounces) fat-free plain yogurt

2 tablespoons canola oil

1 teaspoon vanilla extract

¾ cup whole wheat flour

½ cup buckwheat flour

½ cup yellow cornmeal

2 tablespoons packed brown sugar

1½ teaspoons baking powder

¾ teaspoon baking soda

1 cup sliced strawberries

½ cup maple syrup

1. Preheat the oven to 200°F. Set a griddle or large nonstick skillet coated with cooking spray over medium heat.

2. Whisk together the eggs, ricotta, soymilk, yogurt, oil, and vanilla in a medium bowl until well blended.

3. Whisk together the whole wheat flour, buckwheat flour, cornmeal, brown sugar, baking powder, and baking soda in a large bowl until blended. Stir in the egg mixture just until blended.

4. Drop the batter by heaping ¼ cupful onto the griddle. Cook for 3 minutes, or until bubbles form on the tops and the bottoms brown. Flip and cook for 2 minutes, or until browned and cooked through, reducing the heat if necessary. Remove the pancakes to a heatproof plate and keep warm in the oven. Repeat with the cooking spray and remaining batter. Serve with the strawberries and maple syrup.

Per serving: 292 calories, 9 g fat, 2 g saturated fat, 11 g protein, 44 g carbohydrates, 3 g fiber, 277 mg sodium

Whole Wheat Pancakes with Pecans and Blueberries

To freeze the pancakes, place each pancake between squares of wax paper. Store in a resealable food-storage bag or plastic freezer container for up to 3 months. You can substitute a peeled and chopped apple for the blueberries, and walnuts for the pecans.

Prep time: 15 minutes ⦂ **Cook time:** 15 minutes ⦂ **Total time:** 30 minutes ⦂ MAKES 8 SERVINGS

1 cup white whole wheat flour or whole wheat pastry flour
6 tablespoons buttermilk powder
$\frac{1}{4}$ cup ground flaxseeds
1 teaspoon baking powder
1 teaspoon baking soda
$\frac{1}{2}$ teaspoon ground cinnamon

Pinch of salt
1 large egg
2 tablespoons canola oil
1 cup blueberries
$\frac{1}{4}$ cup chopped pecans
$\frac{3}{4}$ cup pure maple syrup

1. Combine the flour, buttermilk powder, flaxseeds, baking powder, baking soda, cinnamon, and salt in a large bowl. Whisk the egg in a medium bowl. Whisk in $1\frac{1}{2}$ cups of water and the oil. Whisk the egg mixture into the flour mixture just until combined. Stir in the blueberries and pecans. Let sit for 5 minutes.

2. Heat a griddle coated with cooking spray over medium-high heat until hot. Drop the batter by $\frac{1}{4}$ cupful onto the griddle. Cook for 2 minutes, or until bubbles form on the tops and the bottoms brown. Flip and cook for 2 minutes, or until cooked through. Serve with the maple syrup.

Per serving: 244 calories, 9 g fat, 1 g saturated fat, 4 g protein, 39 g carbohydrates, 4 g fiber, 299 mg sodium

French Toast with Raspberries and Almonds

This cinnamon-scented breakfast gets a fresh pick-me-up from tangy-sweet raspberries and sliced almonds.

Prep time: 15 minutes ⁑ **Cook time:** 20 minutes ⁑ **Total time:** 35 minutes ⁑ MAKES 4 SERVINGS

¾ cup fat-free milk

½ cup fat-free egg substitute

1 teaspoon canola oil

½ teaspoon vanilla extract

¼ teaspoon ground cinnamon

8 slices 7-grain bread

¼ cup maple syrup

1 cup raspberries

¼ cup sliced almonds, toasted

1. Combine the milk, egg substitute, oil, vanilla, and cinnamon in a 13" × 9" baking dish. Add the bread in a single layer and soak until most of the liquid is absorbed, turning once.

2. Heat a large nonstick griddle or a large nonstick skillet coated with cooking spray over medium heat. Add the bread slices, in batches if necessary, and cook for 6 minutes, turning once, or until browned on both sides. Place 2 slices on each of 4 plates. Top each serving with 1 tablespoon maple syrup, ¼ cup raspberries, and 1 tablespoon almonds.

Per serving: 282 calories, 7 g fat, 1 g saturated fat, 13 g protein, 44 g carbohydrates, 7 g fiber, 307 mg sodium

Waffle Sandwich with Banana and Strawberries

This filling open-face sandwich makes a great breakfast when you're in a rush in the morning. Assemble it and place in a food-storage container; it's ready to go when you get to work.

Prep time: 5 minutes ❧ **Cook time:** 5 minutes ❧ **Total time:** 10 minutes ❧ MAKES 1 SERVING

1 frozen whole grain waffle, toasted

1 teaspoon unsalted natural peanut butter

2 tablespoons part-skim ricotta cheese

$\frac{1}{2}$ small banana, sliced

3 strawberries, sliced (about $\frac{1}{3}$ cup)

$\frac{1}{2}$ teaspoon honey

Spread the waffle with the peanut butter and then the ricotta. Top with the banana and strawberry slices. Drizzle with the honey.

Per serving: 270 calories, 10 g fat, 3 g saturated fat, 8 g protein, 37 g carbohydrates, 4 g fiber, 260 mg sodium

Whole Wheat Crepes
with Fresh Fruit

To make ahead, cook the crepes, stack and cover with foil, then refrigerate or freeze. Thaw if frozen, then reheat the foil-wrapped stack on a baking sheet at 350°F for 5 minutes, or until the crepes are warm and pliable.

Prep time: 25 minutes ▶ **Cook time:** 35 minutes ▶ **Total time:** 1 hour ▶ MAKES 4 SERVINGS

CREPES

1 cup whole grain pastry flour

1 tablespoon sugar

$\frac{1}{4}$ teaspoon salt

1 large egg

1 cup + 3 tablespoons unsweetened
plain soymilk or whole dairy milk

$1\frac{1}{2}$ teaspoons vanilla extract

2 teaspoons butter

FILLING

$\frac{1}{2}$ cup low-fat plain yogurt

1 banana, cut on the diagonal into
24 slices

2 kiwifruit, peeled and quartered
lengthwise

1 cup sliced strawberries

2 teaspoons fresh lime juice

$\frac{1}{2}$ teaspoon ground cinnamon

1. To make the crepes: Combine the flour, sugar, and salt in a large bowl.

2. Beat the egg, milk, and vanilla in a small bowl. Stir into the flour mixture until blended.

3. Melt $\frac{1}{2}$ teaspoon of the butter in an 8" nonstick skillet over medium heat. Pour 3 tablespoons of the batter into the skillet and tilt the skillet to coat the bottom in a thin layer (if the batter seems too thick, add 1 to 2 tablespoons water). Cook the first side for 2 minutes, or until browned. Turn and cook for 1 minute, or until firm. Slide the crepe onto a plate and cover with foil to keep warm. Continue making crepes in the same fashion, rebuttering the pan after every second crepe, until all the butter and batter are used.

4. To assemble: Place 1 crepe on a plate and spread with 1 tablespoon of the yogurt. Arrange 3 banana slices, 1 kiwi quarter, and 2 tablespoons strawberries in strips one-third of the way from one edge. Sprinkle with $\frac{1}{4}$ teaspoon of the lime juice and a pinch of the cinnamon, and roll up. Repeat with the remaining crepes, serving 2 crepes per person.

Per serving: 262 calories, 7 g fat, 3 g saturated fat, 10 g protein, 42 g carbohydrates, 5 g fiber, 229 mg sodium

Multigrain Cereal with Roasted Soybeans and Apricots

Soybeans are loaded with all three Miracle Minerals—calcium, potassium, and magnesium. They're a Salt Solution Star, and a nutty addition to this good-for-you cereal.

Prep time: 5 minutes ▷ **Cook time:** 5 minutes ▷ **Total time:** 10 minutes ▷ MAKES 1 SERVING

¾ cup unsweetened plain soymilk
2 tablespoons quick-cooking barley
2 tablespoons bulgur
2 tablespoons old-fashioned rolled oats

1 tablespoon chopped dried apricots
1 teaspoon packed brown sugar
1 tablespoon unsalted dry-roasted soy nuts

1. Combine ½ cup of the soymilk, ¼ cup of water, the barley, bulgur, and oats in a micro-waveable 1-quart bowl. Microwave on high power for 2 minutes. Stir in the apricots and microwave on high power for 3 minutes, stirring once, or until the grains are tender but still chewy and the liquid is absorbed.

2. Cover and let stand for 1 minute. Spoon into a bowl. Sprinkle with the brown sugar and soy nuts. Serve with the remaining ¼ cup soymilk.

Per serving: 294 calories, 7 g fat, 1 g saturated fat, 16 g protein, 46 g carbohydrates, 11 g fiber, 27 mg sodium

Oatmeal with Apricots, Almonds, and Brown Sugar

Sliced dried apricots and creamy almond milk are a great way to dress up a boring bowl of oatmeal. A drop of vanilla extract just before serving brings out the brown sugar and cinnamon flavors.

Prep time: 5 minutes ▸ **Cook time:** 5 minutes ▸ **Total time:** 10 minutes ▸ MAKES 2 SERVINGS

  2 cups unsweetened almond milk
  4 teaspoons packed dark brown sugar
  1 cup old-fashioned rolled oats
¼ cup dried apricots, sliced
½ teaspoon vanilla extract
¼ teaspoon ground cinnamon
  2 tablespoons sliced almonds, toasted

1. Combine the almond milk and brown sugar in a small saucepan. Bring to a boil over medium-high heat, stir in the oats and apricots, and reduce the heat to medium.

2. Simmer for 5 minutes, stirring occasionally, or until thickened and the oats are cooked. Remove from the heat and stir in the vanilla and cinnamon. Divide between 2 bowls and top with the almonds.

Per serving: 311 calories, 8 g fat, 0 g saturated fat, 10 g protein, 50 g carbohydrates, 7 g fiber, 184 mg sodium

Breakfast Quinoa with Banana and Pecans

Quinoa is a wonderful grain with a slightly nutty flavor and fluffy texture. Be sure to rinse it thoroughly prior to cooking to remove the saponins, a naturally occurring coating that has a slightly bitter, soapy flavor.

Prep time: 5 minutes ⁑ **Cook time:** 15 minutes ⁑ **Total time:** 20 minutes ⁑ MAKES 4 SERVINGS

  2 cups vanilla rice milk
¾ cup quinoa, rinsed
  2 medium bananas, sliced
¼ cup pecan halves, coarsely chopped
  3 tablespoons raisins
¼ teaspoon vanilla extract

1. Bring the rice milk and quinoa to a simmer in a medium saucepan over medium heat. Reduce the heat to medium-low and cook for 15 minutes, or until the quinoa is tender.

2. Stir in the bananas, pecans, raisins, and vanilla. Divide among 4 bowls.

Per serving: 303 calories, 8 g fat, 1 g saturated fat, 6 g protein, 54 g carbohydrates, 5 g fiber, 48 mg sodium

Fruit and Nut Breakfast Bars

One of these bars and a banana make a great portable breakfast—the banana brings the calories to 240 while keeping the sodium low. The bars can be stored in an airtight plastic container for up to 3 days or frozen for up to 3 months.

Prep time: 15 minutes ⫶ **Cook time:** 20 minutes ⫶ **Total time:** 35 minutes ⫶ MAKES 16 SERVINGS

1 cup quick-cooking oats	$1/2$ cup almonds
$1/3$ cup toasted wheat germ	$1/3$ cup dried cranberries
$1/4$ cup whole wheat flour	$1/3$ cup walnut pieces
1 teaspoon ground cinnamon	$1/4$ cup raw hulled sunflower seeds
$1/2$ cup dried apricots	$1/2$ cup fat-free egg substitute
$1/2$ cup dried figs, stems removed	$1/4$ cup maple syrup
$1/2$ cup golden raisins	2 ounces dark chocolate (70%), melted

1. Preheat the oven to 350°F. Line a 13" × 9" baking pan with foil, letting the foil extend 1" over the sides of the pan. Coat the foil with cooking spray.

2. Combine the oats, wheat germ, flour, and cinnamon in a food processor; pulse a few times to mix. Add the apricots, figs, raisins, almonds, cranberries, walnuts, and sunflower seeds. Pulse for 30 seconds, or until the fruit and nuts are finely ground. The mixture should be ground, but small pieces of nuts and fruit should be discernible.

3. Combine the egg substitute and maple syrup in a large bowl. Add the fruit mixture and stir until blended. Mix with your hands until the mixture comes together into a paste. Place in the prepared pan and press evenly. If the mixture sticks to your hands, rinse with water, shake off the excess, and press.

4. Bake for 20 minutes, or until the edges brown and the top feels firm when pressed. Cool completely in the pan on a rack. To cut into bars, remove from the pan using the foil. Cut lengthwise into 4 strips, then crosswise into 4 strips to make 16 bars. Place the bars on the rack and drizzle with the chocolate.

Per serving: 150 calories, 5 g fat, 1 g saturated fat, 5 g protein, 23 g carbohydrates, 3 g fiber, 15 mg sodium

Maple-Cherry Granola

Packed with the wholesome goodness of seeds, nuts, dried fruit, and soy nuts (a Salt Solution Star), this homemade granola is a surefire way to start the day right.

Prep time: 15 minutes ᨃᐧ **Cook time:** 1 hour 20 minutes ᨃᐧ **Total time:** 1 hour 35 minutes
ᨃᐧ MAKES 16 SERVINGS (SCANT 1 CUP EACH)

5 cups old-fashioned rolled oats
$1/3$ cup slivered almonds
$1/3$ cup pecans, chopped
$1/3$ cup unsalted raw hulled pumpkin seeds
$1/4$ cup unsalted raw hulled sunflower seeds
$1/2$ cup maple syrup

$1/3$ cup unsweetened apple juice
$1/3$ cup packed brown sugar
2 tablespoons canola oil
$1/2$ teaspoon ground cinnamon
$1/2$ cup dried cherries, coarsely chopped
$1/2$ cup dried peaches and/or pears, chopped
$1/2$ cup unsalted dry-roasted soy nuts

1. Preheat the oven to 275°F. Coat a rimmed baking sheet with cooking spray. Combine the oats, almonds, pecans, pumpkin seeds, and sunflower seeds in the pan.

2. Whisk together the maple syrup, apple juice, brown sugar, oil, and cinnamon in a measuring cup until blended. Drizzle over the oat mixture, stirring with a wooden spoon until evenly coated. Spread the oat mixture out on the pan.

3. Bake for 1 hour 20 minutes, stirring 3 times, or until golden brown. Stir in the cherries, peaches and/or pears, and soy nuts. Let cool completely. Store in an airtight container.

Per serving: 266 calories, 10 g fat, 1 g saturated fat, 7 g protein, 40 g carbohydrates, 5 g fiber, 3 mg sodium

Fruit Bowls with Ricotta Cream

The ricotta cream and fruit mixture can be made up to 2 days ahead.

Prep time: 20 minutes ▶ **Total time:** 20 minutes ▶ MAKES 4 **SERVINGS**

$\frac{1}{2}$ cup part-skim ricotta cheese
2 tablespoons sugar
$\frac{3}{4}$ cup 0% plain Greek yogurt
$\frac{1}{2}$ teaspoon grated lime zest
1 mango, cut into chunks
2 peaches, sliced

1 large banana, sliced
1 cup blueberries
1 tablespoon fresh lime juice
2 tablespoons almonds, toasted and coarsely chopped

1 Puree the ricotta and sugar until smooth in a food processor or blender. Scrape into a small bowl. Stir in the yogurt and lime zest.

2. Combine the mango, peaches, banana, blueberries, and lime juice in a large bowl. Divide the fruit, ricotta cream, and almonds among 4 bowls.

Per serving: 224 calories, 5 g fat, 2 g saturated fat, 9 g protein, 40 g carbohydrates, 4 g fiber, 60 mg sodium

Bacon-Cheddar Breakfast Muffins

These muffins can be made ahead and frozen in a resealable food-storage bag. To thaw, microwave on defrost for about 1 minute.

Prep time: 20 minutes ᴥ **Cook time:** 25 minutes ᴥ **Total time:** 45 minutes ᴥ MAKES 12 SERVINGS

2 cups whole wheat pastry flour
1/2 cup unbleached all-purpose flour
1/2 cup yellow cornmeal
2 teaspoons baking powder
1/2 teaspoon baking soda
1/2 teaspoon ground black pepper
1 1/2 cups fat-free buttermilk
2 large eggs
3 tablespoons olive oil

2 tablespoons unsalted butter or margarine, melted
5 scallions, thinly sliced
1/2 red bell pepper, finely chopped
1/2 cup shredded reduced-sodium Cheddar cheese
2 slices (3/4 ounce each) Canadian bacon, finely chopped

1. Preheat the oven to 400°F. Line a 12-cup muffin pan with paper liners or coat with cooking spray.

2. Whisk together the whole wheat flour, all-purpose flour, cornmeal, baking powder, baking soda, and black pepper in a large bowl. Whisk together the buttermilk, eggs, oil, butter or margarine, scallions, bell pepper, cheese, and bacon in a measuring cup. Stir into the flour mixture, just until blended. Spoon the batter into the muffin cups. (The cups will be very full.)

3. Bake for 22 minutes, or until the tops brown lightly and a toothpick inserted in the center of a muffin comes out clean. Remove the muffins from the pan to cool on a rack. Serve warm or at room temperature.

Per serving: 207 calories, 9 g fat, 4 g saturated fat, 8 g protein, 25 g carbohydrates, 3 g fiber, 231 mg sodium

Baked Apples with Cranberries and Yogurt

You can refrigerate these apples if you like for several days. To reheat, place a cooked apple on a work surface and cut into slices or wedges. Place in a microwaveable bowl and drizzle with some of the cooking liquid. Microwave on medium power for 2 minutes, or until warmed through.

Prep time: 15 minutes ▸ **Cook time:** 50 minutes ▸ **Total time:** 1 hour 5 minutes + standing time
▸ MAKES 4 SERVINGS

4 large Granny Smith apples (about 8 ounces each)

1/4 cup dried cranberries

3 tablespoons sugar

2 tablespoons unsalted butter, diced

2 tablespoons chopped walnuts

1/2 teaspoon ground cinnamon

1 cup 0% plain Greek yogurt

1. Preheat the oven to 350°F. Set out a 13" × 9" glass baking dish.

2. Cut each apple in half through the stem end and remove the core with a melon baller. Make V-shaped cuts in the stem and blossom ends to remove. Place the apples skin side down in the baking dish.

3. With your fingers, mix the cranberries, sugar, butter, walnuts, and cinnamon in a small bowl until crumbly. Divide among the apples. Pour 1 cup of water into the baking dish.

4. Bake for 40 minutes, or until the apples are very tender when pierced with a fork. Let stand for 30 minutes before serving. Place 2 apple halves on each of 4 plates and drizzle the cooking juices over each serving. Serve each with 1/4 cup of the yogurt.

Per serving: 282 calories, 9 g fat, 4 g saturated fat, 6 g protein, 50 g carbohydrates, 6 g fiber, 24 mg sodium

Banana-Bran Muffins

Eat one of these grab-and-go muffins with 1 cup of fat-free milk to make this a complete meal.

Prep time: 40 minutes ⁑ **Cook time:** 20 minutes ⁑ **Total time:** 1 hour ⁑ MAKES 12 SERVINGS

$1\frac{1}{2}$ cups shredded bran cereal
$\frac{1}{2}$ cup golden raisins
3 tablespoons canola oil
$\frac{1}{2}$ cup boiling water
1 cup low-fat buttermilk
1 large egg

2 tablespoons light molasses
1 cup whole wheat flour
1 tablespoon packed brown sugar
$1\frac{1}{4}$ teaspoons baking soda
1 large banana, cut into $\frac{1}{2}$" chunks
$\frac{1}{2}$ cup walnuts, chopped

1. Preheat the oven to 400°F. Line a 12-cup muffin pan with paper liners or coat with cooking spray.

2. Combine the cereal, raisins, and oil in a large bowl. Add the boiling water and stir to combine. Let cool for 15 minutes.

3. Beat the buttermilk, egg, and molasses in a measuring cup until blended. Add to the cereal mixture and stir until combined.

4. Whisk together the flour, brown sugar, and baking soda in a small bowl until blended. Stir the flour mixture, banana, and walnuts into the cereal mixture. Stir just until moistened. Cover the bowl and let stand for 15 minutes.

5. Divide the batter among the muffin cups.

6. Bake for 20 minutes, or until a toothpick inserted in the center of a muffin comes out clean. Let cool for 5 minutes in the pan on a rack before removing.

Per serving: 172 calories, 7 g fat, 1 g saturated fat, 5 g protein, 26 g carbohydrates, 4 g fiber, 181 mg sodium

Good Morning Muffins

Drink 1 cup of soy, almond, or fat-free milk with one of these muffins to make a complete breakfast.

Prep time: 10 minutes ▷ **Cook time:** 20 minutes ▷ **Total time:** 30 minutes ▷ MAKES 12 SERVINGS

1/3 cup sugar

2 large eggs

1/4 cup vegetable oil

1 large carrot, grated

1 small Granny Smith apple, unpeeled, grated

1/2 cup golden raisins

1/2 cup pitted prunes, finely chopped

1/3 cup walnuts, chopped

1/2 cup unbleached all-purpose flour

1/2 cup whole wheat flour

1/4 cup quick-cooking oats

1 1/2 teaspoons baking soda

1/2 teaspoon ground cinnamon

1/4 teaspoon ground nutmeg

1/4 teaspoon salt

1. Preheat the oven to 350°F. Line a 12-cup muffin pan with paper liners or coat with cooking spray.

2. Combine the sugar, eggs, oil, carrot, apple, raisins, prunes, and walnuts in a medium bowl.

3. Whisk together the all-purpose flour, whole wheat flour, oats, baking soda, cinnamon, nutmeg, and salt in a large bowl. Stir in the carrot mixture just until blended.

4. Divide the batter among the muffin cups.

5. Bake for 20 minutes, or until a toothpick inserted in the center of a muffin comes out clean. Let cool for 5 minutes in the pan on a rack before removing.

Per serving: 187 calories, 8 g fat, 1 g saturated fat, 3 g protein, 27 g carbohydrates, 2 g fiber, 227 mg sodium

Bacon-Mushroom Breakfast Sandwich

You can cook the bacon the day before and refrigerate it to save time in the morning.

Prep time: 10 minutes ▷ **Cook time:** 10 minutes ▷ **Total time:** 20 minutes ▷ MAKES 4 SERVINGS

4 slices reduced-sodium bacon, halved

2 tablespoons canola mayonnaise

4 slices light whole wheat bread, toasted

8 mushrooms, thinly sliced

¼ teaspoon ground black pepper

1 tomato, cut into 4 slices

4 ounces thinly sliced reduced-fat, low-sodium Swiss cheese

1. Cook the bacon in the microwave according to the package directions.

2. Place a broiler rack in the farthest position from the heat source and preheat the broiler.

3. Spread ½ tablespoon of the mayonnaise on each slice of bread. Place the bread, mayonnaise side up, on a baking sheet. Top with the mushrooms and sprinkle with the pepper. Arrange the tomato slices over the mushrooms. Top with the bacon and cover with the cheese. Broil until the cheese melts.

Per serving: 258 calories, 16 g fat, 6 g saturated fat, 14 g protein, 14 g carbohydrates, 3 g fiber, 263 mg sodium

★ **EDAMAME** ★
(Fresh Soybeans)

Rich in calcium,
magnesium, and potassium

6

Soups, Salads, and Sandwiches

Lentil Soup with Spinach and Butternut Squash

This soup is packed with filling fiber from lentils and vegetables, and it will keep you feeling satisfied for hours.

Prep time: 20 minutes ⁘ **Cook time:** 1 hour ⁘ **Total time:** 1 hour 20 minutes ⁘ MAKES 6 SERVINGS

2 teaspoons olive oil
1 large onion, chopped
2 large carrots, sliced
3 medium ribs celery with leaves, sliced
1½ cups lentils, picked over and rinsed
4 cloves garlic, minced
1½ teaspoons dried thyme
1 teaspoon ground black pepper

½ teaspoon dried marjoram
¼ teaspoon salt
4 cups low-sodium chicken broth
1 package (10 ounces) frozen cubed butternut squash
1 can (14.5 ounces) no-salt-added diced tomatoes
8 ounces baby spinach

1. Heat the oil in a large, heavy Dutch oven over medium heat. Cook the onion, carrots, and celery for 8 minutes, stirring occasionally, or until softened. Stir in the lentils, garlic, thyme, pepper, marjoram, and salt. Cook for 1 minute, stirring.

2. Add the broth and 4 cups water. Bring to a boil over high heat. Reduce the heat to low, cover, and simmer for 25 minutes, or until the lentils are very tender.

3. Stir in the squash and tomatoes and return to a boil, breaking up the tomatoes with the side of a spoon. Cover and simmer for 10 minutes, or until the vegetables are tender. Stir in the spinach and cook for 2 minutes, or until wilted.

Per serving: 293 calories, 3 g fat, 1 g saturated fat, 19 g protein, 50 g carbohydrates, 19 g fiber, 284 mg sodium

Chicken Pho with Buckwheat Noodles

Bok choy is a Chinese cabbage that has a sweet flavor and is packed with beta-carotene, vitamin C, and calcium.

Prep time: 20 minutes ▷ **Cook time:** 15 minutes ▷ **Total time:** 35 minutes ▷ MAKES 4 SERVINGS

4 ounces low-sodium buckwheat (soba) noodles

12 ounces chicken tenders, cut into thin strips

4 cups low-sodium chicken broth

8 baby bok choy, quartered lengthwise

$1/2$ cup shelled edamame

$1/2$ red bell pepper, cut into thin strips

1 small bunch scallions, sliced

1 teaspoon toasted sesame oil

1 teaspoon reduced-sodium soy sauce

$1/2$ cup fresh cilantro, coarsely chopped

Lime wedges, for serving

1. Prepare the noodles according to package directions, omitting the salt and cooking about 1 minute less than directed (about 4 minutes). Drain well.

2. Meanwhile, heat a nonstick saucepan coated with cooking spray over medium-high heat. Cook the chicken for 4 minutes, stirring, or until browned. Add the broth and bring to a boil. Add the bok choy and edamame and simmer for 4 minutes, or until the chicken is cooked through.

3. Stir in the bell pepper and scallions. Cook for 2 minutes. Remove from the heat and stir in the sesame oil, soy sauce, and cilantro. Divide the noodles and soup among 4 bowls. Serve with lime wedges.

Per serving: 273 calories, 6 g fat, 1 g saturated fat, 30 g protein, 29 g carbohydrates, 3 g fiber, 157 mg sodium

White Bean and Escarole Soup

This soup features white beans, a Salt Solution Star. They're packed with fiber, potassium, and folate—and they make this soup delicious!

Prep time: 20 minutes ⁂ **Cook time:** 30 minutes ⁂ **Total time:** 50 minutes ⁂ MAKES 6 SERVINGS

2 teaspoons olive oil

3 cloves garlic, minced

2 carrots, chopped

1 large onion, chopped

¾ pound ground chicken breast

1 teaspoon dried basil

4 cups low-sodium chicken broth

1 head escarole (1 pound), washed well and sliced

2 cans (15 ounces each) no-salt-added cannellini beans, rinsed and drained

8 ounces spinach, chopped

6 tablespoons grated Parmesan cheese

1. Heat the oil in a large saucepan over medium heat. Cook the garlic, carrots, and onion for 6 minutes, or until softened. Add the chicken and basil and cook, breaking up the meat with a spoon, until no longer pink.

2. Stir in the broth and bring to a boil. Stir in the escarole and beans. Reduce the heat to low, cover, and simmer for 25 minutes. Stir in the spinach and cook for 2 minutes. Divide among 6 bowls and sprinkle with the Parmesan.

Per serving: 270 calories, 4 g fat, 1 g saturated fat, 28 g protein, 34 g carbohydrates, 15 g fiber, 271 mg sodium

Okra Gumbo

Who says Southern food has to be unhealthy? This okra gumbo is filled with delicious, low-salt ingredients.

Prep time: 15 minutes ▸ **Cook time:** 45 minutes ▸ **Total time:** 1 hour ▸ MAKES 4 SERVINGS

- 5 cups low-sodium chicken broth
- 2 cups frozen black-eyed peas
- 1 onion, chopped
- 3 large scallions, sliced
- 1 red bell pepper, chopped
- 1 rib celery, sliced
- 2 cloves garlic, chopped
- ¼ cup chopped fresh parsley
- ¼ cup long-grain white rice
- ¼ teaspoon dried thyme
- 1 can (14.5 ounces) no-salt-added stewed tomatoes
- ¾ cup sliced fresh or frozen okra
- ⅛ teaspoon ground black pepper
- ⅛ teaspoon cayenne pepper (optional)
- ¾ pound medium shrimp, peeled and deveined

1. Combine the broth, black-eyed peas, onion, scallions, bell pepper, celery, garlic, parsley, rice, and thyme in a Dutch oven or large saucepan. Bring to a boil over medium-high heat. Reduce the heat, cover, and simmer, stirring occasionally, for 30 minutes.

2. Stir in the tomatoes, okra, black pepper, and cayenne (if using). Cover and simmer, stirring occasionally, for 10 minutes. Stir in the shrimp. Simmer for 2 minutes, or until the shrimp are just opaque.

Per serving: 309 calories, 2 g fat, 0 g saturated fat, 31 g protein, 41 g carbohydrates, 7 g fiber, 249 mg sodium

Chilled Cucumber Soup with Shrimp

Omit the shrimp, and keep this soup on hand for a refreshing pick-me-up on a hot summer's day.

Prep time: 15 minutes ⁘ **Cook time:** 10 minutes ⁘ **Total time:** 25 minutes ⁘ MAKES 4 SERVINGS

3 cups low-fat buttermilk
¾ cup cooked shelled edamame
2 small Kirby cucumbers, peeled, seeded, and chunked
1 tablespoon fresh lime juice
1 teaspoon extra-virgin olive oil

2 tablespoons chopped fresh mint
3 tablespoons chopped chives
6 ounces peeled and deveined cooked medium shrimp
8 rye crispbread crackers
Lime wedges, for serving

1. Blend 1 cup of the buttermilk and ½ cup of the edamame in a blender until smooth. Add the cucumbers, lime juice, oil, and remaining 2 cups buttermilk. Blend until smooth. Add the mint and 2 tablespoons of the chives. Blend until the herbs are finely chopped. Divide the mixture among 4 bowls.

2. Set aside 4 shrimp for garnish and coarsely chop the remaining shrimp. Divide the chopped shrimp and remaining ¼ cup edamame among the bowls. Garnish with the whole shrimp and remaining 1 tablespoon chives. Serve with the crispbreads and lime wedges.

Per serving: 278 calories, 7 g fat, 2 g saturated fat, 23 g protein, 30 g carbohydrates, 5 g fiber, 338 mg sodium

New England Fish Chowder

Clam juice is the secret ingredient in this chowder. It adds a rich, savory flavor to soups and stews.

Prep time: 10 minutes ⁑ **Cook time:** 30 minutes ⁑ **Total time:** 40 minutes ⁑ MAKES 4 SERVINGS

$\frac{1}{2}$ teaspoon olive oil

2 onions, chopped

1 rib celery, chopped

2 tablespoons unbleached all-purpose flour

1 bottle (8 ounces) clam juice

3 sweet potatoes ($1\frac{1}{2}$ pounds), peeled and cut into $\frac{3}{4}$" cubes

2 teaspoons dried thyme

1 bay leaf

4 cups unsweetened plain soymilk

$\frac{3}{4}$ pound cod or haddock, cut into 1" pieces

$\frac{1}{8}$ teaspoon ground black pepper

1. Heat the oil in a large saucepan over medium heat. Add the onions and celery. Cook for 10 minutes, stirring occasionally, or until the onions are softened.

2. Meanwhile, whisk together the flour and clam juice in a measuring cup. Stir the clam juice mixture, sweet potatoes, thyme, bay leaf, and 1 cup water into the saucepan. Bring to a simmer, cover, and cook for 12 minutes, or until the potatoes are almost tender when pierced. Remove the bay leaf.

3. Gradually stir the soymilk into the pan, and bring the mixture just to a simmer. (Do not boil or the milk could separate.) Add the fish and cook for 5 minutes, or until the fish just flakes. Season with the pepper.

Per serving: 293 calories, 5 g fat, 0 g saturated fat, 26 g protein, 34 g carbohydrates, 4 g fiber, 318 mg sodium

Creamy Tomato and Tofu Soup

Here's a great way to sneak protein into your family's diet.

Prep time: 15 minutes ⁑ **Cook time:** 10 minutes ⁑ **Total time:** 25 minutes ⁑ MAKES 4 SERVINGS

1 teaspoon canola oil
2 medium onions, chopped
8 ounces lite silken tofu, drained and crumbled
1 clove garlic, minced
2 teaspoons dried basil
¼ teaspoon dried thyme
1 cup low-sodium chicken broth

1 can (14.5 ounces) no-salt-added diced tomatoes
1½ cups canned no-salt-added tomato puree
1 tablespoon honey
¼ teaspoon salt
2 teaspoons balsamic vinegar

1. Heat the oil in a large nonstick saucepan over medium heat. Cook the onions for 5 minutes, stirring occasionally, or until softened. Add the tofu, garlic, basil, and thyme. Cook for 2 minutes, stirring occasionally.

2. Add the broth, tomatoes, tomato puree, honey, and salt. Bring to a simmer over medium-low heat. Cook for 10 minutes, or until flavored through. Stir in the vinegar.

3. Working in batches, ladle the soup into a blender or food processor and blend until smooth. Pour into bowls to serve.

Per serving: 166 calories, 2 g fat, 0 g saturated fat, 6 g protein, 30 g carbohydrates, 3 g fiber, 287 mg sodium

 MAKE IT A SALT SOLUTION MEAL: Serve with 1 medium apple and ½ tablespoon unsalted peanut butter (285 calories and 291 mg sodium total).

Russian Beet and Bean Soup

This soup is great served hot or cold. If you make it ahead, taste and adjust the seasoning, adding a drizzle of vinegar or a pinch of fresh dill, if needed.

Prep time: 10 minutes ⁑ **Cook time:** 50 minutes ⁑ **Total time:** 1 hour ⁑ MAKES 6 SERVINGS

1 teaspoon olive oil
2 small onions, finely chopped
2 cloves garlic, finely chopped
3 cups low-sodium chicken broth
1 cup no-salt-added tomato puree
3 medium beets, peeled and diced
2 tablespoons honey
½ teaspoon dried thyme

6 ounces beet greens, chopped
1 cup no-salt-added canned kidney
  beans, rinsed and drained
2 tablespoons cider vinegar
¼ teaspoon salt
1 tablespoon chopped fresh dill or
  1 teaspoon dried dillweed
3 tablespoons 0% plain Greek yogurt

1. Heat the oil in a large saucepan over medium-high heat. Add the onions and garlic. Cook for 5 minutes, stirring occasionally, or until softened.

2. Add the broth, tomato puree, beets, honey, and thyme. Bring to a boil. Reduce the heat to low, cover, and simmer for 30 minutes, or until the beets are very soft when pierced with a sharp knife.

3. Stir in the beet greens, beans, vinegar, and salt. Simmer for 10 minutes, or until the greens are tender. Stir in the dill. Ladle into bowls and top each serving with ½ tablespoon yogurt.

Per serving: 156 calories, 2 g fat, 0 g saturated fat, 8 g protein, 29 g carbohydrates, 7 g fiber, 276 mg sodium

 MAKE IT A SALT SOLUTION MEAL: Serve with 1 slice low-sodium sprouted wheat bread and 1 medium pear (316 calories and 281 mg sodium total).

Veggie Gazpacho with Red Lentils

Lentils are not only packed with fiber, protein, and B vitamins, but they can help lower cholesterol and keep blood sugar stable.

Prep time: 15 minutes ⊪ **Cook time:** 20 minutes ⊪ **Total time:** 35 minutes + chilling time
⊪ MAKES 4 SERVINGS

¾ cup red lentils
5 large tomatoes, peeled and cut into 1" chunks
1 English (seedless) cucumber, peeled and cut into 1" chunks
1 large red bell pepper, cut into 1" chunks
2 ribs celery, cut into 1" chunks
1 small white onion, chopped
2 cloves garlic, minced

¾ cup reduced-sodium tomato juice
1 cup fat-free, reduced-sodium beef broth
¼ cup chopped fresh parsley
1 tablespoon balsamic vinegar
2 teaspoons extra-virgin olive oil
2 dashes hot-pepper sauce
8 wheat and rye crispbread crackers
Parsley sprigs, for garnish

1. Bring 2 cups of water to a boil in a small saucepan. Add the lentils and return to a boil. Reduce the heat to low, cover, and simmer for 20 minutes, or until tender. Rinse in a colander under cold water and drain well.

2. Meanwhile, working in small batches in a food processor, pulse the tomatoes, cucumber, bell pepper, celery, onion, and garlic to a chunky puree. Transfer the mixture to a large bowl.

3. Stir in the tomato juice, broth, chopped parsley, vinegar, oil, hot-pepper sauce, and drained lentils. Cover and refrigerate for at least 2 hours. Serve with the crispbreads and garnish with the parsley sprigs.

Per serving: 290 calories, 5 g fat, 1 g saturated fat, 16 g protein, 49 g carbohydrates, 11 g fiber, 264 mg sodium

Mexican Black Bean Soup

Make this a vegan meal by substituting low-sodium vegetable broth for the chicken broth. To have this on hand for a quick lunch or dinner, portion the soup out and freeze in individual containers.

Prep time: 10 minutes ⁑ **Cook time:** 30 minutes ⁑ **Total time:** 40 minutes ⁑ MAKES 6 SERVINGS

1 teaspoon olive oil

2 medium onions, finely chopped

2 cloves garlic, chopped

2 cups low-sodium chicken broth

2 cans (15.5 ounces each) no-salt-added black beans, rinsed and drained

1 can (14.5 ounces) no-salt-added stewed tomatoes, chopped, with juices

2 teaspoons salt-free chili powder

1 teaspoon ground cumin

1 cup frozen corn kernels

1 cup loose-packed frozen cut-leaf spinach

$\frac{1}{4}$ + $\frac{1}{8}$ teaspoon salt

2 tablespoons balsamic or red wine vinegar

3 tablespoons reduced-fat sour cream

1. Heat the oil in a large saucepan over medium heat. Cook the onions for 7 minutes, stirring occasionally, or until softened. Stir in the garlic and cook for 1 minute.

2. Add the broth, beans, tomatoes, chili powder, and cumin. Bring to a boil over medium-high heat. Reduce the heat to medium, cover, and simmer for 15 minutes. Stir in the corn, spinach, and salt. Bring to a simmer and cook for 5 minutes.

3. Stir in the vinegar. Divide the soup and sour cream among 6 bowls.

Per serving: 200 calories, 2.5 g fat, 1 g saturated fat, 12 g protein, 32 g carbohydrates, 8 g fiber, 280 mg sodium

 MAKE IT A SALT SOLUTION MEAL: Serve with 1 medium orange (280 calories and 280 mg sodium total).

SOUPS, SALADS, AND SANDWICHES ⬇

Grilled Steak and Peach Salad

If peaches are out of season, make this salad with fresh pineapple or mango for a refreshing change.

Prep time: 10 minutes ▷ **Cook time:** 10 minutes ▷ **Total time:** 20 minutes ▷ MAKES 4 SERVINGS

$1\frac{1}{2}$ tablespoons white wine vinegar

1 tablespoon olive oil

1 tablespoon orange juice

$\frac{1}{2}$ teaspoon grated fresh ginger

$\frac{1}{4}$ teaspoon salt

2 large peaches, halved

1 small sirloin steak (8 ounces), trimmed of external fat

$\frac{1}{4}$ teaspoon ground black pepper

1 red bell pepper, cut into thin, short strips

1 bag (5 ounces) baby spinach

3 tablespoons toasted sliced almonds

$\frac{1}{4}$ cup fresh basil leaves, torn

4 slices sodium-free sprouted wheat bread, toasted

1. Heat a grill or grill pan to medium.

2. Whisk together the vinegar, oil, orange juice, ginger, and salt in a medium bowl. Set the dressing aside. Coat the cut surfaces of the peaches with olive oil cooking spray. Season the steak with the black pepper.

3. Place the steak and peaches (cut side down) on the grill or grill pan. Grill the peaches for 6 minutes, or until soft. Grill the steak for 8 minutes, turning once, or until a thermometer inserted in the center registers 145°F for medium-rare/160°F for medium/165°F for well-done. Let stand for 5 minutes before thinly slicing.

4. Slice the peaches into wedges. Add the bell pepper and spinach to the bowl of dressing and toss to coat. Transfer to 4 plates. Top with sliced steak and peaches. Sprinkle with the almonds and basil leaves. Serve with the toast.

Per serving: 274 calories, 9 g fat, 2 g saturated fat, 19 g protein, 30 g carbohydrates, 7 g fiber, 235 mg sodium

Moroccan Chicken and Couscous Salad

This salad keeps fantastically. Make it the day before and enjoy it for lunch right out of the fridge, warmed in the microwave, or at room temperature.

Prep time: 15 minutes ⠿ **Cook time:** 5 minutes ⠿ **Total time:** 20 minutes + chilling time
⠿ MAKES 4 SERVINGS

1 cup boiling water
1 cup whole wheat couscous
¼ cup orange juice
2 tablespoons red wine vinegar
1 tablespoon honey
1½ teaspoons olive oil
¼ teaspoon salt
2 cups diced cooked chicken

½ pint pear tomatoes, halved
1 yellow or red bell pepper, finely chopped
1 carrot, shredded
2 tablespoons thinly sliced dried apricots
Baby spinach, for serving (optional)

1. Combine the boiling water and couscous in a large bowl. Cover and set aside for 5 minutes. Fluff with a fork, cover, and refrigerate for at least 30 minutes.

2. Meanwhile, whisk together the orange juice, vinegar, honey, oil, and salt in a small bowl.

3. Add the chicken, tomatoes, bell pepper, carrot, apricots, and dressing to the couscous and toss to coat well. Serve over baby spinach, if desired.

Per serving: 292 calories, 5 g fat, 1 g saturated fat, 27 g protein, 36 g carbohydrates, 5 g fiber, 215 mg sodium

Quinoa and Chicken Salad

To save time, substitute $1\frac{1}{2}$ cups canned no-sugar-added mandarin orange segments for the 2 oranges.

Prep time: 20 minutes ⊪ **Cook time:** 20 minutes ⊪ **Total time:** 40 minutes ⊪ MAKES 4 SERVINGS

1 cup quinoa
$\frac{1}{3}$ cup frozen lima beans
2 navel oranges
$1\frac{1}{2}$ tablespoons sherry vinegar or red
    wine vinegar
1 teaspoon extra-virgin olive oil
$\frac{1}{8}$ teaspoon salt

$\frac{1}{4}$ teaspoon ground black pepper
$1\frac{1}{2}$ cups shredded cooked chicken
1 large red bell pepper, chopped
3 scallions, thinly sliced
$\frac{1}{4}$ cup fresh basil leaves, coarsely
    chopped

1. Place the quinoa in a skillet over medium heat and cook for 5 minutes, or until golden and fragrant, shaking the pan and stirring occasionally. Add $1\frac{1}{2}$ cups of water and bring to a boil. Add the lima beans. Reduce the heat to low, cover, and simmer for 15 minutes, or until the quinoa is tender. Fluff with a fork and set aside for at least 15 minutes to cool.

2. Meanwhile, grate 1 teaspoon of zest from one of the oranges into a medium bowl. Remove the peel and pith from both oranges. Cut the flesh into segments, cutting them out at the membrane, and slice the segments crosswise. Add to the bowl, along with the vinegar, oil, salt, and black pepper. Stir to combine.

3. Add the chicken, bell pepper, scallions, basil, and quinoa. Toss until evenly coated.

Per serving: 318 calories, 6 g fat, 1 g saturated fat, 25 g protein, 42 g carbohydrates, 6 g fiber, 270 mg sodium

Asian Chicken and Melon Salad

Try this salad with grilled shrimp in place of the chicken.

Prep time: 15 minutes ⁑ **Cook time:** 10 minutes ⁑ **Total time:** 25 minutes ⁑ MAKES 4 SERVINGS

2 cups (6 ounces) sugar snap peas or snow pea pods, strings removed, halved crosswise

1½ tablespoons fresh lime juice

2 tablespoons chopped fresh cilantro

2 teaspoons toasted sesame oil

1 teaspoon grated fresh ginger

⅛ teaspoon salt

8 ounces cooked boneless, skinless chicken breast, shredded

2 cups honeydew melon balls

1 red bell pepper, cut into thin, short strips

1 bag (5 ounces) baby spinach

¼ cup unsalted dry-roasted cashews (optional)

1. Bring a small saucepan of water to a boil over high heat. Cook the sugar snaps or snow peas for 4 minutes, or until tender-crisp. Drain and rinse under cold water; drain well.

2. Whisk together the lime juice, 1 tablespoon of water, the cilantro, sesame oil, ginger, and salt in a large bowl. Add the chicken, melon, bell pepper, spinach, and sugar snaps or snow peas. Toss to coat well. Divide among 4 plates and sprinkle with the cashews (if using).

Per serving: 267 calories, 11 g fat, 2 g saturated fat, 21 g protein, 23 g carbohydrates, 5 g fiber, 162 mg sodium

Greek Chicken Salad

If you want to make this salad ahead, prepare the yogurt mixture, chicken, and cucumbers, then store separately up to 1 day in advance. Toss together right before serving.

Prep time: 20 minutes ▸ **Total time:** 20 minutes ▸ MAKES 4 SERVINGS

½ cup 0% plain Greek yogurt
¼ cup reduced-fat sour cream
1½ teaspoons grated lemon zest
1 clove garlic, minced
3 tablespoons chopped fresh mint
2 scallions, thinly sliced

3½ cups chopped cooked chicken breast
¾ cup cooked shelled edamame
1 large cucumber, peeled, seeded, and chopped
Lettuce leaves, for serving

1. Stir together the yogurt, sour cream, lemon zest, garlic, mint, and scallions in a large bowl. Add the chicken, edamame, and cucumber. Toss to coat well.

2. Serve the chicken mixture on a bed of lettuce.

Per serving: 286 calories, 7 g fat, 2 g saturated fat, 44 g protein, 7 g carbohydrates, 2 g fiber, 266 mg sodium

Salad Niçoise with Basil Vinaigrette

Enjoy this low-salt, protein-packed salad—it'll make you feel like you're on a trip to France!

Prep time: 15 minutes ⁂ **Total time:** 15 minutes + chilling time ⁂ MAKES 4 SERVINGS

SALAD

 8 Boston lettuce leaves, torn

12 ounces green beans, steamed

 4 small Yukon Gold potatoes, cooked and sliced

 2 plum tomatoes, sliced

 2 cans (6.5 ounces each) no-salt-added water-packed tuna, drained

 4 scallions, thinly sliced

BASIL VINAIGRETTE

2 tablespoons Dijon mustard

1 tablespoon chopped fresh basil

1 tablespoon fresh lemon juice

1 tablespoon red wine vinegar

2 teaspoons olive oil

$\frac{1}{2}$ teaspoon ground black pepper

1. To make the salad: Toss the lettuce, beans, potatoes, tomatoes, tuna, and scallions in a large bowl. Cover and refrigerate for 20 minutes.

2. To make the basil vinaigrette: Whisk together 2 tablespoons of water, the mustard, basil, lemon juice, vinegar, oil, and pepper in a small bowl. Drizzle the dressing over the salad just before serving.

Per serving: 314 calories, 5 g fat, 1 g saturated fat, 27 g protein, 41 g carbohydrates, 8 g fiber, 288 mg sodium

Italian Sardine Salad

Sardines are a Salt Solution Star, for good reason. These small fish are packed with potassium, iron, and omega-3 fatty acids (the best fats). Canned sardines are inexpensive and can keep for months in your pantry.

Prep time: 10 minutes ⁛ **Total time:** 10 minutes ⁛ MAKES 2 SERVINGS

1 tablespoon balsamic vinegar

1 tablespoon apple juice or water

2 teaspoons extra-virgin olive oil

Pinch of ground black pepper

3 cups baby spinach

¼ large fennel bulb, thinly sliced

½ cup thinly sliced yellow bell pepper

1 plum tomato, sliced

½ cup very thinly sliced red onion

¼ cup no-salt-added canned chickpeas, rinsed and drained

1 can (4.375 ounces) water-packed sardines, drained and patted dry

2 rye crispbread crackers

1. Whisk together the vinegar, apple juice or water, oil, and black pepper in a small bowl.

2. Divide the spinach, fennel, bell pepper, tomato, onion, chickpeas, and sardines between 2 plates. Drizzle with the dressing and serve with the crispbreads.

Per serving: 277 calories, 5 g fat, 1 g saturated fat, 19 g protein, 28 g carbohydrates, 7 g fiber, 321 mg sodium

Crab and Apple Slaw

Try this slaw with small, whole cooked shrimp or shredded chicken for a change of pace.

Prep time: 20 minutes ❖ **Total time:** 20 minutes + chilling time ❖ MAKES 4 SERVINGS

$\frac{1}{2}$ cup reduced-fat sour cream

$\frac{1}{4}$ cup orange juice

3 tablespoons white wine vinegar

4 teaspoons sugar

1 teaspoon olive oil

1 package (16 ounces) shredded cabbage

2 large apples, cut into matchsticks

1 large carrot, shredded

3 scallions, thinly sliced

6 ounces canned crabmeat, well drained

$\frac{1}{2}$ honeydew melon, peeled and seeded

1. Whisk together the sour cream, orange juice, vinegar, sugar, and oil in a large bowl. Add the cabbage, apples, carrot, scallions, and crabmeat. Toss until well combined. For best flavor, chill the slaw for at least 30 minutes.

2. Cut the melon into $\frac{1}{4}$"-thick wedge-shaped slices; cut in half crosswise. Arrange the melon slices on each of 4 salad plates in a starburst pattern. Top with the slaw mixture.

Per serving. 200 calories, 0 g fat, 0 g saturated fat, 13 g protein, 46 g carbohydrates, 7 g fiber, 304 mg sodium

Middle Eastern Rice Salad

Add leftover ends and leaves of celery to the lentils for a boost of flavor. Look for precooked French lentils to save even more time. If you have fresh mint on hand, add some chopped leaves to the salad. Serve at room temperature or chilled.

Prep time: 10 minutes ⧉ **Cook time:** 15 minutes ⧉ **Total time:** 25 minutes ⧉ MAKES 4 SERVINGS

1 cup brown lentils
3 tablespoons fresh lemon juice
2 teaspoons extra-virgin olive oil
1 teaspoon grated lemon zest
$1/2$ teaspoon smoked paprika
$1/4$ teaspoon salt
$1/8$ teaspoon cayenne pepper

$1^1/_2$ cups cooked brown rice (cooked without salt)
2 carrots, shredded
2 ribs celery, chopped
2 tomatoes, seeded and chopped
1 small red onion, chopped
$3/4$ cup chopped fresh parsley leaves

1. Bring 4 cups of water to a boil in a large saucepan. Add the lentils and reduce to a simmer. Cook for 15 minutes, or just until tender. Drain well and cool.

2. Meanwhile, whisk together the lemon juice, oil, zest, paprika, salt, and cayenne in a large bowl. Add the rice, carrots, celery, tomatoes, onion, parsley, and cooled lentils. Stir to combine.

Per serving: 305 calories, 4 g fat, 1 g saturated fat, 16 g protein, 54 g carbohydrates, 15 g fiber, 204 mg sodium

Cucumber, Cantaloupe, and Tomato Salad

Edamame are fresh soybeans, a Salt Solution Star. These nutritional powerhouses are rich in calcium, potassium, and magnesium.

Prep time: 25 minutes ▷ **Total time:** 25 minutes ▷ MAKES 4 SERVINGS

2 tablespoons fresh lime juice
2 tablespoons white wine vinegar
2 teaspoons extra-virgin olive oil
1 teaspoon sugar
¼ teaspoon salt
¼ teaspoon ground black pepper
1 large English (seedless) cucumber, peeled and chopped

1 cantaloupe, scooped into balls or cubed
2 tomatoes, coarsely chopped
1½ cups cooked shelled edamame
2 bunches arugula (8 ounces)
½ cup basil leaves
12 wheat and rye crispbread crackers

1. Whisk together the lime juice, vinegar, oil, sugar, salt, and pepper in a small bowl.

2. Combine the cucumber, cantaloupe, tomatoes, edamame, arugula, and basil in a large bowl. Toss with the dressing and serve with the crispbreads.

Per serving: 289 calories, 7 g fat, 1 g saturated fat, 14 g protein, 43 g carbohydrates, 9 g fiber, 305 mg sodium

Spinach, Chicken, and Mandarin Orange Salad

This Asian-inspired salad can be assembled in a flash by making the dressing ahead of time.

Prep time: 20 minutes ⁂ **Total time:** 20 minutes ⁂ MAKES 4 SERVINGS

$1\frac{1}{2}$ tablespoons Dijon mustard

1 tablespoon honey

1 tablespoon fresh lemon juice

1 tablespoon orange juice

8 cups baby spinach

1 red onion, thinly sliced and separated into rings

4 ounces sliced mushrooms

3 cups shredded cooked chicken breast

$\frac{1}{2}$ cup no-salt-added canned kidney beans, rinsed and drained

1 cup canned water- or juice-packed mandarin orange segments, drained

$1\frac{1}{2}$ tablespoons sliced almonds, toasted

1. Whisk together the mustard, honey, lemon juice, and orange juice in a large bowl.

2. Add the spinach, onion, mushrooms, chicken, and kidney beans to the dressing. Toss until well blended. Divide the salad among 4 plates. Top with the mandarin oranges and almonds.

Per serving: 284 calories, 5 g fat, 1 g saturated fat, 38 g protein, 21 g carbohydrates, 5 g fiber, 269 mg sodium

SOUPS, SALADS, AND SANDWICHES ⩔

129

Moroccan Turkey Pitas

Prepare the ingredients before assembling up to 1 day in advance. To serve, simply microwave the turkey mixture right before serving. Serve the meat mixture open-face style, piling it on top of the pita and drizzling with the sauce. Or if you prefer, spoon the meat mixture into halved and split pita rounds.

Prep time: 20 minutes ▷ **Cook time:** 10 minutes ▷ **Total time:** 30 minutes ▷ MAKES 4 SERVINGS

1 lemon
½ cup 0% plain Greek yogurt
4 scallions, thinly sliced
⅓ cup chopped fresh mint
¾ pound 99% fat-free ground turkey breast
2 cloves garlic, chopped
1½ teaspoons ground cumin

¼ teaspoon ground allspice
¼ teaspoon dried oregano
⅛ teaspoon cayenne pepper
1 cup no-salt-added canned chickpeas, rinsed and drained
¼ cup no-salt-added tomato puree
⅛ teaspoon salt
4 whole wheat pitas (4" diameter)

1. Grate 1 teaspoon of zest from the lemon; juice one half and cut the remaining into 4 wedges. Place the yogurt in a small bowl. Stir in 2 tablespoons of the scallions, 2 tablespoons of the mint, and ½ teaspoon of the lemon zest; set aside.

2. Combine the turkey, garlic, cumin, allspice, oregano, and cayenne in a nonstick skillet over medium-high heat. Cook for 6 minutes, stirring and breaking up the meat with a spoon, or until no longer pink.

3. Stir in the chickpeas, tomato puree, salt, and remaining scallions. Cook for 2 minutes, or until heated through. Remove from the heat and stir in the lemon juice, remaining ½ teaspoon lemon zest, and the remaining mint. Spoon onto the pitas and serve with the yogurt sauce and lemon wedges.

Per serving: 279 calories, 2 g fat, 0 g saturated fat, 31 g protein, 35 g carbohydrates, 6 g fiber, 300 mg sodium

Grilled Chicken and Portobello Panini

This warm sandwich is perfect on a cold day—and the extra potassium, magnesium, and calcium from spinach, a Salt Solution Star, makes it even better.

Prep time: 15 minutes ⊳ **Cook time:** 10 minutes ⊳ **Total time:** 25 minutes ⊳ MAKES 2 SERVINGS

3 tablespoons balsamic vinegar
$\frac{1}{2}$ teaspoon salt-free seasoning blend
2 large portobello mushrooms
$\frac{1}{2}$ large red onion, cut into two $\frac{1}{2}$" slices

4 slices thin-sliced whole wheat bread
1 cup sliced cooked chicken breast
$\frac{1}{2}$ cup baby spinach

1. Whisk together 2 tablespoons of the vinegar and the seasoning blend in a shallow bowl. Add the mushrooms and onion slices, turning to coat. Let stand for 10 minutes.

2. Lay 2 slices of the bread on a work surface. Top each with half the chicken, 1 onion slice, and 1 mushroom. Top each with $\frac{1}{4}$ cup baby spinach and the remaining bread slices.

3. Coat the top slices with cooking spray and place sprayed-side down onto a grill pan or skillet. Coat the other piece of bread with cooking spray. Place a heavy pan over the top of the sandwiches. Cook over medium heat, turning once, for 4 minutes, or until browned.

Per serving: 311 calories, 5 g fat, 1 g saturated fat, 30 g protein, 33 g carbohydrates, 6 g fiber, 267 mg sodium

Turkey, Apple, and Chutney Sandwiches

The creamy chutney spread takes this sandwich from ordinary to exciting. If you don't have chutney on hand, substitute 1 tablespoon apricot jam and a pinch of curry powder.

Prep time: 15 minutes ⁛ **Total time:** 15 minutes ⁛ MAKES 2 SERVINGS

1 tablespoon chutney

1 tablespoon reduced-fat sour cream

1 teaspoon fresh lemon juice

4 slices thin-sliced 100% whole wheat bread

½ cup baby spinach

3 ounces cooked unsalted sliced turkey breast

1 ounce sliced reduced-fat Swiss cheese

1 small Granny Smith apple, thinly sliced

1. Finely chop any large chunks in the chutney. Stir together the chutney, sour cream, and lemon juice in a small bowl until combined.

2. Spread the chutney cream on 2 slices of the bread. Top each with the spinach, turkey, cheese, apple, and remaining bread slices. Cut in half to serve.

Per serving: 250 calories, 6 g fat, 3 g saturated fat, 21 g protein, 30 g carbohydrates, 7 g fiber, 331 mg sodium

MAKE IT A SALT SOLUTION MEAL: Serve with 1 tangerine (295 calories and 331 mg sodium total).

Turkey Sloppy Joes

Sloppy Joes don't have to be junk food—these are made with healthy ground turkey breast and low- and no-sodium condiments. Dig in!

Prep time: 10 minutes ▶ **Cook time:** 25 minutes ▶ **Total time:** 35 minutes ▶ MAKES 6 SERVINGS

1 onion, chopped
1 green bell pepper, chopped
1 carrot, chopped
3 cloves garlic, chopped
1¼ pounds ground turkey breast
⅓ cup no-salt-added ketchup
1 tablespoon reduced-sodium Worcestershire sauce

1 can (8 ounces) no-salt-added tomato sauce
½ teaspoon ground cumin
¼ teaspoon cayenne pepper
6 whole wheat hamburger buns, split and toasted

1. Heat a large nonstick skillet coated with cooking spray over medium-high heat. Add the onion, bell pepper, carrot, and garlic. Cook, stirring, for 3 minutes. Add the turkey. Cook for 3 minutes, stirring and breaking up the meat with a spoon, or until the turkey begins to brown.

2. Stir in the ketchup, Worcestershire sauce, tomato sauce, cumin, and cayenne. Cover and cook for 20 minutes, stirring occasionally, or until thick. Serve on the buns.

Per serving: 268 calories, 3 g fat, 0 g saturated fat, 28 g protein, 34 g carbohydrates, 5 g fiber, 276 mg sodium

Tuna Tacos

To take these tacos on the road, make the salad mixture ahead and pack in mounds in a shallow container, along with the lettuce and tomatoes. Assemble them right before eating.

Prep time: 20 minutes ⁙ **Total time:** 20 minutes ⁙ MAKES 2 SERVINGS

1 cup no-salt-added canned cannellini beans, rinsed and drained

1 can (6 ounces) low-sodium water-packed chunk white tuna, well drained

$1/3$ cup 0% plain Greek yogurt

2 teaspoons fresh lemon juice

1 small carrot, shredded

$1/4$–$1/2$ teaspoon salt-free extra-spicy seasoning blend

$1/8$ teaspoon salt

2 large romaine lettuce leaves, thinly sliced

1 tomato, chopped

4 low-salt taco shells (look for brand with the lowest sodium)

1. Place the beans in a medium bowl and mash with the back of a large spoon. Stir in the tuna, yogurt, lemon juice, carrot, seasoning, and salt until combined.

2. Divide the tuna mixture, lettuce, and tomato among the taco shells.

Per serving. 283 calories, 0 g fat, 2 g saturated fat, 19 g protein, 40 g carbohydrates, 9 g fiber, 247 mg sodium

Curried Tuna and Apple Salad Sandwich

Try this with firm-ripe pears in place of the apples.

Prep time: 20 minutes ⁘ **Total time:** 20 minutes ⁘ MAKES 2 SERVINGS

2 tart green apples, halved

½ cup no-salt-added canned white beans, rinsed and drained

3 tablespoons 0% plain Greek yogurt

2 tablespoons reduced-fat sour cream

2 teaspoons fresh lemon juice

1 teaspoon honey

1 teaspoon curry powder

1 can (6 ounces) low-sodium water-packed chunk white tuna, drained

1 rib celery, chopped

½ cup baby spinach

1 tomato, thinly sliced

4 slices thin-sliced whole grain bread

1. Chop ½ apple and set aside for the salad. Cut the remaining 1½ apples into wedges for serving.

2. Place the beans in a medium bowl and mash with the back of a spoon or a potato masher. Add the yogurt, sour cream, lemon juice, honey, and curry powder. Stir until combined.

3. Add the tuna, celery, and chopped apple. Stir until combined. Arrange the spinach and tomato on 2 slices of the bread. Top with the tuna and remaining bread slices. Cut the sandwiches in half and serve with the apple wedges.

Per serving: 298 calories, 4 g fat, 2 g saturated fat, 16 g protein, 52 g carbohydrates, 9 g fiber, 228 mg sodium

Salmon and White Bean Stuffed Pitas

These stuffed pitas feature white beans, Salt Solution Stars. You can make the filling ahead of time and stuff the pitas when you're ready to eat.

Prep time: 15 minutes ⟩· **Cook time:** 5 minutes ⟩· **Total time:** 20 minutes ⟩· MAKES 2 SERVINGS

 5 ounces skinless salmon fillet
$\frac{1}{2}$ teaspoon grated lemon zest
 1 tablespoon fresh lemon juice
$\frac{1}{4}$ teaspoon ground black pepper
   Pinch of salt
$\frac{1}{2}$ cup no-salt-added canned cannellini beans, rinsed and drained

$\frac{1}{2}$ small red bell pepper, chopped
$\frac{1}{2}$ cup chopped arugula
 2 whole wheat pitas (4" diameter), halved crosswise

1. Heat a small nonstick skillet coated with cooking spray over medium heat. Add the salmon and cook for 6 minutes, turning once, or until browned and just opaque throughout. Set aside to cool for 10 minutes, then break into chunks.

2. Whisk together the lemon zest, lemon juice, black pepper, and salt in a medium bowl. Toss in the beans, bell pepper, arugula, and salmon until combined. Spoon the mixture into the split pitas.

Per serving: 270 calories, 7 g fat, 1 g saturated fat, 24 g protein, 27 g carbohydrates, 5 g fiber, 284 mg sodium

Veggie Sandwich with Edamame Hummus

Served with knife and fork, this filling sandwich will satisfy your lunchtime cravings. Wrap each half separately if you're taking this sandwich on the go.

Prep time: 20 minutes ⫶ **Total time:** 20 minutes ⫶ MAKES 2 SERVINGS

¾ cup frozen shelled edamame

⅓ cup 0% plain Greek yogurt

1 tablespoon fresh lemon juice

3 tablespoons chopped fresh parsley

2 tablespoons chopped fresh chives

1 teaspoon honey mustard

Generous pinch of salt

4 slices thin-sliced whole wheat bread, toasted

¾ cup baby spinach

1 tomato, sliced

1 Kirby cucumber, sliced

1. Bring a small saucepan of water to a boil. Add the edamame and cook for 5 minutes, or until tender. Drain well. Place in a mini-processor and blend until finely chopped. Add the yogurt, lemon juice, parsley, chives, mustard, and salt. Process until smooth.

2. Spread 2 tablespoons of the edamame hummus on each slice of bread. Top with the spinach. Spoon on ½ tablespoon of the hummus on top. Top with the sliced tomato and cucumber and a final dollop of hummus. Serve 2 open-face sandwiches per person.

Per serving: 224 calories, 4 g fat, 0 g saturated fat, 15 g protein, 36 g carbohydrates, 11 g fiber, 380 mg sodium

 MAKE IT A SALT SOLUTION MEAL: Serve with 1 small banana (310 calories and 391 mg sodium total).

Chicken Summer Rolls

If you want, use large soft lettuce leaves in place of the rice wrappers. Set out bowls of the vegetables and have everyone make his or her own rolls.

Prep time: 20 minutes ⁂ **Total time:** 20 minutes ⁂ MAKES 4 SERVINGS

SAUCE
- $\frac{1}{3}$ cup low-sodium chicken broth
- 1 tablespoon reduced-sodium soy sauce
- 1 tablespoon fresh lime juice
- 1 teaspoon white wine vinegar
  Pinch of cayenne pepper

ROLLS
- 2 ounces low-sodium buckwheat noodles, cooked and drained
- 8 round rice paper wrappers (8" diameter)
- $\frac{1}{4}$ cup chopped fresh mint leaves
- $\frac{1}{4}$ cup chopped fresh cilantro
- $\frac{1}{2}$ avocado, cut into 8 thin slices
- 1 cup fresh spinach, cut into strips
- 1 red bell pepper, cut into thin strips
- 1 carrot, shredded
- $1\frac{1}{2}$ cups shredded cooked chicken breast

1. To make the sauce: Whisk together the broth, soy sauce, lime juice, vinegar, and cayenne in a medium bowl.

2. To make the rolls: Prepare the buckwheat noodles according to the package directions, omitting the salt. Rinse under cold running water and drain well. Soak 1 rice paper wrapper in warm water for 30 to 60 seconds, or until soft. Carefully transfer to a clean towel and blot dry.

3. Place $\frac{1}{2}$ tablespoon mint and $\frac{1}{2}$ tablespoon cilantro along the bottom third of the wrapper. Top with one-eighth of the noodles, avocado, spinach, bell pepper, carrot, and chicken.

4. Fold the bottom of the rice paper up and over the filling. Fold in the sides and continue rolling until the roll is sealed completely. Repeat with the remaining wrappers and fillings. Cut each roll in half crosswise and serve 2 rolls per person, with the sauce.

Per serving: 267 calories, 5 g fat, 1 g saturated fat, 22 g protein, 31 g carbohydrates, 4 g fiber, 245 mg sodium

Mushroom and Zucchini Pizzas

Pizza doesn't have to be bad for you! Ours is packed with fresh veggies and naturally low-salt ingredients.

Prep time: 10 minutes ▷ **Cook time:** 20 minutes ▷ **Total time:** 30 minutes ▷ MAKES 4 SERVINGS

4 cups thinly sliced cremini mushrooms (about 8 ounces)

Yellow cornmeal, for sprinkling

1/2 8-ounce package whole wheat pizza dough, fresh or thawed frozen

1 medium zucchini, thinly sliced

1 cup thinly sliced sweet onion (such as Vidalia)

2 teaspoons fresh thyme leaves, chopped

Pinch of kosher salt

Pinch of ground black pepper

1/3 cup grated Gruyère cheese

4 apples

1. Preheat the oven to 475°F.

2. Heat a large nonstick skillet coated with cooking spray over medium-high heat. Cook the mushrooms for 5 minutes, or until golden brown.

3. Sprinkle two ungreased baking sheets with the cornmeal. Divide the pizza dough into 4 equal portions, each about the size of a large egg. On a well-floured surface, pat each portion into 6" to 7" rounds. Transfer to the baking sheets.

4. Arrange the mushrooms on the dough. Top with the zucchini and onion. Sprinkle with the thyme, salt, and pepper. Bake for 12 minutes, or until golden brown around the edges. Remove from the oven and top with the cheese. Bake for 2 minutes, or until the cheese melts. Serve with the apples.

Per serving: 294 calories, 6 g fat, 2 g saturated fat, 10 g protein, 58 g carbohydrates, 10 g fiber, 321 mg sodium

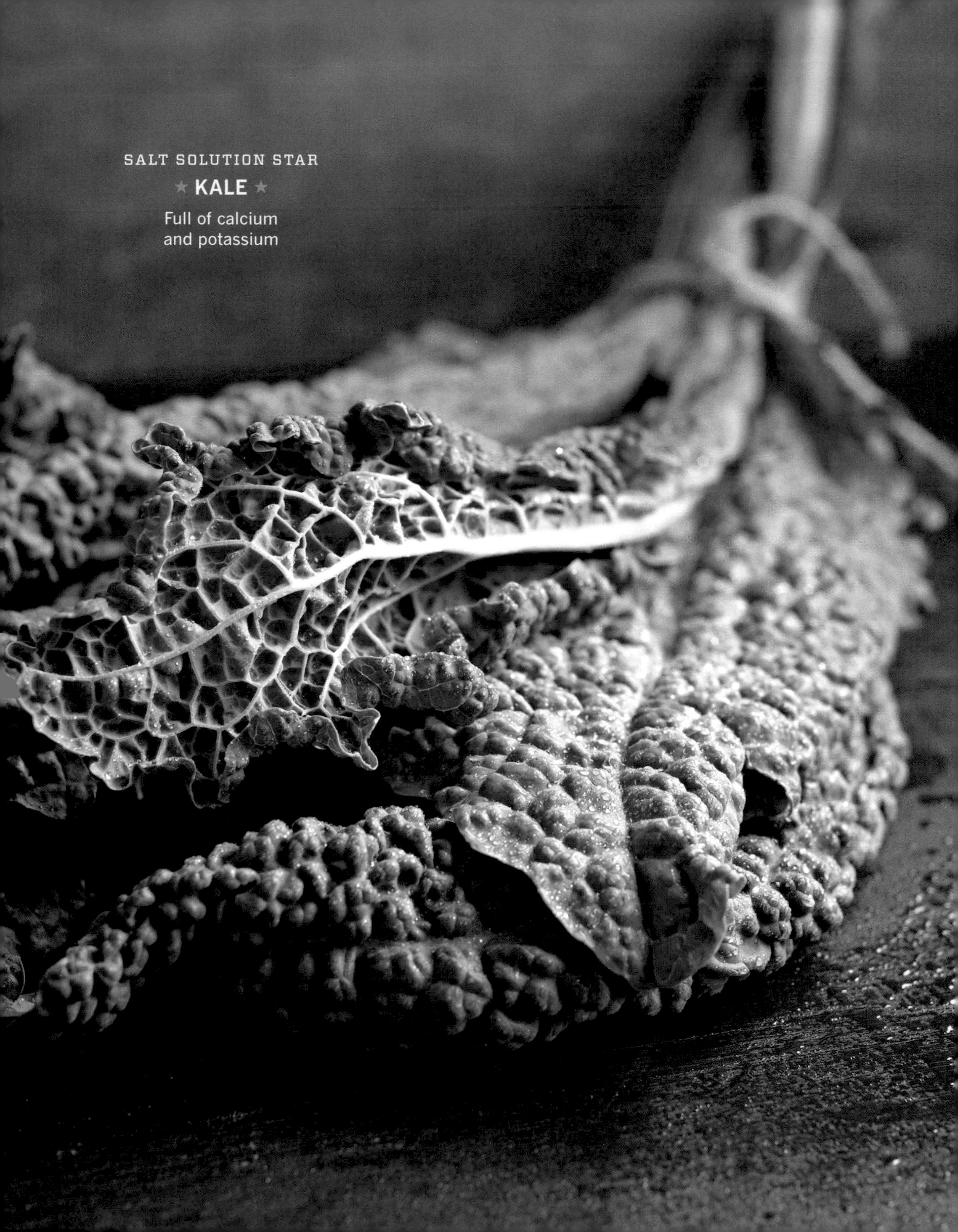

SALT SOLUTION STAR

★ **KALE** ★

Full of calcium
and potassium

Meat

Marinated Broiled Flank Steak with Sweet and Sour Beet Greens

This highly flavorful but simple marinade also works wonderfully on boneless, skinless chicken breasts or thighs and pork.

Prep time: 20 minutes ▷ **Cook Time:** 10 minutes ▷ **Total Time:** 30 minutes + marinating time
▷ MAKES 4 SERVINGS

- 1 pound flank steak, trimmed of all visible fat
- 1 large shallot, finely chopped
- 3 cloves garlic, minced
- 1 teaspoon chopped fresh thyme leaves
- 1 teaspoon extra-virgin olive oil
- 4 tablespoons balsamic vinegar
- $\frac{1}{8}$ teaspoon salt
- $\frac{1}{8}$ teaspoon ground black pepper
- 10 cups beet greens, washed, chopped, and left damp
- 1 tablespoon sugar
- 2 teaspoons grated lemon zest
- 2 cups cooked couscous

1. Combine the flank steak, shallot, garlic, thyme, oil, and 3 tablespoons of the vinegar in a resealable plastic bag. Turn the bag several times to coat the steak and refrigerate for 1 to 24 hours, turning occasionally.

2. Preheat the broiler. Coat a broiler pan with cooking spray.

3. Remove the steak from the plastic bag and wipe off the excess marinade. Set the steak on the pan and sprinkle with the salt and pepper. Broil 5" from the heat for 10 minutes, turning once, or until a thermometer inserted in the center registers 145°F for medium-rare/160°F for medium/or 165°F for well-done. Place on a cutting board and let stand for 10 minutes before thinly slicing across the grain.

4. Meanwhile, heat a large nonstick skillet coated with cooking spray over medium-high heat. Add the beet greens and cook, stirring often, for 2 minutes, or until starting to wilt. Pour in the remaining 1 tablespoon vinegar and the sugar; cook for 2 minutes, stirring, or until wilted. Remove from the heat and stir in the lemon zest. Divide the steak, greens, and couscous among 4 plates.

Per serving: 313 calories, 8 g fat, 3 g saturated fat, 30 g protein, 30 g carbohydrates, 4 g fiber, 316 mg sodium

Savory Pot Roast

The slow cooker makes this dish an easy dinner at the end of a long day.

Prep time: 15 minutes ⫶ **Cook time:** 8 hours ⫶ **Total time:** 8 hours 15 minutes ⫶ MAKES 6 SERVINGS

1²/₃ cups low-sodium beef broth

½ cup all-purpose flour

3 tablespoons no-salt-added tomato paste

1 teaspoon dried thyme

⅛ teaspoon salt

¼ teaspoon ground black pepper

2 pounds boneless beef chuck roast, trimmed of all visible fat

8 ounces baby carrots

4 ribs celery, chopped

1 medium onion, chopped

¾ pound small red-skinned potatoes

1. Coat a 4- to 6-quart slow cooker with cooking spray. Add the broth and flour and whisk until smooth. Whisk in the tomato paste, thyme, salt, and pepper. Add the beef, carrots, celery, onion, and potatoes. Spoon some of the liquid over the beef to moisten. Cover and cook on low for 8 hours, or until the meat is fork-tender.

2. Transfer the beef to a cutting board, cover loosely with foil, and let stand for 10 minutes before slicing. Divide the meat and vegetables among 6 dinner plates. Top with the sauce.

Per serving: 323 calories, 7 g fat, 3 g saturated fat, 38 g protein, 25 g carbohydrates, 4 g fiber, 300 mg sodium

Beef and Bean Stew

Slow simmering helps to build and intensify the flavor in this easy crowd-pleasing dish.

Prep time: 15 minutes ▷ **Cook time:** 1 hour 35 minutes ▷ **Total time:** 1 hour 50 minutes
▷ MAKES 4 SERVINGS

1 tablespoon olive oil

¾ pound extra-lean beef top round, cut into 1" cubes

1 large onion, chopped

2 medium carrots, chopped

2 ribs celery, chopped

8 ounces mushrooms, quartered

4 cloves garlic, minced

1 teaspoon fresh thyme leaves

1½ cups low-sodium beef broth

½ cup red wine

3 tablespoons no-salt-added tomato paste

3 tablespoons chopped fresh parsley

1 can (15 ounces) no-salt-added red kidney beans, rinsed and drained

¼ teaspoon salt

¼ teaspoon ground black pepper

1. Heat 2 teaspoons of the oil in a Dutch oven over medium-high heat. Add the beef and cook for 5 minutes, turning occasionally, or until browned. Transfer to a plate and set aside.

2. Heat the remaining 1 teaspoon oil in the same pan. Cook the onion, carrots, celery, mushrooms, garlic, and thyme for 6 minutes, stirring occasionally, or until slightly softened. Stir in the beef, broth, wine, tomato paste, and parsley. Bring to a boil, reduce the heat to medium-low, cover, and simmer for 1 hour.

3. Stir in the beans, return to a simmer, and cook for 20 minutes, or until the beef is tender. Remove from the heat and stir in the salt and pepper.

Per serving: 293 calories, 7 g fat, 2 g saturated fat, 29 g protein, 29 g carbohydrates, 9 g fiber, 273 mg sodium

Greek-Seasoned Filet of Beef with Cucumber Tzatziki, Broccoli, and Pita

As an alternative, slice the steaks and serve with tomato and lettuce to create a deconstructed souvlaki.

Prep time: 10 minutes ▷ **Cook time:** 15 minutes ▷ **Total time:** 25 minutes ▷ MAKES 4 SERVINGS

4 beef filet steaks (about 3 ounces each)
2 tablespoons fresh lemon juice
1 teaspoon dried oregano
2 cloves garlic, minced
1 cup 0% plain Greek yogurt
¾ medium cucumber, peeled, seeded, grated, and excess liquid squeezed out

6 cups broccoli florets
⅛ teaspoon salt
⅛ teaspoon ground black pepper
4 whole wheat pitas (4" diameter), toasted

1. Combine the beef, lemon juice, oregano, and half the garlic in a bowl. Turn to coat and let stand for 10 minutes.

2. Meanwhile, to make the tzatziki, combine the yogurt, cucumber, and remaining garlic in a bowl.

3. Set a steamer basket in a large saucepan with 2" of water. Bring to a boil, add the broccoli, and steam for 4 minutes, or until tender-crisp. Remove from the heat and keep warm.

4. Remove the beef from the marinade and sprinkle with the salt and pepper. Coat a nonstick grill pan with cooking spray and heat over medium-high heat. Cook the beef for 8 minutes, turning once, or until a thermometer inserted in the center registers 145°F for medium-rare/160°F for medium/or 165°F for well-done.

5. To serve, place 1 steak on each of 4 plates with ¼ cup cucumber tzatziki, 1½ cups broccoli, and 1 pita.

Per serving: 278 calories, 7 g fat, 2 g saturated fat, 30 g protein, 25 g carbohydrates, 6 g fiber, 321 mg sodium

MEAT

Gingered Beef with Broccolini and Walnuts

Broccolini is similar to broccoli but with smaller florets and thinner, more tender stalks. It is a cross between regular broccoli and Chinese broccoli.

Prep time: 5 minutes ❧ **Cook time:** 10 minutes ❧ **Total time:** 15 minutes ❧ MAKES 4 SERVINGS

½ cup long-grain white rice
2 tablespoons grated fresh ginger
1 tablespoon oyster sauce
2 teaspoons less-sodium soy sauce
1 teaspoon no-salt-added tomato paste
2 teaspoons toasted sesame oil
1½ pounds broccolini, trimmed and cut into bite-size pieces

¾ pound flank steak, trimmed of all visible fat, cut across the grain into thin strips
6 scallions, cut into 1" pieces
¼ cup walnut halves, coarsely chopped

1. Bring 1 cup of water to a boil in a small saucepan over medium-high heat. Add the rice, reduce the heat to medium-low, cover, and simmer for 20 minutes, or until the water is absorbed.

2. Combine the ginger, oyster sauce, soy sauce, tomato paste, and 2 tablespoons of water in a small bowl.

3. Heat the sesame oil in a large nonstick skillet over high heat. Add the broccolini and cook, stirring frequently, for 3 minutes. Add 3 tablespoons of water and cook for 2 minutes. Add the steak, scallions, and ginger mixture. Cook for 2 minutes, stirring constantly, or until the beef is cooked through but still slightly pink. Stir in the walnuts and serve over the rice.

Per serving: 324 calories, 11 g fat, 3 g saturated fat, 27 g protein, 31 g carbohydrates, 6 g fiber, 319 mg sodium

Beef and Vegetable Medley

Earthy mushrooms and a sweet sauce add flavor and bulk to this family favorite.

Prep time: 10 minutes ⊳ **Cook time:** 10 minutes ⊳ **Total time:** 20 minutes ⊳ MAKES 4 SERVINGS

1 cup quick-cooking brown rice
¾ pound extra-lean ground beef
1 medium onion, chopped
1 green bell pepper, chopped
4 ounces sliced mushrooms
1 clove garlic, minced

¾ teaspoon chili powder
¾ teaspoon ground cumin
¾ cup no-salt-added ketchup
1 tablespoon packed dark brown sugar
1 teaspoon Worcestershire sauce

1. Prepare the rice according to package directions, omitting any salt or fat.

2. Meanwhile, heat a large nonstick skillet over medium-high heat. Add the beef and cook for 4 minutes, breaking it up with a wooden spoon, or until no longer pink. Stir in the onion, bell pepper, mushrooms, garlic, chili powder, and cumin. Cook for 5 minutes, stirring occasionally, or until the vegetables are tender. Stir in the ketchup, brown sugar, and Worcestershire sauce. Cook for 2 minutes, stirring, or until slightly thickened.

3. Divide the rice among 4 dinner plates and top with the beef mixture.

Per serving: 296 calories, 5 g fat, 2 g saturated fat, 22 g protein, 44 g carbohydrates, 4 g fiber, 92 mg sodium

Meatloaf with Mushroom Gravy

Dried porcini mushrooms, usually found in the produce section of the grocery store, have a very intense earthy taste that helps add a lot of flavor to lean ground beef.

Prep time: 30 minutes ▷ **Cook time:** 2 hours ▷ **Total time:** 2 hours 30 minutes ▷ MAKES 8 SERVINGS

MEATLOAF

1 ounce dried mushrooms, such as porcini
1½ cups hot water
2 slices multigrain bread
1 can (8 ounces) no-salt-added tomato sauce
½ cup low-sodium beef broth
½ cup bulgur
1½ pounds extra-lean ground beef
2 large egg whites
2 medium onions, finely chopped
2 cloves garlic, minced
1 tablespoon fresh thyme leaves, chopped
1 tablespoon chopped fresh oregano
¼ teaspoon + ⅛ teaspoon salt
½ teaspoon ground black pepper

GRAVY

2 teaspoons olive oil
1 small onion, chopped
8 ounces mushrooms, sliced
2 cloves garlic, minced
1½ cups low-sodium beef broth
½ cup white wine
1 tablespoon fresh thyme leaves, chopped
¼ teaspoon salt
1 tablespoon cornstarch

1. To make the meatloaf: Combine the dried mushrooms with 1 cup of the hot water in a small bowl and let soak for 20 minutes. Drain, reserving ¼ cup of the liquid. Combine the bulgur and the remaining ½ cup water in a large bowl and let stand for 30 minutes, or until the liquid is absorbed. Place the bread slices in a food processor and process to crumbs.

2. Preheat the oven to 375°F. Coat a 9" × 5" × 3" loaf pan with cooking spray.

3. Add the drained mushrooms, tomato sauce, and broth to the bulgur and mix well. Add the beef, bread crumbs, egg whites, onions, garlic, thyme, oregano, salt, and pepper. Gently mix to combine. Transfer the mixture to the loaf pan. Bake for 1 hour 15 minutes, or until a thermometer inserted in the center registers 160°F and the meat is no longer pink.

4. Meanwhile, to make the gravy: Heat the oil in a medium nonstick skillet over medium heat. Add the onion and cook for 3 minutes, stirring occasionally, or until starting to soften. Add the mushrooms and garlic. Cook for 5 minutes, stirring occasionally, or until the mushrooms start to soften. Stir in the broth, wine, thyme, salt, and reserved mushroom liquid. Bring to a boil, reduce the heat to medium-low, cover, and simmer for 10 minutes. Stir 2 tablespoons of water into the cornstarch in a small bowl. Add to the skillet, increase the heat to medium-high, bring to a boil, and cook for 1 minute, or until thickened.

5. Remove the meatloaf from the pan and transfer to a cutting board. Cut into 16 slices and serve 2 per person, topped with gravy.

Per serving: 240 calories, 6 g fat, 2 g saturated fat, 23 g protein, 20 g carbohydrates, 4 g fiber, 286 mg sodium

 MAKE IT A SALT SOLUTION MEAL: Serve with a salad made from 2 cups spinach, 1 teaspoon olive oil, and 1 teaspoon fresh lemon juice (294 calories and 333 mg sodium total).

Salt Solution Burger

Sure, you can still enjoy a juicy burger. Just a touch of salty steak sauce is balanced with garlic, onion powder, and cracked black pepper, giving delicious flavor to this American classic while keeping the sodium in check.

Prep time: 10 minutes ▸ **Cook time:** 30 minutes ▸ **Total time:** 40 minutes ▸ MAKES 4 SERVINGS

2 medium red onions, sliced

2 tablespoons low-sodium beef broth

2 teaspoons balsamic vinegar

1 pound extra-lean ground beef

2 cloves garlic, minced

1 teaspoon steak sauce

$\frac{1}{2}$ teaspoon onion powder

$\frac{1}{2}$ teaspoon cracked black pepper

4 thin slices ($\frac{1}{2}$ ounce each) reduced-sodium cheese, such as Cheddar, American, or Swiss

4 bagel "thins"

Lettuce leaves (optional)

Tomato slices (optional)

1. Heat a medium nonstick skillet coated with cooking spray over medium-high heat. Cook the onions for 5 minutes, or until lightly browned. Add the broth and vinegar and cook, stirring, for 1 minute. Reduce the heat to low, cover, and simmer for 15 minutes, or until browned and tender.

2. Preheat the broiler or grill.

3. Combine the beef, garlic, steak sauce, onion powder, and cracked pepper in a large bowl. Form the mixture into 4 patties. Broil or grill for 7 minutes, turning once, or until a thermometer inserted in the center registers 160°F. During the last minute of cooking, top each burger with a slice of cheese.

4. Divide the bagel thins among 4 plates. Place the lettuce and tomato (if using) on the bagel and top with a burger and onions.

Per serving: 338 calories, 11 g fat, 5 g saturated fat, 34 g protein, 28 g carbohydrates, 6 g fiber, 99 mg sodium

Spaghetti and Meatballs

Extra-lean ground beef and an egg white help to lighten this classic Italian favorite.

Prep time: 20 minutes ▷ **Cook time:** 40 minutes ▷ **Total time:** 1 hour ▷ MAKES 4 SERVINGS

6 ounces spaghetti
½ slice whole wheat bread
½ pound extra-lean ground beef
2 tablespoons minced onion + 1 small onion, chopped
2 cloves garlic, minced
½ teaspoon dried basil
½ teaspoon dried oregano

Dash of cayenne pepper
1 large egg white
½ cup reduced-sodium chicken broth
2 red bell peppers, finely chopped
4 large tomatoes, seeded and chopped
¼ cup canned tomato sauce
⅛ teaspoon salt

1. Prepare the spaghetti according to package directions, omitting the salt.

2. Meanwhile, place the bread in a food processor and pulse to make fine crumbs. Add the beef, minced onion, garlic, basil, oregano, and cayenne and pulse until just combined. Add the egg white and pulse until well blended. Form into 2" balls.

3. Heat a large nonstick skillet coated with cooking spray over medium heat. Add the meatballs and cook for 6 minutes, turning often, or until browned. Transfer to a platter and set aside.

4. Return the skillet to medium-high heat and pour in the broth, scraping up any browned bits with a wooden spoon. Add the chopped onion and bell peppers. Cook for 5 minutes, stirring often, or until softened. Stir in the tomatoes, tomato sauce, and salt. Bring to a boil, reduce the heat to medium-low, cover, and simmer for 10 minutes, stirring often. Add the meatballs and cook for 10 minutes, or until the meatballs are cooked through.

5. Divide the spaghetti among 4 plates and top with the meatballs and sauce.

Per serving: 306 calories, 4 g fat, 1 g saturated fat, 21 g protein, 48 g carbohydrates, 6 g fiber, 280 mg sodium

Broiled Lamb Chops with Spinach and White Bean Sauté

Rosemary and spinach give the beans a fresh, light flavor that plays nicely off the hearty taste of the lamb.

Prep time: 10 minutes ▷ **Cook time:** 20 minutes ▷ **Total time:** 30 minutes ▷ MAKES 4 SERVINGS

1 tablespoon extra-virgin olive oil
1 large onion, thinly sliced
2 teaspoons sugar
1 teaspoon chopped fresh rosemary
3 cloves garlic, sliced
$\frac{3}{4}$ cup low-sodium beef broth
1 can (15 ounces) no-salt-added cannellini beans, rinsed and drained

6 cups baby spinach
$\frac{1}{4}$ teaspoon + $\frac{1}{8}$ teaspoon salt
$\frac{1}{4}$ teaspoon ground black pepper
4 loin lamb chops, trimmed of all visible fat
$\frac{1}{2}$ teaspoon fennel seeds, crushed

1. Preheat the broiler. Coat a broiler pan with cooking spray.

2. Heat the oil in a large nonstick skillet over medium-high heat. Add the onion, sugar, and rosemary and cook for 7 minutes, stirring occasionally, or until starting to brown. Add the garlic and cook for 2 minutes.

3. Stir in the broth, bring to a boil, and cook for 1 minute. Stir in the beans and cook for 2 minutes. Add the spinach and cook for 1 minute, stirring, or until wilted. Remove from the heat and stir in $\frac{1}{4}$ teaspoon of the salt and $\frac{1}{8}$ teaspoon of the pepper. Keep warm.

4. Sprinkle the lamb chops with the fennel seeds and remaining $\frac{1}{8}$ teaspoon salt and $\frac{1}{8}$ teaspoon pepper. Place on the broiler pan and broil 4" from the heat for 6 minutes, turning once, or until browned and a thermometer inserted in the center registers 145°F for medium-rare. Serve with the bean mixture.

Per serving: 273 calories, 9 g fat, 2 g saturated fat, 24 g protein, 25 g carbohydrates, 6 g fiber, 313 mg sodium

Shepherd's Pie

The earthy bite of turnips adds a bit of intrigue to the traditional creamy potato topping.

Prep time: 15 minutes ⁘ **Cook time:** 1 hour 5 minutes ⁘ **Total time:** 1 hour 20 minutes
⁘ MAKES 6 SERVINGS

1 pound russet (baking) potatoes, peeled and chopped

3 small white turnips, peeled and chopped

$\frac{1}{3}$ cup fat-free milk

2 tablespoons trans-free margarine

1$\frac{1}{4}$ pounds extra-lean ground beef

1 large onion, chopped

1 cup frozen peas and carrots

2 cloves garlic, minced

1 can (14.5 ounces) no-salt-added diced tomatoes

$\frac{1}{2}$ cup low-sodium chicken broth

3 tablespoons no-salt-added tomato paste

1 teaspoon chopped fresh thyme

$\frac{1}{4}$ teaspoon salt

$\frac{1}{4}$ teaspoon ground black pepper

1. Combine the potatoes and turnips in a large pot with enough water to cover by 2". Bring to a boil over high heat, reduce the heat to medium-low, cover, and simmer for 20 minutes, or until tender. Drain and return to the pot. Place over low heat and add the milk and margarine. Mash with a potato masher until smooth. Cover and remove from the heat.

2. Meanwhile, heat a large nonstick skillet over medium-high heat. Add the beef, onion, peas and carrots, and garlic. Cook for 7 minutes, breaking up the beef with a wooden spoon, or until the beef is browned and the onion is soft. Stir in the tomatoes, broth, tomato paste, thyme, salt, and pepper. Reduce the heat to medium-low and cook for 30 minutes, stirring occasionally, or until the mixture is very thick.

3. Spread the potato mixture over the beef mixture in the skillet to within 1" of the skillet sides and serve. For a crispy topping, preheat the broiler and broil 4" from the heat for 2 minutes, or until the top is lightly browned.

Per serving: 278 calories, 8 g fat, 4 g saturated fat, 23 g protein, 29 g carbohydrates, 4 g fiber, 246 mg sodium

MEAT

159

Roast Pork Tenderloin with Sherry, Cream, and Almonds

No need to fall off the 4-Week Shake the Salt Meal Plan when entertaining. This dish is elegant enough to serve at a dinner party. It pairs perfectly with steamed spinach.

Prep time: 25 minutes ▷ **Cook time:** 40 minutes ▷ **Total time:** 1 hour 5 minutes ▷ MAKES 4 SERVINGS

1 pound pork tenderloin, trimmed of all visible fat

$3/4$ teaspoon paprika

$1/2$ teaspoon ground black pepper

$1/4$ teaspoon + $1/8$ teaspoon salt

1 tablespoon whole wheat flour

$3/4$ pound small red-skinned potatoes, scrubbed

3 teaspoons olive oil

2 large shallots, thinly sliced

$1/3$ cup sherry

$1/3$ cup low-sodium chicken broth

$1/4$ cup half-and-half

2 tablespoons sliced almonds

1. Preheat the oven to 350°F.

2. Sprinkle the pork with the paprika, pepper, and $1/4$ teaspoon of the salt. Rub with the flour to coat. Combine the potatoes, 1 teaspoon of the oil, and the remaining $1/8$ teaspoon salt in a bowl. Toss well to coat.

3. Heat the remaining 2 teaspoons oil in a large ovenproof skillet over medium heat. Add the pork and cook for 5 minutes, turning often, or until browned on all sides. Add the shallots and cook for 1 minute. Add the potatoes, sherry, and broth and transfer to the oven.

4. Roast for 25 minutes, turning the pork and stirring the vegetables once or twice, or until a thermometer inserted in the center of the pork reaches 155°F and the juices run clear. Transfer the pork to a cutting board and the potatoes to a platter. Let the pork stand for 10 minutes.

5. Meanwhile, place the skillet over medium-low heat and stir in the half-and-half. Cook for 2 minutes, stirring occasionally, or until slightly thickened. Slice the pork on a slight diagonal. Divide the pork and potatoes among 4 plates. Spoon the sauce over the pork and sprinkle with the almonds.

Per serving: 288 calories, 9 g fat, 3 g saturated fat, 28 g protein, 19 g carbohydrates, 2 g fiber, 298 mg sodium

Swedish Lamb and Lentils

Marjoram is an aromatic herb that is often confused with oregano. It has a slightly sweeter flavor with a hint of pine.

Prep time: 10 minutes ▸ **Cook time:** 1 hour 30 minutes ▸ **Total time:** 1 hour 40 minutes + standing time ▸ MAKES 8 SERVINGS

1½ cups lentils
1½ tablespoons unsalted butter
1 large onion, sliced
1½ pounds lamb stew meat
3 cups low-sodium beef broth

½ teaspoon salt
¼ teaspoon ground black pepper
1 bay leaf
1 teaspoon dried marjoram
2 tablespoons chopped fresh parsley

1. Combine the lentils in a large bowl with enough cold water to cover by 2". Let stand for 3 hours. Drain.

2. Melt 1 tablespoon of the butter in a large saucepan or Dutch oven over medium heat. Cook the onion for 8 minutes, stirring occasionally, or until softened. Transfer to a bowl.

3. Melt the remaining ½ tablespoon butter in the same pan over medium-high heat. Add the lamb and cook for 8 minutes, turning occasionally, or until browned. Stir in the onion, broth, salt, and pepper. Bring to a boil, reduce the heat to medium, and simmer for 30 minutes.

4. Add the lentils, bay leaf, and marjoram. Return to a simmer and cook for 45 minutes, stirring occasionally, or until the lamb is tender and the lentils are cooked through. Discard the bay leaf and sprinkle with the parsley.

Per serving: 276 calories, 8 g fat, 3 g saturated fat, 29 g protein, 23 g carbohydrates, 9 g fiber, 248 mg sodium

Pork Roast with Pears

Pork is ideally suited for pairing with fruit. The sweetness in the pears and cranberries in this dish enhances the natural flavor of the pork tenderloin.

Prep time: 10 minutes ▹ **Cook time:** 20 minutes ▹ **Total time:** 30 minutes ▹ MAKES 4 SERVINGS

1 pound pork tenderloin, trimmed of all visible fat
1 teaspoon ground cumin
½ teaspoon ground coriander
½ teaspoon paprika
1 teaspoon packed light brown sugar

¼ teaspoon + ⅛ teaspoon salt
2 teaspoons trans-free margarine
3 medium pears, cut into ½" wedges
½ cup dried cranberries
¼ cup almonds, chopped

1. Halve the pork crosswise to create two equal pieces. Combine the cumin, coriander, paprika, brown sugar, and ¼ teaspoon of the salt in a small bowl. Rub the mixture over each half of the pork.

2. Melt 1 teaspoon of the margarine in a nonstick skillet over medium-high heat. Reduce the heat to medium, add the pork, and cook for 4 minutes, turning occasionally, or until browned on all sides. Cover and cook for 12 minutes longer, turning occasionally, or until a thermometer inserted into the center registers 155°F. Transfer the pork to a cutting board, cover with foil, and let stand for 10 minutes.

3. Meanwhile, melt the remaining 1 teaspoon margarine in the same skillet over medium-high heat. Add the pears and cook for 3 minutes, tossing occasionally, or until starting to brown slightly. Reduce the heat to medium and add ½ cup of water, the cranberries, and the remaining ⅛ teaspoon salt. Bring to a boil and cook for 10 minutes, stirring occasionally, or until the liquid has almost evaporated and the pears are tender. Stir in the almonds and cook for 1 minute longer.

4. Cut the pork crosswise into 12 medallions and divide among 4 plates. Top the pork with the pear mixture and serve.

Per serving: 321 calories, 9 g fat, 1 g saturated fat, 26 g protein, 37 g carbohydrates, 7 g fiber, 296 mg sodium

Savory Pork Stew

Balsamic vinegar lends a slightly sweet yet tangy note to this appetizing stew.

Prep time: 20 minutes ⁞▸ **Cook time:** 2 hours 10 minutes ⁞▸ **Total time:** 2 hours 30 minutes
⁞▸ MAKES 4 SERVINGS

¼ cup unbleached all-purpose flour
¼ teaspoon salt
½ teaspoon ground black pepper
1 pound pork tenderloin, trimmed of all visible fat, cut into ¾" cubes
2 tablespoons olive oil
1 medium onion, chopped
6 cloves garlic, minced

1 can (14.5 ounces) no-salt-added diced tomatoes
½ pound red-skinned potatoes, cut into ½" cubes
8 ounces mushrooms, halved
2 carrots, sliced
2 tablespoons balsamic vinegar
½ teaspoon dried thyme

1. Combine the flour, salt, and pepper in a bowl. Add the pork and toss well to coat.

2. Heat the oil in a large saucepot or Dutch oven over medium-high heat. Add the pork and cook for 5 minutes, stirring occasionally, or until browned. Add the onion and garlic. Cook for 3 minutes, stirring occasionally, or until slightly softened.

3. Stir in the tomatoes, potatoes, mushrooms, carrots, vinegar, and thyme. Bring to a boil, reduce the heat to medium-low, cover, and simmer for 2 hours, or until the pork and vegetables are tender.

Per serving: 325 calories, 10 g fat, 2 g saturated fat, 30 g protein, 30 g carbohydrates, 5 g fiber, 296 mg sodium

Ma Pu Tofu with Ground Pork

Ground pork is used as a condiment in this dish rather than the main protein. A small amount helps to add a lot of flavor to the tofu as well as a nice textural contrast.

Prep time: 10 minutes ▷ **Cook time:** 10 minutes ▷ **Total time:** 20 minutes ▷ MAKES 4 SERVINGS

½ cup quick-cooking brown rice
1 package (14 ounces) lite firm tofu
½ cup low-sodium chicken broth
1 tablespoon oyster sauce
1 tablespoon cornstarch
1 teaspoon toasted sesame oil
2 ounces ground pork

6 scallions, chopped
1 red bell pepper, chopped
2 cloves garlic, minced
1 tablespoon grated fresh ginger
2 tablespoons unsalted peanuts, chopped

1. Prepare the rice according to package directions, omitting any salt or fat.

2. Meanwhile, place the tofu on a paper towel on a dinner plate. Top with a second paper towel and plate and let stand for 10 minutes. Cut the tofu into ½" cubes. Combine the broth, oyster sauce, and cornstarch in a bowl and mix well.

3. Heat the sesame oil in a large nonstick skillet over medium-high heat. Cook the pork for 3 minutes, breaking it up with a wooden spoon, or until browned. Add the scallions, bell pepper, garlic, and ginger. Cook for 3 minutes, stirring. Add the tofu and cook for 3 minutes, stirring often, or until lightly browned. Add the broth mixture and cook for 1 minute, or until the sauce thickens. Stir in the peanuts. Divide the rice and pork mixture among 4 plates.

Per serving: 273 calories, 9 g fat, 2 g saturated fat, 15 g protein, 32 g carbohydrates, 4 g fiber, 286 mg sodium

Asparagus, Red Pepper, and Pork Stir-Fry over Quinoa

Quinoa is a great substitute for rice. It is high in protein and has a pleasantly light texture.

Prep time: 15 minutes ⊳ **Cook time:** 25 minutes ⊳ **Total time:** 40 minutes ⊳ MAKES 4 SERVINGS

²/₃ cup quinoa, rinsed

1 pound pork tenderloin, trimmed of all visible fat, cut into ³/₄" chunks

2 tablespoons less-sodium soy sauce

2 tablespoons hoisin sauce

1 tablespoon toasted sesame oil

1 medium onion, chopped

2 cloves garlic, minced

1 tablespoon grated fresh ginger

1 medium red bell pepper, cut into thin strips

³/₄ pound asparagus, cut into 2" pieces

4 scallions, cut into 1" pieces

1. Bring the quinoa and 1¹/₃ cups of water to a boil in a small saucepan over medium-high heat. Reduce the heat to medium, cover, and simmer for 20 minutes, or until the liquid is absorbed and the quinoa is tender. Remove from the heat and keep warm.

2. Meanwhile, combine the pork and 1 tablespoon of the soy sauce in a medium bowl, tossing to coat well. Combine the hoisin sauce and the remaining 1 tablespoon soy sauce in a small bowl.

3. Heat 1 teaspoon of the sesame oil in a large nonstick skillet over medium-high heat. Cook the pork for 5 minutes, stirring occasionally, or until lightly browned. Transfer to a plate.

4. Heat the remaining 2 teaspoons sesame oil in the same skillet over medium-high heat. Cook the onion, garlic, and ginger for 1 minute, stirring often. Add the bell pepper and asparagus. Cook for 3 minutes, stirring occasionally, or until tender-crisp. Stir in the scallions, soy sauce mixture, and the pork with any juices that have accumulated. Cook for 1 minute, stirring, or until heated through. Serve over the quinoa.

Per serving: 315 calories, 10 g fat, 2 g saturated fat, 25 g protein, 33 g carbohydrates, 5 g fiber, 282 mg sodium

Pan-Grilled Pork Loin Chops with Braised Dried Plums

Pork and fruit have a natural affinity for each other. The intensely tangy sweet plums play nicely against the grilled flavor of the chops.

Prep time: 15 minutes ▷ **Cook time:** 30 minutes ▷ **Total time:** 45 minutes ▷ MAKES 4 SERVINGS

4 lean loin pork chops (4 ounces each), trimmed of all visible fat
2 teaspoons olive oil
2 cloves garlic, minced
1 teaspoon chopped fresh rosemary
1½ cups dried plums (prunes)

1 cup calcium-enriched orange juice
1 medium onion, chopped
¼ cup balsamic vinegar
1 tablespoon sugar
¼ teaspoon salt
⅛ teaspoon ground black pepper

1. Combine the pork chops, oil, garlic, and rosemary in a medium bowl. Refrigerate for 30 minutes.

2. Meanwhile, combine the dried plums, orange juice, onion, vinegar, and sugar in a medium saucepan over medium-high heat. Bring to a boil, reduce the heat to medium, and simmer for 20 minutes, or until the plums are very tender. Transfer the plums to a bowl with a slotted spoon. Increase the heat under the saucepan to medium-high and boil for 3 minutes, or until the liquid is slightly thickened. Remove from the heat and keep warm.

3. Heat a nonstick grill pan coated with cooking spray over medium-high heat. Remove the pork chops from the bowl and sprinkle with the salt and pepper. Grill for 8 minutes, turning once, or until a thermometer inserted into the center of a chop registers 160°F and the juices run clear.

4. Place 1 chop on each of 4 plates. Divide the plums among the plates and spoon the braising liquid over the plums. Serve hot.

Per serving: 304 calories, 6 g fat, 2 g saturated fat, 20 g protein, 43 g carbohydrates, 4 g fiber, 187 mg sodium

Pork Chops with Apricots

If you can't find boneless center-cut loin chops, pork tenderloin cut into medallions and pounded to a ¾" thickness makes a great substitution.

Prep time: 10 minutes ※ **Cook time:** 25 minutes ※ **Total time:** 35 minutes ※ MAKES 4 SERVINGS

8 ounces green beans, trimmed

4 boneless center-cut loin pork chops (4 ounces each), trimmed of all visible fat

1 teaspoon ground cinnamon

¼ teaspoon ground black pepper

¼ teaspoon + ⅛ teaspoon salt

1 medium onion, thinly sliced crosswise and separated into rings

1 tablespoon grated fresh ginger

¾ cup unsweetened apple juice

½ cup coarsely chopped drained canned apricot halves

2 cups hot cooked bulgur

1 tablespoon sliced almonds

1. Bring a large saucepan of water to a boil over medium-high heat. Add the green beans, return to a boil, and cook for 3 minutes. Drain.

2. Meanwhile, sprinkle the pork chops with the cinnamon, pepper, and ¼ teaspoon of the salt. Heat a large nonstick skillet over medium heat until hot. Cook the onion, ginger, and 3 tablespoons of the apple juice for 5 minutes, or until the onion is slightly softened and the juice has evaporated. Transfer to a plate.

3. Coat the same skillet with cooking spray and heat over medium-high heat. Cook the pork chops for 3 minutes per side. Stir in the onion mixture, apricots, and the remaining apple juice and ⅛ teaspoon salt. Reduce the heat to medium-low, cover, and simmer for 10 minutes, or until the sauce has thickened slightly, the pork juices run clear, and a thermometer inserted into the center of a chop registers 160°F.

4. Divide the bulgur among 4 plates and top with the pork and onion mixture. Sprinkle with the almonds and serve with the green beans.

Per serving: 288 calories, 7 g fat, 2 g saturated fat, 26 g protein, 32 g carbohydrates, 8 g fiber, 274 mg sodium

Linguine with Braised Kale, Garlic, and Sausage

Braising the sausage along with the kale allows its flavor to permeate the whole dish.

Prep time: 10 minutes ▷ **Cook time:** 20 minutes ▷ **Total time:** 30 minutes ▷ MAKES 4 SERVINGS

6 ounces linguine

1 teaspoon olive oil

6 ounces sweet Italian sausage, removed from the casings

4 cloves garlic, sliced

6 cups chopped kale

1 cup low-sodium chicken broth

2 plum tomatoes, seeded and chopped

1/4 cup fresh basil leaves, sliced

2 teaspoons grated Parmesan cheese

Red-pepper flakes (optional)

1. Prepare the linguine according to package directions, omitting the salt.

2. Meanwhile, heat the oil in a large nonstick skillet over medium-high heat. Cook the sausage for 5 minutes, breaking it up with a wooden spoon, or until no longer pink. Stir in the garlic and kale. Cook for 2 minutes, or until the kale starts to wilt. Add 1/2 cup of the broth, reduce the heat to medium-low, cover, and simmer for 5 minutes.

3. Increase the heat to medium-high, uncover, and add the tomatoes and remaining 1/2 cup broth. Cook for 5 minutes. Stir in the linguine and cook for 1 minute, stirring, or until heated through. Stir in the basil. Divide among 4 bowls and sprinkle each with 1/2 teaspoon of the cheese and some red-pepper flakes (if using).

Per serving: 296 calories, 6 g fat, 2 g saturated fat, 17 g protein, 45 g carbohydrates, 4 g fiber, 320 mg sodium

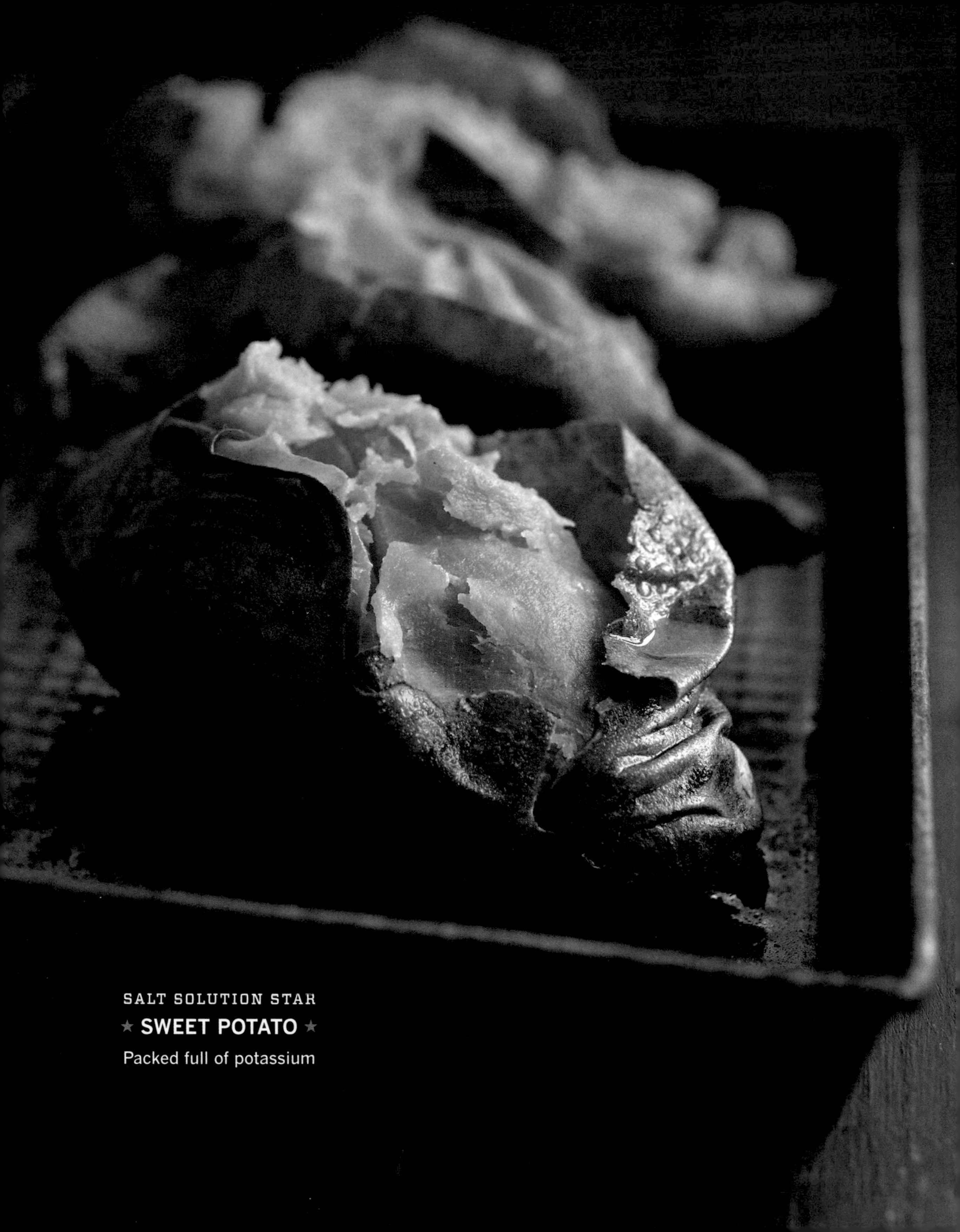

SALT SOLUTION STAR

★ **SWEET POTATO** ★

Packed full of potassium

Poultry

8

Rosemary Roasted Chicken and Vegetables

This chicken dish is fancy enough for a dinner party—but requires only 15 minutes of prep time.

Prep time: 15 minutes ⧽ **Cook time:** 45 minutes ⧽ **Total time:** 1 hour ⧽ MAKES 4 SERVINGS

2 small sweet potatoes (¾ pound), peeled and cut into 1" chunks

2 red bell peppers, cut into ¾" chunks

1 sweet onion, cut into ¾" chunks, layers separated

1 package (10 ounces) frozen artichoke hearts

⅛ teaspoon salt

¼ teaspoon ground black pepper

½ teaspoon olive oil

2 teaspoons chopped fresh rosemary

2 boneless, skinless chicken breast halves (5 ounces each), cut in half crosswise

1 teaspoon grated lemon zest

Lemon wedges, for serving

1. Preheat the oven to 425°F. Place the sweet potatoes in a shallow microwaveable bowl and microwave on high power for 2 minutes. Coat a roasting pan or large baking dish with cooking spray.

2. Combine the sweet potatoes, bell peppers, onion, and artichoke hearts in the pan. Sprinkle with the salt, black pepper, ¼ teaspoon of the oil, and 1¼ teaspoons of the rosemary. Stir together until combined. Move the vegetables to the sides, leaving a 4" path down the center of the pan.

3. Place the chicken down the center of the pan. Brush with the remaining ¼ teaspoon oil and sprinkle on the remaining ¾ teaspoon rosemary.

4. Bake for 45 minutes, or until a thermometer inserted into the thickest part of a breast registers 160°F. Transfer the chicken to a plate. Stir the lemon zest into the roasted vegetables to combine and serve with the chicken and lemon wedges.

Per serving: 295 calories, 5 g fat, 1 g saturated fat, 19 g protein, 27 g carbohydrates, 8 g fiber, 196 mg sodium

Chicken Stew with Cider and Herbs

This stew features sweet potatoes, the Salt Solution Stars that are an excellent source of potassium.

Prep time: 20 minutes ▷ **Cook time:** 55 minutes ▷ **Total time:** 1 hour 15 minutes ▷ MAKES 4 SERVINGS

1 teaspoon olive oil

2 bone-in, skinless chicken breast halves (about 1½ pounds), cut in half crosswise

2 large onions, thinly sliced

2 cups sliced mushrooms

8 whole dried apricots, sliced

1 clove garlic, minced

2 bay leaves

½ teaspoon ground nutmeg

½ teaspoon dried thyme

2 cups apple cider

2 medium sweet potatoes, peeled and cut into ¾" chunks

¼ teaspoon salt

2 tablespoons cornstarch

1. Preheat the oven to 400°F. Heat the oil in a Dutch oven over medium heat. Add the chicken and cook for 8 minutes, turning once, or until browned. Transfer to a plate.

2. Add ½ cup of water to the pan and scrape the bottom with a wooden spoon to loosen any browned bits. Bring the water to a simmer and add the onions. Cover and simmer for 10 minutes, or until the onions are softened. Add the mushrooms, apricots, garlic, bay leaves, nutmeg, and thyme. Cover and cook for 10 minutes, or until the vegetables are softened.

3. Add the cider and chicken to the pan. Cover and place in the oven. Bake for 20 minutes, or until a thermometer inserted into the thickest part of a breast (not touching bone) registers 160°F.

4. Transfer the chicken to a serving platter and cover loosely with foil to keep warm. Discard the bay leaves. Add the reserved cornstarch mixture and the salt to the liquid in the pan. Stir over medium heat until thickened.

Per serving: 314 calories, 4 g fat, 1 g saturated fat, 22 g protein, 48 g carbohydrates, 5 g fiber, 244 mg sodium

Chicken Breasts Marrakesh

This Moroccan-inspired dish will wow you with its delicious spices. And the edamame, a Salt Solution Star, will give you a dose of calcium, potassium, and magnesium.

Prep time: 15 minutes ⁑ **Cook time:** 40 minutes ⁑ **Total time:** 55 minutes ⁑ MAKES 4 SERVINGS

1 can (28 ounces) no-salt-added diced tomatoes
1 large onion, quartered
1 green bell pepper, quartered
2 cloves garlic, minced
1 teaspoon ground cumin
1/2 teaspoon ground coriander
1/2 teaspoon ground black pepper
1/4 teaspoon ground cinnamon

1/4 cup chopped fresh cilantro
4 boneless, skinless chicken breast halves (4 ounces each)
1/2 package (12 ounces) frozen okra
1/2 cup frozen shelled edamame
1/4 teaspoon hot-pepper sauce, or to taste
3/4 cup low-sodium chicken broth
2 tablespoons dried currants or raisins
1/2 cup whole wheat couscous

1. Combine the tomatoes, onion, bell pepper, garlic, cumin, coriander, black pepper, cinnamon, and 2 tablespoons of the cilantro in a large Dutch oven. Bring to a boil over medium-high heat.

2. Place the chicken in the pot and cover with the sauce. Return to a boil, then immediately reduce the heat to low, cover, and simmer for 15 minutes, or until the chicken is no longer pink in the center. Transfer the chicken to a warm plate and set aside.

3. Increase the heat to high and add the okra, edamame, and hot-pepper sauce. Boil the sauce, stirring frequently, for 10 minutes, or until thick. Reduce the heat to low, return the chicken to the pot, and cover with the sauce.

4. Meanwhile, combine the broth and currants or raisins a small saucepan and bring to a boil over medium-high heat. Remove from the heat and stir in the couscous. Cover and let stand for 5 minutes, or until the liquid is absorbed. Fluff with a fork. Serve with the chicken, sauce, and remaining 2 tablespoons cilantro.

Per serving: 309 calories, 3 g fat, 1 g saturated fat, 30 g protein, 38 g carbohydrates, 7 g fiber, 256 mg sodium

Cajun Chicken with Okra and Beans

Like spicy food? Add as much hot sauce as you'd like to this Cajun dish.

Prep time: 15 minutes ⫸ **Cook time:** 25 minutes ⫸ **Total time:** 40 minutes ⫸ MAKES 4 SERVINGS

1¼ pounds boneless, skinless chicken breasts, cut into thin strips

1½ teaspoons salt-free Cajun seasoning blend

1 tablespoon hot-pepper sauce

⅛ teaspoon salt

1½ teaspoons olive oil

1 large red bell pepper, cut into thin strips

1 large green bell pepper, cut into thin strips

2 large onions, cut into thin wedges

2 cups frozen cut green beans

1 cup frozen okra

2 cups cherry tomatoes, halved

1. Heat a large skillet coated with cooking spray over medium heat. Add the chicken, seasoning, hot-pepper sauce, and salt. Cook for 5 minutes, stirring, or until the chicken is no longer pink. Transfer to a plate and keep warm.

2. Heat the oil in the same skillet over medium heat. Add the bell peppers and onion. Cook for 5 minutes, stirring occasionally, or until the peppers begin to soften. Add the beans, okra, and ¼ cup of water. Cover and cook for 10 minutes, or until the vegetables are just tender.

3. Stir in the chicken and tomatoes and cook for 2 minutes, or until heated through.

Per serving: 272 calories, 5 g fat, 1 g saturated fat, 37 g protein, 20 g carbohydrates, 6 g fiber, 279 mg sodium

Chicken Breasts Stuffed with Goat Cheese and Quinoa

Goat cheese adds a creamy note to these chicken breasts, and kale, a Salt Solution Star, adds calcium, potassium, vitamin C, beta-carotene, and iron.

Prep time: 20 minutes ⦂ **Cook time:** 15 minutes ⦂ **Total time:** 35 minutes ⦂ MAKES 4 SERVINGS

2 ounces soft reduced-fat goat cheese, cut into pieces
$\frac{1}{2}$ cup cooked quinoa
$\frac{1}{4}$ cup chopped fresh parsley
1 clove garlic, minced
4 boneless, skinless chicken breast halves (6 ounces each)

$\frac{1}{8}$ teaspoon salt
$\frac{1}{8}$ teaspoon ground black pepper
1 teaspoon extra-virgin olive oil
$\frac{3}{4}$ cup low-sodium chicken broth
2 packages (10 ounces each) frozen kale, cooked according to package directions

1. Stir together the cheese, quinoa, parsley, and garlic in a small bowl.

2. Using a sharp knife, cut a horizontal slit through the thickest portion of each chicken breast to form a deep pocket. Stuff each pocket with an equal amount of the cheese mixture. Press the edges of the pocket together to seal. Season the chicken with salt and pepper.

3. Heat the oil in a large nonstick skillet over medium-high heat. Add the chicken and cook for 8 minutes turning once, or until lightly browned. Reduce the heat to medium. Add the broth, cover, and simmer for 6 minutes, or until the chicken is just cooked through and still juicy. Serve with the kale.

Per serving: 299 calories, 6 g fat, 2 g saturated fat, 47 g protein, 13 g carbohydrates, 4 g fiber, 256 mg sodium

Tequila Lime Chicken with Avocado-Black Bean Salsa

For added heat to the salsa, chop some of the ribs and seeds of the jalapeño and add to taste.

Prep time: 30 minutes ▷ **Cook time:** 10 minutes ▷ **Total time:** 40 minutes ▷ MAKES 4 SERVINGS

CHICKEN AND MARINADE
- ⅓ cup orange juice
- 3 tablespoons tequila or orange juice
- 1 teaspoon grated lime zest
- 2 cloves garlic, chopped
- 1 teaspoon ground cumin
- 4 boneless, skinless chicken breast halves (5 ounces each)

SALSA
- 2 tomatoes, chopped
- 1 avocado, peeled, seeded, and chopped
- ¾ cup no-salt-added canned black beans, rinsed and drained
- 2 tablespoons chopped fresh cilantro
- 2 teaspoons chopped jalapeño chile pepper (wear plastic gloves when handling)
- 2 tablespoons fresh lime juice
- ¼ teaspoon ground cumin
- ⅛ teaspoon salt

1. *To make the chicken and marinade:* Combine the orange juice, tequila or additional orange juice, lime zest, garlic, and cumin in a large resealable food-storage bag. Shake to combine. Add the chicken, push out all air, and seal. Marinate in the refrigerator for 30 minutes.

2. Preheat a grill or grill pan coated with cooking spray to medium. Grill the chicken for 8 minutes, turning once, or until a thermometer inserted in the thickest portion registers 160°F and the juices run clear.

3. *To make the salsa:* Toss together the tomatoes, avocado, beans, cilantro, jalapeño, lime juice, cumin, and salt in a bowl until combined. Serve with the chicken.

Per serving: 280 calories, 9 g fat, 2 g saturated fat, 37 g protein, 14 g carbohydrates, 6 g fiber, 250 mg sodium

Jerk Chicken with Plantains

When selecting a ripe plantain for this dish, look for the skin to be mottled with black and yellow.

Prep time: 15 minutes ⁘ **Cook time:** 30 minutes ⁘ **Total time:** 45 minutes ⁘ MAKES 4 SERVINGS

2 teaspoons salt-free jerk seasoning blend

4 boneless, skinless chicken breast halves (4 ounces each)

$1\frac{1}{2}$ teaspoons olive oil

1 large onion, chopped

1 tablespoon no-salt-added tomato paste

1 can (15 ounces) no-salt-added whole tomatoes

1 green bell pepper, chopped

1 ripe plantain, cut into $\frac{3}{4}$" chunks

2 small zucchini, halved lengthwise and sliced crosswise

$\frac{1}{2}$ cup frozen peas

2 teaspoons balsamic vinegar

3 tablespoons chopped fresh parsley

2 cups cooked brown rice

1. Sprinkle $\frac{1}{2}$ teaspoon of the jerk seasoning on both sides of the chicken breasts. Heat $\frac{3}{4}$ teaspoon of the oil in a nonstick deep skillet or shallow Dutch oven over medium-high heat. Add the chicken and cook for 5 minutes, turning once. Set aside on a plate.

2. Add the remaining $\frac{3}{4}$ teaspoon oil to the pan. Add the onion and 2 tablespoons of water. Cook for 5 minutes, stirring occasionally, or until softened. Stir in the tomato paste and cook for 30 seconds, stirring. Stir in the tomatoes, breaking them up with the side of a spoon. Add the bell pepper, plantain, zucchini, and the remaining $1\frac{1}{2}$ teaspoons of the jerk seasoning. Cover and simmer for 10 minutes.

3. Add the chicken and any accumulated juices, pushing the meat down into the mixture. Cover and simmer for 5 minutes. Stir in the peas and simmer for 5 minutes, or until a thermometer inserted in the thickest portion of a chicken breast registers 160°F and the juices run clear.

4. Stir in the vinegar and parsley and serve with the rice.

Per serving: 296 calories, 3 g fat, 1 g saturated fat, 10 g protein, 59 g carbohydrates, 8 g fiber, 267 mg sodium

Garlicky Chicken Adobo

The paprika adds a smoky, but not spicy, flavor to this Spanish dish.

Prep time: 10 minutes ⊳ **Cook time:** 20 minutes ⊳ **Total time:** 30 minutes ⊳ MAKES 4 SERVINGS

- 2 red bell peppers, cut into thin strips
- 1 box (8 ounces) sliced mushrooms
- 1 teaspoon olive oil
- 1 pound boneless, skinless chicken breasts, cut into strips
- 4 large cloves garlic, minced
- 2 tablespoons medium-dry sherry (optional)

- 2 tablespoons fresh lemon juice
- 1 tablespoon smoked paprika
- $\frac{1}{2}$ teaspoon ground black pepper
- 4 cups frozen leaf spinach, steamed and drained

1. Heat a large, deep, heavy skillet coated with cooking spray over medium heat. Add the bell peppers and mushrooms. Cook, stirring occasionally, for 6 minutes. Transfer to a plate.

2. Heat the oil in the same skillet over medium heat. Add the chicken and garlic. Cook for 6 minutes, stirring occasionally. Add the sherry (if using), lemon juice, paprika, and black pepper. Cook for 1 minute, stirring, or until the pan juices are bubbling and thickened.

3. Return the mushroom mixture to the pan and cook for 3 minutes, stirring, or until heated through. Serve the chicken and vegetables with the cooked spinach.

Per serving: 310 calories, 4 g fat, 1 g saturated fat, 33 g protein, 34 g carbohydrates, 6 g fiber, 249 mg sodium

Chicken Tostadas with Beans

You'd never guess this cheesy Mexican dish is healthy—but it's packed with fiber and low-sodium ingredients.

Prep time: 10 minutes ❧ **Cook time:** 10 minutes ❧ **Total time:** 20 minutes ❧ MAKES 4 SERVINGS

- 4 corn tortillas (6" diameter)
- 2 cups shredded cooked chicken
- 1 cup no-salt-added canned pinto beans, rinsed and drained
- 2 tablespoons shredded reduced-fat Mexican-blend cheese
- 2 tomatoes, diced
- 3 scallions, sliced
- 2 cups shredded iceberg lettuce
- 2 tablespoons reduced-fat sour cream

1. Preheat the oven to 400°F. Coat the tortillas with olive oil cooking spray and place on a baking sheet. Bake for 6 minutes, or until dry and crisp.

2. Top with the chicken, beans, and cheese. Bake for 5 minutes, or until heated through. Top with the tomatoes, scallions, lettuce, and sour cream.

Per serving: 320 calories, 6 g fat, 2 g saturated fat, 30 g protein, 35 g carbohydrates, 7 g fiber, 171 mg sodium

Chicken with Smashed Peas and Edamame

Smash this minty pea mixture with a potato masher or, for a velvety smooth texture, use a hand blender or mini-processor.

Prep time: 25 minutes ⟩ **Cook time:** 10 minutes ⟩ **Total time:** 35 minutes ⟩ MAKES 4 SERVINGS

1 teaspoon grated lemon zest
1/4 cup fresh lemon juice
3 cloves garlic, chopped
1/8 teaspoon ground black pepper
1/4 cup chopped fresh mint
4 boneless, skinless chicken breast halves (4 ounces each)

2 parsnips, peeled, hard cores removed, coarsely chopped
1 cup frozen peas
2/3 cup frozen shelled edamame
3 scallions, sliced
1/4 teaspoon salt
3 tablespoons reduced-fat sour cream

1. Stir together the lemon zest, juice, garlic, pepper, and 2 tablespoons of the mint in a medium bowl. Add the chicken, tossing to coat. Cover and refrigerate for 15 to 30 minutes.

2. Preheat a grill or grill pan coated with cooking spray to medium. Grill the chicken for 8 minutes, turning once, or until a thermometer inserted in the thickest portion registers 160°F and the juices run clear.

3. Meanwhile, bring 2 cups of water to a boil in a medium saucepan. Add the parsnips and cook for 6 minutes, or until almost tender. Add the peas and edamame. Reduce to a simmer and cook for 5 minutes, or until the vegetables are tender. Stir in the scallions and remove from the heat. Reserving 1/4 cup of the cooking liquid, drain the vegetables and return to the pan.

4. Mash the vegetables with a potato masher. For a softer texture, add the reserved cooking liquid. Stir in the salt, sour cream, and remaining 2 tablespoons mint. Serve with the grilled chicken.

Per serving: 299 calories, 5 g fat, 1 g saturated fat, 39 g protein, 25 g carbohydrates, 6 g fiber, 303 mg sodium

BBQ Chicken with Watermelon Salad

When fresh corn is in season, grill 2 ears of corn, then cut the kernels off the cob to use in the salad.

Prep time: 20 minutes ▸ **Cook time:** 15 minutes ▸ **Total time:** 35 minutes ▸ MAKES 4 SERVINGS

BBQ SAUCE
- ½ cup no-salt-added tomato puree
- ⅓ cup no-salt-added ketchup
- 3 tablespoons cider vinegar
- 1 tablespoon molasses
- 2 teaspoons Worcestershire sauce
- ½ onion, grated
- 1 teaspoon salt-free chili powder
- ½ teaspoon smoked paprika
- ¼ teaspoon mustard powder
- ¼ teaspoon salt

CHICKEN AND SALAD
- 4 boneless, skinless chicken breast halves (4 ounces each)
- 2 cups cubed watermelon
- 1 cup frozen corn kernels, thawed
- ½ cup shelled edamame, cooked
- 1 tablespoon fresh lime juice
- 1 tablespoon honey

1. *To make the BBQ sauce:* Combine the tomato puree, ketchup, vinegar, molasses, Worcestershire sauce, onion, chili powder, paprika, mustard powder, and salt in a deep nonreactive saucepan. Bring to a simmer and cook for 15 minutes, stirring occasionally, or until thickened and reduced to about ¾ cup. Place half the sauce in a serving bowl.

2. *To make the chicken and salad:* Preheat a grill or grill pan coated with cooking spray to medium. Grill the chicken for 8 minutes, turning once, or until a thermometer inserted in the thickest portion registers 160°F and the juices run clear. Brush the chicken with half of the BBQ sauce during the last 4 minutes of cooking.

3. Meanwhile, toss together the watermelon, corn, edamame, lime juice, and honey in a medium bowl. Serve the salad with the grilled chicken and the remaining BBQ sauce for topping.

Per serving: 320 calories, 5 g fat, 1 g saturated fat, 37 g protein, 36 g carbohydrates, 3 g fiber, 290 mg sodium

Chicken Tikka with Green Rice

If you don't care to prepare skewers for this recipe, cut the chicken lengthwise into ³⁄₄" strips and the peppers into 2" slabs. Grill as directed and serve with the cherry tomatoes.

Prep time: 5 minutes ⁑ **Cook time:** 55 minutes ⁑ **Total time:** 1 hour ⁑ MAKES 4 SERVINGS

CHICKEN

¹⁄₄ cup fat-free plain yogurt

1 tablespoon chopped fresh ginger

1 teaspoon ground coriander

³⁄₄ teaspoon curry powder

1 pound boneless, skinless chicken breasts, cut into ³⁄₄" cubes

3 yellow or green bell peppers, cut into ³⁄₄" pieces

16 cherry tomatoes

RICE

1 onion, chopped

2 teaspoons chopped fresh ginger

1 teaspoon ground coriander

¹⁄₂ teaspoon salt-free extra-spicy seasoning blend

¹⁄₂ cup long-grain brown rice

1 bag (12 ounces) frozen cut-leaf spinach, thawed

2 tablespoons fresh lemon juice

1. *To make the chicken:* Stir together the yogurt, ginger, coriander, and curry powder in a medium bowl until combined. Stir in the chicken and refrigerate for 30 minutes. Thread the chicken, bell peppers, and cherry tomatoes onto four 12" skewers.

2. *Meanwhile, to make the rice:* Heat a nonstick medium saucepan coated with cooking spray over medium heat. Cook the onion for 6 minutes, or until softened. Stir in the ginger, coriander, and seasoning blend. Cook for 1 minute.

3. Stir in the brown rice and cook for 1 minute. Add 1¹⁄₂ cups of water, bring to a simmer, and cook, covered, for 25 minutes. Place the spinach on top of the rice and cook, covered, for 10 minutes, or until the rice is cooked through.

4. Meanwhile, preheat a grill or grill pan coated with cooking spray to medium. Grill the skewers for 8 minutes, turning once, or until the chicken is no longer pink and the juices run clear. Stir the lemon juice into the rice and serve with the skewers.

Per serving: 301 calories, 3 g fat, 1 g saturated fat, 33 g protein, 33 g carbohydrates, 5 g fiber, 220 mg sodium

Santa Fe Chicken

This delicious Southwestern dish features spinach, a Salt Solution Star that's packed with potassium, magnesium, calcium, vitamin C, beta-carotene, and folate.

Prep time: 15 minutes ⁛ **Cook time:** 20 minutes ⁛ **Total time:** 35 minutes ⁛ MAKES 4 SERVINGS

1 teaspoon olive oil
1 small red bell pepper, chopped
1 small green bell pepper, chopped
¾ pound boneless, skinless chicken breasts, cut into ¾" cubes
4 scallions, thinly sliced
1 can (14.5 ounces) no-salt-added diced tomatoes
1½ cups frozen corn kernels, thawed

1 cup no-salt-added canned black beans, rinsed and drained
2 teaspoons salt-free chili powder
1 teaspoon cumin seeds, crushed
2 cups frozen spinach leaves
Dash of cayenne pepper
¼ cup chopped fresh cilantro
2 tablespoons reduced-fat sour cream

1. Heat the oil in a large saucepan over medium-high heat. Cook the bell peppers, stirring frequently, for 5 minutes, or until the vegetables are soft.

2. Add the chicken and scallions. Cook for 5 minutes, stirring occasionally. Add the tomatoes, corn, black beans, chili powder, and cumin seeds. Bring to a simmer and cook, covered, for 5 minutes.

3. Stir in the spinach and cook for 5 minutes, or until tender. Stir in the cayenne and cilantro. Serve with the sour cream.

Per serving: 305 calories, 4 g fat, 1 g saturated fat, 30 g protein, 34 g carbohydrates, 8 g fiber, 299 mg sodium

Asian Chicken Stir-Fry

In a hurry? This chicken stir-fry dish comes together in no time—faster than delivery!

Prep time: 15 minutes ▸ **Cook time:** 15 minutes ▸ **Total time:** 30 minutes ▸ MAKES 4 SERVINGS

1 cup reduced-sodium chicken broth

4 teaspoons cornstarch

2 teaspoons less-sodium soy sauce

1 teaspoon toasted sesame oil

4 scallions, finely chopped

1 pound boneless, skinless chicken breasts, thinly sliced crosswise

1 large clove garlic, minced

2 teaspoons grated fresh ginger

1 pound broccoli, cut into bite-size pieces

1 large red bell pepper, cut into squares

¼ cup chopped fresh cilantro

2 cups hot cooked brown rice

1. Whisk together the broth, cornstarch, and soy sauce in a small bowl. Stir in the scallions and set aside.

2. Heat the oil in a wok or large nonstick skillet over medium-high heat. Add the chicken, garlic, and ginger. Cook, stirring constantly, for 3 minutes, or until the chicken is no longer pink. Transfer to a bowl and set aside.

3. Add the reserved broth mixture to the wok or skillet. Cook for 2 minutes, stirring constantly, or until thickened. Add the broccoli and bell pepper, cover, and simmer over low heat for 8 minutes, or until the broccoli is bright green and tender-crisp. Stir in the reserved chicken. Cook for 2 minutes, or until the chicken is hot. Stir in the cilantro.

4. Serve the stir-fry over the brown rice.

Per serving: 321 calories, 6 g fat, 1 g saturated fat, 31 g protein, 36 g carbohydrates, 6 g fiber, 305 mg sodium

Chicken Fajita Sauté

For a spicier version, add a few shakes of hot-pepper sauce to the marinating liquid in step 1.

Prep time: 15 minutes + 30 minutes marinating ▷ **Cook time:** 15 minutes ▷ **Total time:** 1 hour
▷ MAKES 4 SERVINGS

½ cup low-sodium chicken broth
1 clove garlic, minced
1 teaspoon chili powder
¾ teaspoon ground cumin
¼ teaspoon salt
½ teaspoon reduced-sodium Worcestershire sauce
¾ pound boneless, skinless chicken breasts, cut into strips

½ cup chopped fresh cilantro
1 large red bell pepper, cut into strips
1 large zucchini, cut into strips
1 sweet onion, cut into thin strips
1 can (15.5 ounces) no-salt-added kidney beans, rinsed and drained
3 tablespoons fresh lime juice
8 warmed corn tortillas (6" diameter)
4 tablespoons fat-free sour cream

1. Stir together the broth, garlic, chili powder, cumin, salt, and Worcestershire sauce in a medium bowl. Stir in the chicken and cilantro until coated. Cover and refrigerate for 30 minutes.

2. Heat a large nonstick skillet coated with cooking spray over medium-high heat. Add the chicken mixture and cook for 4 minutes, stirring, or until the chicken is no longer pink. Transfer to a large bowl and keep warm.

3. Add the bell pepper and zucchini to the skillet. Cook for 6 minutes, stirring, or until the peppers are tender-crisp. Transfer to the bowl with the chicken.

4. Add the onion to the skillet. Cook for 3 minutes, stirring, or until the onions are tender-crisp. Add the beans and cook for 1 minute. Return the chicken and vegetables to the skillet. Drizzle the lime juice over the mixture and stir until combined. Remove from the heat and serve with the tortillas and sour cream.

Per serving: 333 calories, 4 g fat, 1 g saturated fat, 30 g protein, 46 g carbohydrates, 9 g fiber, 286 mg sodium

Southern-Style Chicken and Kale

This delicious dish features two Salt Solution Stars—cannellini beans and kale.

Prep time: 5 minutes ⁘ **Cook time:** 30 minutes ⁘ **Total time:** 35 minutes ⁘ MAKES 4 SERVINGS

$1\frac{1}{2}$ teaspoons olive oil

2 onions, chopped

1 can (14.5 ounces) no-salt-added stewed tomatoes

1 cup no-salt-added tomato puree

$1\frac{1}{2}$ teaspoons Italian seasoning blend

$\frac{1}{4}$ teaspoon salt

$\frac{1}{4}$ teaspoon red-pepper flakes

1 package (10 ounces) frozen kale

1 pound boneless, skinless chicken breasts, cut into $\frac{3}{4}$" cubes

1 can (15 ounces) no-salt-added cannellini beans, rinsed and drained

$\frac{1}{2}$ cup frozen corn kernels

1 tablespoon balsamic vinegar

1. Heat the oil in a large nonstick skillet or Dutch oven over medium heat. Add the onions and cook for 5 minutes, or until softened. Stir in the tomatoes, tomato puree, seasoning, salt, and red-pepper flakes. Push the vegetables to the outside of the pan and add the kale. Cover and cook for 15 minutes, stirring occasionally to break up the kale.

2. Stir in the chicken and beans. Reduce the heat to low, cover, and simmer for 5 minutes. Stir in the corn and cook for 5 minutes, or until the vegetables are tender and the chicken is no longer pink. Stir in the vinegar.

Per serving: 307 calories, 4 g fat, 1 g saturated fat, 30 g protein, 38 g carbohydrates, 9 g fiber, 299 mg sodium

Chicken, Corn, and Black Bean Pizza

Yes, pizza—we've cut the salt and amped up the vitamins, minerals, and fiber, but it's still gooey and cheesy!

Prep time: 10 minutes ⁛ **Cook time:** 20 minutes ⁛ **Total time:** 30 minutes ⁛ MAKES 2 SERVINGS

- 2 sandwich thins, split
- ¼ cup low-sodium marinara sauce
- 1 small red bell pepper, sliced
- 2 scallions, sliced
- ¼ cup frozen corn kernels
- ⅓ cup no-salt-added canned black beans, rinsed and drained
- ⅔ cup diced cooked chicken breast
- 3 tablespoons shredded reduced-fat Cheddar cheese
- 3 cups frozen broccoli and cauliflower, cooked according to package directions

1. Preheat the oven to 375°F. Place the sandwich thins on a large baking sheet.

2. Spread the sauce onto the sandwich thins. Top with the bell pepper, scallions, corn, black beans, chicken, and cheese.

3. Bake for 20 minutes, or until the cheese is melted and the vegetables are heated through. Serve with the cooked broccoli and cauliflower.

Per serving: 267 calories, 4 g fat, 1 g saturated fat, 25 g protein, 33 g carbohydrates, 9 g fiber, 272 mg sodium

Brazil Nut-Crusted Oven-Fried Chicken

Brazil nuts have about 2,500 times as much selenium as other nuts! Selenium is a powerful antioxidant that may help protect against heart disease and some types of cancer.

Prep time: 20 minutes ▷ **Cook time:** 20 minutes ▷ **Total time:** 40 minutes ▷ MAKES 4 SERVINGS

1¼ pounds chicken tenders
½ cup low-fat buttermilk
4 tablespoons bread crumbs
3 tablespoons finely chopped Brazil nuts
12 ounces frozen kale

1 can (14.5 ounces) no-salt-added diced tomatoes
2 cloves garlic, slivered
¾ teaspoon Italian seasoning blend
⅛ teaspoon salt

1. Preheat the oven to 425°F. Line a baking sheet with foil.

2. Combine the chicken with the buttermilk in a medium bowl. Stir together the bread crumbs and nuts in a shallow dish or pie plate. Shake off the excess buttermilk and dip the chicken into the crumb mixture. Place on the baking sheet and mist the chicken with olive oil cooking spray. Bake for 20 minutes, or until golden and the juices run clear.

3. Meanwhile, combine the kale, tomatoes, garlic, seasoning, salt, and ½ cup of water in a medium saucepan over medium-high heat. Simmer for 15 minutes, or until tender. Serve with the chicken.

Per serving: 280 calories, 10 g fat, 2 g saturated fat, 38 g protein, 13 g carbohydrates, 3 g fiber, 290 mg sodium

Creamy Cucumber-Dill Gyros

Yogurt, a Salt Solution Star, adds protein, calcium, and magnesium to these delicious chicken gyros.

Prep time: 15 minutes ⁖ **Total time:** 15 minutes ⁖ MAKES 4 SERVINGS

- ⅓ English (seedless) cucumber, chopped
- 3 scallions, thinly sliced
- 1 small red bell pepper, finely chopped
- ½ cup 0% plain Greek yogurt
- 1 tablespoon fresh lemon juice
- 2 teaspoons chopped fresh dill or ¼ teaspoon dried dillweed

- ¼ teaspoon ground black pepper
- 4 whole wheat pitas (6" diameter), halved and lightly toasted
- 8 Boston lettuce leaves
- 2 cups shredded cooked chicken breast
- 1 bag (12 ounces) frozen broccoli steamers, cooked according to package directions

1. Toss together the cucumber, scallions, bell pepper, yogurt, lemon juice, dill, and black pepper in a medium bowl. Open the pita halves and spread the interiors with half of the yogurt sauce.

2. Place the lettuce leaves and chicken in the pita halves. Spoon the remaining sauce on top. Serve with the broccoli.

Per serving: 277 calories, 4 g fat, 1 g saturated fat, 35 g protein, 34 g carbohydrates, 13 g fiber, 344 mg sodium

Chicken Chili Verde

A poblano pepper adds a spicy note to this chili. If you like, substitute a green bell pepper and half of a seeded chopped jalapeño pepper for the poblano.

Prep time: 15 minutes ▷ **Cook time:** 35 minutes ▷ **Total time:** 50 minutes ▷ MAKES 4 SERVINGS

- 1 teaspoon olive oil
- 2 onions, chopped
- 1 pound ground chicken breast
- 3 cloves garlic, chopped
- 2 cups low-sodium chicken broth
- 8 tomatillos (¾ pound), husked and chopped
- 1 poblano or green bell pepper, chopped
- 2 teaspoons ground cumin
- 1 teaspoon chili powder
- ¼ teaspoon salt
- 1 can (15 ounces) no-salt-added cannellini beans, rinsed and drained
- 1 tablespoon yellow cornmeal
- ¼ cup chopped fresh cilantro
- ¼ cup reduced-fat sour cream
  Lime wedges, for serving

1. Heat the oil in a Dutch oven over medium-high heat. Cook the onions for 5 minutes, or until softened. Add the chicken and garlic. Cook for 5 minutes, breaking up the meat with a wooden spoon. Add the broth, tomatillos, pepper, cumin, chili powder, and salt.

2. Bring to a simmer and cook for 15 minutes. Stir in the beans and cornmeal. Cook, stirring occasionally, for 10 minutes longer, or until flavored throughout. Serve with the cilantro, sour cream, and lime wedges.

Per serving: 300 calories, 5 g fat, 2 g saturated fat, 35 g protein, 31 g carbohydrates, 12 g fiber, 281 mg sodium

Chicken Tacos
with Cilantro Cream

Fill the tacos and serve with mounds of lettuce and chopped fresh tomatoes. There's ample sauce to dress the leftover salad ingredients.

Prep time: 20 minutes ▷ **Cook time:** 10 minutes ▷ **Total time:** 30 minutes ▷ MAKES 4 SERVINGS

¼ cup fat-free plain yogurt

¼ cup reduced-fat sour cream

3 tablespoons chopped fresh cilantro

¼ teaspoon salt

1 pound ground chicken breast

1 small onion, finely chopped

2 teaspoons chili powder

1 teaspoon ground cumin

½ cup no-salt-added tomato puree

2 tablespoons no-salt-added ketchup

8 low-salt taco shells (look for brand with the lowest sodium)

4 cups shredded iceberg lettuce

2 tomatoes, chopped

Lime wedges, for serving

1. Stir together the yogurt, sour cream, cilantro, and a pinch of the salt in a small bowl. Set aside for topping.

2. Set a nonstick skillet over medium-high heat. Add the chicken, onion, chili powder, cumin, and remaining salt. Cook for 7 minutes, breaking up the meat with a wooden spoon, or until no longer pink. Add the tomato puree and ketchup. Cook for 2 minutes, or until thickened.

3. To serve, spoon the chicken mixture into the taco shells and serve with shredded lettuce, chopped tomatoes, lime wedges, and the cilantro cream.

Per serving: 290 calories, 7 g fat, 3 g saturated fat, 29 g protein, 30 g carbohydrates, 4 g fiber, 260 mg sodium

Chicken Burgers with Spinach and Quinoa

A low-salt burger? Yes—and spinach and quinoa are added for a host of vitamins, minerals, protein, fiber, and flavor.

Prep time: 15 minutes ⁝▷ **Cook time:** 15 minutes ⁝▷ **Total time:** 30 minutes ⁝▷ MAKES 4 SERVINGS

1¼ pounds ground chicken breast
1 package (10 ounces) frozen chopped spinach, thawed and squeezed dry
½ cup cooked quinoa
2 cloves garlic, minced
1 scallion, finely chopped
1 teaspoon smoked paprika

¾ teaspoon ground black pepper
½ cup 2% plain Greek yogurt
1 English (seedless) cucumber, chopped
8 slices thin-sliced whole wheat bread, toasted
4 tomato slices

1. Preheat a grill or grill pan to medium. Stir together the chicken, spinach, quinoa, garlic, scallion, paprika, and pepper in a large bowl. Shape into 4 burgers.

2. Grill the burgers for 10 minutes, turning once, or until no longer pink.

3. Toss together the yogurt and cucumber in a small bowl. Top 4 slices of the bread with a burger and a slice of tomato. Drizzle with the yogurt-cucumber mixture and top with a slice of bread.

Per serving: 295 calories, 3 g fat, 0 g saturated fat, 39 g protein, 26 g carbohydrates, 5 g fiber, 364 mg sodium

Turkey Cutlets Chimichurri

Salt-free seasoning blends abound. If you don't have any on hand, you can substitute ¼ teaspoon thyme, ¼ teaspoon oregano, ⅛ teaspoon onion powder, and ⅛ teaspoon ground black pepper.

Prep time: 20 minutes ▸ **Cook time:** 20 minutes ▸ **Total time:** 40 minutes ▸ MAKES 4 SERVINGS

3 cloves garlic

1–2 teaspoons chopped seeded jalapeño chile pepper (wear plastic gloves when handling)

¾ cup fresh parsley

¾ cup fresh cilantro

3 tablespoons fresh lime juice

2 teaspoons olive oil

¾ teaspoon dried oregano

¼ teaspoon salt

¾ pound fresh kale, chopped (6 cups)

2 teaspoons salt-free all-purpose seasoning

1 can (15 ounces) no-salt-added kidney beans, rinsed and drained

2 teaspoons red wine vinegar

4 turkey cutlets (4 ounces each)

1. Place the garlic in a small dish with water to cover. Microwave for 30 seconds and drain. Combine the garlic, pepper, parsley, and cilantro in a food processor. Pulse until chopped. Add ½ cup of water, the lime juice, oil, oregano, and ⅛ teaspoon of the salt. Process until blended. Set the chimichurri sauce aside.

2. Combine the kale, seasoning, and ½ cup of water in a medium saucepan. Bring to a simmer, cover, and cook for 10 minutes, or until almost tender. Stir in the beans, vinegar, and the remaining ⅛ teaspoon salt. Cook for 2 minutes and remove from the heat.

3. Meanwhile, heat a nonstick skillet coated with cooking spray over medium heat. Cook the turkey for 6 minutes, turning once, or until browned and the juices run clear. Serve the turkey with the kale and chimichurri sauce.

Per serving: 269 calories, 4 g fat, 0 g saturated fat, 37 g protein, 24 g carbohydrates, 10 g fiber, 301 mg sodium

Tandoori Turkey with Curried Yogurt Sauce

The quick and tasty curry-ginger mixture does double duty as the flavoring agent for both the marinade and sauce. There's ample sauce to drizzle on both the turkey and the spinach mixture.

Prep time: 20 minutes ▷ **Cook time:** 10 minutes ▷ **Total time:** 30 minutes ▷ MAKES 4 SERVINGS

2 teaspoons curry powder
2 teaspoons grated fresh ginger
$\frac{1}{2}$ teaspoon turmeric
$\frac{1}{2}$ teaspoon ground cumin
$\frac{1}{8}$ teaspoon salt
1 teaspoon white wine vinegar
4 teaspoons honey

$\frac{3}{4}$ cup 0% plain Greek yogurt
2 scallions, green parts only, chopped
2 tablespoons chopped fresh cilantro
$1\frac{1}{4}$ pounds turkey tenders
3 cups frozen chopped broccoli
2 cups frozen leaf spinach

1. Stir together the curry powder, ginger, turmeric, cumin, salt, vinegar, honey, and 1 teaspoon of water in a medium microwaveable bowl. Microwave on high power for 30 seconds. Remove 2 teaspoons of the mixture and combine with the yogurt, scallion greens, and cilantro in a small bowl. Set aside.

2. Add the turkey to the bowl and toss with the curry mixture until evenly coated. Heat a grill or grill pan to medium.

3. Meanwhile, combine the broccoli, spinach, and $\frac{1}{4}$ cup water in a medium saucepan. Bring to a simmer, cover, and cook for 5 minutes, or until tender.

4. Grill the tenders for 5 minutes, turning once, or until no longer pink and the juices run clear. Serve with the spinach mixture and the curried yogurt sauce.

Per serving: 260 calories, 2 g fat, 0 g saturated fat, 44 g protein, 17 g carbohydrates, 5 g fiber, 270 mg sodium

Farfalle with Beet Greens, Mango, and Turkey

Farfalle gets a fun twist with tangy beet greens and sweet mango cubes.

Prep time: 15 minutes ⁓ **Cook time:** 20 minutes ⁓ **Total time:** 35 minutes ⁓ MAKES 4 SERVINGS

6 ounces farfalle pasta
4 teaspoons extra-virgin olive oil
$3/4$ pound turkey breast cutlets, cut into thin strips
$1/4$ teaspoon salt

4 cups beet greens, coarsely chopped
2 cloves garlic, minced
$1/2$ cup low-sodium chicken broth
$1/2$ mango, chopped
$1/8$ teaspoon ground black pepper

1. Prepare the pasta according to package directions, omitting the salt.

2. Meanwhile, heat 2 teaspoons of the oil in a large nonstick skillet over medium-high heat. Sprinkle the turkey with $1/8$ teaspoon of the salt and add to the skillet. Cook for 5 minutes, stirring occasionally, or until browned and cooked through. Transfer to a plate.

3. Return the skillet to the heat and add the remaining 2 teaspoons oil. Stir in the greens and garlic. Cook for 2 minutes, tossing often, or until wilted. Add the broth, bring to a boil, and cook for 1 minute. Stir in the pasta, turkey, mango, remaining $1/8$ teaspoon salt, and pepper. Cook for 1 minute, or until hot. Divide among 4 bowls.

Per serving: 317 calories, 6 g fat, 1 g saturated fat, 27 g protein, 38 g carbohydrates, 3 g fiber, 278 mg sodium

Spaghetti Squash with Turkey Meatballs Marinara

Spaghetti squash is a magic vegetable—it looks just like pasta, but it's a low-carb, fiber-packed alternative.

Prep time: 5 minutes ❖ **Cook time:** 45 minutes ❖ **Total time:** 50 minutes ❖ MAKES 6 SERVINGS

- 1 large spaghetti squash (3 pounds), halved and seeded
- 1½ pounds extra-lean ground turkey breast
- 2 large egg whites
- ½ cup toasted wheat germ
- ¼ cup quick-cooking oats
- 1 tablespoon ground flaxseeds
- 1 tablespoon grated Parmesan cheese
- ½ teaspoon salt-free all-purpose seasoning
- ¼ teaspoon ground black pepper
- 1 jar (16 ounces) no salt-added marinara sauce

1. Preheat the oven to 375°F. Lightly coat a baking sheet with olive oil cooking spray.

2. Pierce the outside of each half of the squash a few times with a fork. Place the squash cut side down on the baking sheet and bake for 45 minutes, or until very tender when pierced with a fork. Cool slightly.

3. Meanwhile, combine the turkey, egg whites, wheat germ, oats, flaxseeds, cheese, seasoning, and pepper in a large bowl and mix until well blended. Shape into 18 golf ball–size meatballs.

4. Heat a large nonstick skillet over medium-high heat. Cook the meatballs for 10 minutes, turning occasionally, or until browned. Add the sauce and cook for 15 minutes, or until the flavors meld.

5. When the squash has cooled, use a fork to scrape the spaghetti-like threads of squash into a large, shallow serving bowl. (Discard the shell.) Top the spaghetti squash with the meatballs and sauce.

Per serving: 314 calories, 5 g fat, 0 g saturated fat, 36 g protein, 37 g carbohydrates, 7 g fiber, 128 mg sodium

SALT SOLUTION STAR
★ **SARDINES** ★
Loaded with potassium
and calcium

9

Seafood

Salmon with White Bean and Citrus Salad

Citrus is a great way to add a burst of flavor to a dish without adding a lot of calories or salt.

Prep time: 15 minutes ▸ **Cook time:** 20 minutes ▸ **Total time:** 35 minutes ▸ MAKES 4 SERVINGS

- 1 tablespoon olive oil
- 1 red onion, thinly sliced
- 1 can (15.5 ounces) no-salt-added cannellini beans, rinsed and drained
- 2 teaspoons grated lemon zest
- 1/4 teaspoon salt
- 1/4 teaspoon ground black pepper
- 1 pink grapefruit, peeled and cut into segments
- 1 navel orange, peeled and cut into segments
- 1/4 cup chopped fresh parsley
- 1 tablespoon fresh lemon juice
- 4 center-cut salmon fillets (4 ounces each)

1. Heat 1½ teaspoons of the oil in a medium nonstick skillet over medium heat. Cook the onion for 5 minutes, stirring, or until softened. Stir in the beans, lemon zest, ⅛ teaspoon of the salt, and ⅛ teaspoon of the pepper. Cook for 5 minutes, stirring often, or until heated through. Transfer to a medium bowl and stir in the grapefruit and orange segments, parsley, and lemon juice. Set aside.

2. Sprinkle the salmon with the remaining ⅛ teaspoon salt and ⅛ teaspoon pepper. Heat the remaining 1½ teaspoons oil in a large nonstick skillet over medium-high heat. Starting with the salmon flesh side down, cook for 5 minutes, turning once, or until lightly browned and just opaque. Divide the salmon and salad among 4 plates.

Per serving: 302 calories, 8 g fat, 1 g saturated fat, 30 g protein, 30 g carbohydrates, 9 g fiber, 229 mg sodium

Salmon with Pesto

Freshly made pesto pairs wonderfully with the rich flavor of salmon.

Prep time: 20 minutes ❧ **Cook time:** 20 minutes ❧ **Total time:** 40 minutes ❧ MAKES 4 SERVINGS

1¼ cups fresh basil leaves
1 clove garlic
⅓ cup low-sodium chicken broth
1 tablespoon fresh lemon juice
2 teaspoons extra-virgin olive oil
2 teaspoons slivered almonds

1 teaspoon grated Parmesan cheese
¼ teaspoon salt
¼ teaspoon ground black pepper
4 salmon fillets (3 ounces each)
⅔ cup quick-cooking brown rice
4 cups broccoli florets

1. Combine the basil, garlic, broth, lemon juice, oil, almonds, cheese, salt, and pepper in a blender; puree. Place the salmon on a plate and spoon 3 tablespoons of the pesto over the salmon and turn to coat. Cover with plastic wrap and let stand for 15 minutes. Set the remaining pesto aside.

2. Meanwhile, prepare the rice according to package directions, omitting any salt or fat. Set a steamer basket in a large saucepan with 2" of water in the bottom. Bring to a boil, add the broccoli, cover, and cook for 4 minutes, or until bright green and tender-crisp. Remove from the heat and keep warm.

3. Preheat the broiler. Coat a broiler pan with cooking spray.

4. Place the salmon on the pan and broil 5" from the heat for 6 minutes, or until the fish is just opaque. Place the salmon on 4 plates and top with the reserved pesto. Serve with the rice and broccoli.

Per serving: 306 calories, 10 g fat, 2 g saturated fat, 25 g protein, 29 g carbohydrates, 4 g fiber, 217 mg sodium

Salmon and Artichoke Hash

This hearty hash is chockful of omega-3 fatty acids, a beneficial type of fat that may protect against coronary artery disease.

Prep time: 10 minutes ⁑ **Cook time:** 35 minutes ⁑ **Total time:** 45 minutes ⁑ MAKES 4 SERVINGS

1 pound potatoes, cut into $\frac{1}{2}$" cubes
1 tablespoon olive oil
1 large leek, white and light green parts, chopped
6 ounces wild sockeye smoked salmon, cut into 1" pieces

1 package (10 ounces) frozen artichoke hearts, thawed and patted dry
$\frac{1}{2}$ teaspoon ground black pepper
$\frac{1}{4}$ teaspoon salt
1 medium tomato, seeded and chopped
1 tablespoon chopped fresh dill

1. Preheat the oven to 400°F. Line a baking sheet with foil.

2. Arrange the potatoes on the baking sheet in a single layer and coat with cooking spray. Bake for 25 minutes, or until lightly browned and cooked through.

3. Meanwhile, heat 1$\frac{1}{2}$ teaspoons of the oil in a large nonstick skillet over medium heat. Add the leek and cook for 3 minutes, or until softened. Transfer to a large bowl. Stir in the potatoes, salmon, artichokes, pepper, and salt.

4. Heat the remaining 1$\frac{1}{2}$ teaspoons oil in the same skillet over medium-high heat. Add the salmon mixture. Cover and cook for 4 minutes, or until lightly browned and crisp on the bottom. Using a metal spatula, cut the hash into 4 sections and flip each. Cook for 4 minutes, or until lightly browned and crisp. Transfer to 4 plates and sprinkle each serving with the tomato and dill.

Per serving: 320 calories, 9 g fat, 2 g saturated fat, 31 g protein, 31 g carbohydrates, 7 g fiber, 225 mg sodium

Grilled Tuna Steaks Topped with Lemony Artichoke Hearts

Browning the artichoke hearts with the onions brings out a level of sweetness that balances well against the tanginess of the lemon.

Prep time: 10 minutes ▷ **Cook time:** 20 minutes ▷ **Total time:** 30 minutes ▷ MAKES 4 SERVINGS

¾ cup couscous

4 teaspoons extra-virgin olive oil

12 ounces frozen artichoke hearts, thawed

1 medium onion, chopped

½ teaspoon dried basil

3 cloves garlic, minced

2 tablespoons fresh lemon juice

¼ teaspoon salt

¼ teaspoon ground black pepper

4 yellowfin tuna steaks (4 ounces each)

1 teaspoon ground coriander

1. Bring 1 cup of water to a boil in a small saucepan over medium-high heat. Stir in the couscous, cover, and remove from the heat. Let stand for 5 minutes and then fluff with a fork. Keep warm.

2. Heat 3 teaspoons of the oil in a large nonstick skillet over medium-high heat. Cook the artichokes, onion, and basil for 5 minutes, stirring occasionally, or until the artichokes are browned. Add the garlic and cook for 4 minutes, or until the onion is lightly browned. Stir in the lemon juice and cook for 30 seconds. Remove from the heat and stir in ⅛ teaspoon of the salt and ⅛ teaspoon of the pepper. Keep warm.

3. Coat a grill pan with cooking spray and heat over medium-high heat. Rub the tuna with the remaining 1 teaspoon oil. Sprinkle with the coriander and the remaining ⅛ teaspoon salt and ⅛ teaspoon pepper. Cook the tuna for 8 minutes, turning once, or until the fish is just opaque. Serve with the couscous and artichokes.

Per serving: 310 calories, 6 g fat, 1 g saturated fat, 32 g protein, 29 g carbohydrates, 7 g fiber, 248 mg sodium

Tuna with Lemon Broccoli

Fresh tuna steaks have a fresher taste and slightly firmer texture than the canned version. Look for steaks that are about ¾" thick.

Prep time: 15 minutes ▷ **Cook time:** 35 minutes ▷ **Total time:** 50 minutes ▷ MAKES 4 SERVINGS

½ bunch broccoli, cut into florets
Grated zest and juice of 1 lemon
4 yellowfin tuna steaks (4 ounces each), halved crosswise
¾ cup fat-free evaporated milk

2 tablespoons unbleached all-purpose flour
½ cup shredded reduced-fat Cheddar cheese
2 cups hot cooked bulgur

1. Preheat the oven to 350°F. Coat an 8" × 8" baking dish with cooking spray.

2. Set a steamer basket in a large saucepan with 2" of water in the bottom. Bring to a boil, add the broccoli, cover, and cook for 5 minutes, or until bright green and tender-crisp. Transfer to a colander and rinse under cold water. Drain well, place in a medium bowl, and toss with the lemon zest and juice.

3. Arrange 4 pieces of the tuna in the baking dish. Top each piece with the broccoli, spreading it in an even layer. Top the broccoli with the remaining 4 tuna pieces.

4. Whisk together the evaporated milk and flour in a small saucepan. Cook over medium heat for 5 minutes, whisking constantly, or until the mixture is thickened. Remove from the heat and stir in the cheese until smooth. Pour the mixture over the tuna.

5. Bake for 25 minutes, or until the fish is just opaque. Serve with the bulgur.

Per serving: 304 calories, 3 g fat, 1 g saturated fat, 39 g protein, 32 g carbohydrates, 7 g fiber, 213 mg sodium

Halibut en Papillote with Asparagus, Onions, and Lemon

Cooking *en papillote* means to cook something in a packet. Usually done in parchment, you may substitute sheets of aluminum foil, which work just as well and are easier to seal when the packets are formed.

Prep time: 20 minutes ▷ **Cook time:** 15 minutes ▷ **Total time:** 35 minutes ▷ MAKES 4 SERVINGS

1 medium red onion, very thinly sliced	1 plum tomato, seeded and diced
4 teaspoons extra-virgin olive oil	2 tablespoons fresh lemon juice
4 skinless halibut fillets (6 ounces each)	¼ teaspoon salt
	⅛ teaspoon ground black pepper
¾ pound asparagus, trimmed	¼ cup fresh basil leaves, thinly sliced

1. Preheat the oven to 450°F. Cut off four 18" × 12" sheets of parchment paper or foil.

2. Arrange the paper with the long side facing you. Coat with cooking spray. Fold the sheet in half from short end to short end, then open like a book. Place one-fourth of the onion in the center of the right half of the sheet. Drizzle with ¼ teaspoon of the oil. Top the onion with a halibut fillet. Place one-fourth of the asparagus next to the halibut and sprinkle diced tomato over both. Drizzle with ¾ teaspoon oil and ½ tablespoon lemon juice. Repeat with the remaining parchment, onion, oil, halibut, asparagus, tomato, and lemon juice. Sprinkle all the packets with the salt and pepper. Fold the parchment over the halibut mixture, like closing a book, then tightly crimp the edges to seal the packets.

3. Place the packets on a large baking sheet and bake for 12 minutes, or until the packets have expanded and are puffy. Remove from the oven and set one packet onto each of 4 serving plates. Make a cross in the top of each packet with the tip of a knife and carefully fold back the foil, being mindful of the steam, and sprinkle with the basil.

Per serving: 255 calories, 9 g fat, 1 g saturated fat, 37 g protein, 6 g carbohydrates, 2 g fiber, 240 mg sodium

Pan-Seared Halibut with Stone Fruit Salsa

While we used peaches and nectarines in our salsa, any stone fruit, such as apricots or plums, could easily be substituted with equally successful results.

Prep time: 15 minutes ▷ **Cook time:** 10 minutes ▷ **Total time:** 25 minutes ▷ MAKES 4 SERVINGS

2 medium peaches, chopped into $\frac{1}{4}$" pieces

2 medium nectarines, chopped into $\frac{1}{4}$" pieces

3 tablespoons finely chopped red onion

$\frac{1}{2}$ jalapeño chile pepper, seeded and minced (wear plastic gloves when handling)

1 tablespoon fresh lime juice

1 tablespoon chopped fresh cilantro

$\frac{1}{8}$ teaspoon + $\frac{1}{4}$ teaspoon salt

1 tablespoon olive oil

4 skinless halibut fillets (6 ounces each)

$\frac{1}{8}$ teaspoon ground black pepper

1. Combine the peaches, nectarines, onion, jalapeño, lime juice, cilantro, and $\frac{1}{8}$ teaspoon of the salt in a bowl.

2. Heat the oil in a large nonstick skillet over medium-high heat. Sprinkle the halibut with the pepper and the remaining $\frac{1}{4}$ teaspoon salt. Cook for 10 minutes, turning once, or until the fish flakes easily. Serve with the salsa.

Per serving: 282 calories, 8 g fat, 1 g saturated fat, 37 g protein, 16 g carbohydrates, 3 g fiber, 310 mg sodium

Halibut Curry with Brown Basmati Rice

Lite coconut milk, found in the Asian foods section of most grocery stores, lends a lot of flavor without a lot of fat. Be careful not to let it boil or it may separate.

Prep time: 10 minutes ▷ **Cook time:** 1 hour ▷ **Total time:** 1 hour 10 minutes ▷ MAKES 4 SERVINGS

²/₃ cup brown basmati rice

2 teaspoons canola oil

4 skinless halibut fillets (4 ounces each)

1 tablespoon grated fresh ginger

1 tablespoon curry powder

½ teaspoon ground cumin

¾ cup lite coconut milk

1 tablespoon packed light brown sugar

1 tablespoon fresh lime juice

¼ teaspoon cayenne pepper

2 tablespoons chopped fresh cilantro

¼ teaspoon salt

1. Prepare the rice according to package directions, omitting any salt or fat.

2. Meanwhile, heat 1 teaspoon of the oil in a large nonstick skillet over medium-high heat. Cook the halibut for 10 minutes, turning once, or until the fish flakes easily. Transfer to a plate and keep warm.

3. Heat the remaining 1 teaspoon oil in the same skillet over medium heat. Cook the ginger, curry powder, and cumin for 30 seconds, stirring, or until fragrant. Add the coconut milk, brown sugar, lime juice, and cayenne. Cook for 3 minutes, stirring often, or until heated through. Remove from the heat and stir in the cilantro and salt. Add the halibut fillets and turn to coat. Divide the halibut and rice among 4 plates.

Per serving: 302 calories, 9 g fat, 3 g saturated fat, 27 g protein, 28 g carbohydrates, 3 g fiber, 221 mg sodium

Roasted Cod Topped with Sautéed Tomato and Spinach

Cod is a flaky, light, delicately flavored fish that lends itself to savory sauces and toppings. The key is not to overcook it, so the rule of thumb is 10 minutes cooking time per inch of thickness.

Prep time: 20 minutes ▷ **Cook time:** 30 minutes ▷ **Total time:** 50 minutes ▷ MAKES 4 SERVINGS

$\frac{2}{3}$ cup quick-cooking barley

4 skinless cod fillets (6 ounces each)

5 teaspoons extra-virgin olive oil

$\frac{1}{4}$ teaspoon salt

$\frac{1}{8}$ teaspoon ground black pepper

1 medium onion, chopped

2 cloves garlic, minced

1 teaspoon dried basil

$\frac{1}{4}$ teaspoon dried thyme

4 medium tomatoes, seeded and chopped

6 cups baby spinach

1. Preheat the oven to 425°F. Coat a large baking sheet with cooking spray.

2. Bring $1\frac{1}{3}$ cups water to a boil in a small saucepan over medium-high heat. Stir in the barley and reduce the heat to medium-low. Cover and simmer for 10 minutes, or until tender and the water is almost completely absorbed. Remove from the heat and let stand for 5 minutes.

3. Meanwhile, rub the cod fillets with 2 teaspoons of the oil and sprinkle with $\frac{1}{8}$ teaspoon of the salt and the pepper. Place on the baking sheet. Roast for 10 minutes, or until the fish flakes easily. Remove from the oven and keep warm.

4. While the fish cooks, heat the remaining 1 tablespoon oil in a large nonstick skillet over medium-high heat. Cook the onion, garlic, basil, and thyme for 3 minutes, stirring occasionally, or until starting to soften. Stir in the tomatoes and cook for 3 minutes, stirring occasionally, or until the tomatoes are softened. Add the spinach and cook for 2 minutes, stirring, or until the spinach is wilted. Stir in the remaining $\frac{1}{8}$ teaspoon salt.

5. Divide the cod, barley, and spinach mixture among 4 plates.

Per serving: 319 calories, 8 g fat, 1 g saturated fat, 31 g protein, 32 g carbohydrates, 6 g fiber, 282 mg sodium

Mango Salsa Grouper

Grouper is a white-fleshed fish with a firm texture and a large flake. Its flavor is similar to sea bass but milder.

Prep time: 15 minutes ⊱ **Cook time:** 10 minutes ⊱ **Total time:** 25 minutes + chilling time
⊱ MAKES 4 SERVINGS

1 medium mango, chopped
$\frac{1}{2}$ cup chopped fresh cilantro
$\frac{1}{2}$ medium red bell pepper, chopped
$\frac{1}{2}$ medium green bell pepper, chopped
1 small red onion, chopped

$\frac{1}{4}$ cup rice vinegar
$\frac{1}{8}$ teaspoon salt
2 teaspoons olive oil
4 grouper fillets (6 ounces each)
4 corn tortillas (6" diameter)

1. Combine the mango, cilantro, bell peppers, onion, vinegar, and salt in a medium bowl. Toss well, cover, and refrigerate for 2 hours.

2. Preheat the grill to medium-high. Coat a large piece of foil with cooking spray and place on the grill rack.

3. Rub the oil over the fish and set on the foil over the coolest part of the grill. Cook for 8 minutes, or until the fish flakes easily. Warm the tortillas according to package directions. Place one fillet on each of 4 plates and serve with the mango salsa and tortillas.

Per serving: 301 calories, 5 g fat, 1 g saturated fat, 35 g protein, 29 g carbohydrates, 3 g fiber, 310 mg sodium

Fish and Chips

This recipe features two fun twists on the age-old classic. One is panko bread crumbs, which give an excellent crunch to the oven-fried halibut. The second is sweet potatoes, which are packed with fiber, beta-carotene, and a ton of flavor.

Prep time: 20 minutes ⁑ **Cook time:** 45 minutes ⁑ **Total time:** 1 hour 5 minutes ⁑ MAKES 4 SERVINGS

2 medium sweet potatoes, peeled and cut lengthwise into wedges
$1\frac{1}{2}$ teaspoons olive oil
$\frac{1}{2}$ teaspoon smoked paprika
$\frac{1}{8}$ teaspoon salt
$\frac{1}{4}$ teaspoon ground black pepper
2 large egg whites

1 teaspoon Dijon mustard
$\frac{1}{8}$ teaspoon cayenne pepper
1 cup panko bread crumbs
$\frac{1}{2}$ teaspoon dried thyme
4 skinless halibut fillets (6 ounces each)
Lemon wedges or malt vinegar, for serving (optional)

1. Preheat the oven to 425°F. Coat 2 large baking sheets with cooking spray.

2. Combine the sweet potatoes, oil, paprika, salt, and $\frac{1}{8}$ teaspoon of the black pepper in a large bowl, tossing well to coat. Arrange on one of the baking sheets in a single layer. Bake for 30 minutes, turning once, or until browned and cooked through. Remove from the oven and keep warm.

3. Meanwhile, whisk the egg whites, mustard, cayenne, and remaining $\frac{1}{8}$ teaspoon black pepper in a medium bowl. Combine the bread crumbs and thyme in a shallow dish. Working with one fillet at a time, dip the halibut in the egg white mixture, shaking off the excess, then roll in the bread crumb mixture to coat. Place on the second baking sheet. Repeat with the remaining halibut fillets.

4. Bake the halibut for 12 minutes, turning once, or until the crumbs are golden and the fish flakes easily. Divide the fish and sweet potatoes among 4 plates. Serve with lemon wedges or malt vinegar, if desired.

Per serving: 302 calories, 6 g fat, 1 g saturated fat, 39 g protein, 20 g carbohydrates, 3 g fiber, 319 mg sodium

Broiled Pollock with Lemon and Olive Oil

Sautéing sliced garlic in extra-virgin olive oil with a little added lemon juice gives light-tasting pollock a scampi-like flavor.

Prep time: 10 minutes ⁘ **Cook time:** 15 minutes ⁘ **Total time:** 25 minutes ⁘ MAKES 4 SERVINGS

$\frac{1}{2}$ pound green beans, trimmed and halved crosswise

1 teaspoon unsalted butter

2 cups fresh corn kernels, cut from 3 medium ears

$\frac{1}{4}$ teaspoon salt

4 skinless pollock fillets (6 ounces each)

$\frac{1}{8}$ teaspoon ground black pepper

4 teaspoons extra-virgin olive oil

4 cloves garlic, sliced

2 tablespoons fresh lemon juice

1. Preheat the broiler. Coat a broiler pan with cooking spray.

2. Bring a large saucepan of water to a boil. Add the beans, return to a boil, and cook for 2 minutes. Drain.

3. Melt the butter in a large nonstick skillet over medium-high heat. Cook the corn for 3 minutes, stirring occasionally, or until bright yellow. Stir in the beans and cook for 1 minute. Remove from the heat and stir in $\frac{1}{8}$ teaspoon of the salt. Keep warm.

4. Place the fillets on the broiler pan. Coat with cooking spray and broil for 8 minutes, or until the fish flakes easily. Place 1 fillet on each of 4 serving plates.

5. Meanwhile, heat the oil in a small nonstick skillet over medium-high heat. Add the garlic and cook for 1 minute, or until lightly browned. Remove from the heat, stir in the lemon juice, remaining salt and pepper, and spoon over the pollock. Serve with the corn mixture.

Per serving: 297 calories, 8 g fat, 2 g saturated fat, 37 g protein, 20 g carbohydrates, 4 g fiber, 307 mg sodium

Grilled Fresh Sardines over Wilted Spinach

Fresh sardines and potatoes are a classic Portuguese combination.

Prep time: 15 minutes ▷ **Cook time:** 25 minutes ▷ **Total time:** 40 minutes ▷ MAKES 4 SERVINGS

12 fresh sardines, cleaned

1¼ pounds potatoes, cut into ¼"-thick wedges

2 tablespoons fresh lemon juice

2 teaspoons olive oil

1 cup grape tomatoes, halved

8 cups baby arugula

1 teaspoon balsamic vinegar

1. Preheat the grill to medium-high.

2. Coat a grill rack with cooking spray. Grill the sardines for 10 minutes, turning once, or until the fish flakes easily. Transfer to a plate and keep warm. Coat the potato wedges with cooking spray and place on the grill rack. Grill for 4 minutes, or until browned and tender. Transfer to a bowl and toss with 2 teaspoons of the lemon juice. Keep warm. Drizzle the sardines with the remaining 4 teaspoons lemon juice.

3. Meanwhile, heat the oil in a large nonstick skillet over medium-high heat. Add the tomatoes and cook for 3 minutes, or until softened. Add the arugula and vinegar. Cook for 1 minute, stirring, or until just wilted. Divide among 4 plates and serve with potato wedges and 3 sardines.

Per serving: 265 calories, 9 g fat, 1 g saturated fat, 18 g protein, 30 g carbohydrates, 3 g fiber, 304 mg sodium

Salt Solution Cioppino

Cioppino, a fisherman's stew hailing from San Francisco, could be considered a rustic American version of the more refined French bouillabaisse.

Prep time: 15 minutes ❧ **Cook time:** 45 minutes ❧ **Total time:** 1 hour ❧ MAKES 4 SERVINGS

- 1 tablespoon extra-virgin olive oil
- 3 cloves garlic, minced
- 1 medium onion, chopped
- 1 medium red bell pepper, chopped
- 1/2 medium fennel bulb, sliced
- 1 teaspoon dried basil
- 1/8 teaspoon saffron threads, lightly crushed (optional)
- 3/4 cup white wine
- 1/2 pound red-skinned potatoes, cut into 1" pieces

- 1 can (14.5 ounces) no-salt-added diced tomatoes
- 1 cup low-sodium chicken broth
- 16 small mussels, scrubbed
- 1/2 pound peeled and deveined medium shrimp
- 1/2 pound skinless cod fillet, cut into 1 1/2" pieces

1. Heat the oil in a large saucepot or Dutch oven over medium-high heat. Cook the garlic, onion, bell pepper, fennel, basil, and saffron (if using) for 4 minutes, stirring occasionally. Pour in the wine, bring to a boil, and cook for 3 minutes, or until reduced by one-fourth. Add the potatoes, tomatoes, broth, and 1/2 cup of water. Bring to a boil, reduce the heat to medium-low, cover, and simmer for 25 minutes, stirring occasionally.

2. Stir in the mussels, shrimp, and cod. Cover, return to a simmer, and cook for 7 minutes, or until the mussels open, the shrimp are opaque, and the cod flakes easily. (Discard any mussels that have not opened.) Remove from the heat and ladle into 4 bowls to serve.

Per serving: 301 calories, 6 g fat, 1 g saturated fat, 29 g protein, 23 g carbohydrates, 4 g fiber, 307 mg sodium

Seafood Arrabbiata

The sweet taste of sea scallops is the perfect foil to the spicy tomato sauce in this dish. When buying scallops, give them a sniff: They shouldn't smell fishy at all but have a fresh scent of the sea.

Prep time: 10 minutes ❧ **Cook time:** 25 minutes ❧ **Total time:** 35 minutes ❧ MAKES 4 SERVINGS

6 ounces penne
3 teaspoons extra-virgin olive oil
¾ pound sea scallops
1 large onion, chopped
3 cloves garlic, minced
¼ teaspoon red-pepper flakes
1 red bell pepper, chopped

1 can (14.5 ounces) no-salt-added diced tomatoes
3 tablespoons no-salt-added tomato paste
⅛ teaspoon salt
¼ cup chopped fresh basil

1. Prepare the penne according to package directions, omitting the salt.

2. Meanwhile, heat 2 teaspoons of the oil in a large nonstick skillet over medium-high heat. Cook the scallops for 5 minutes, turning once, or until just opaque. Transfer the scallops to a plate and set aside.

3. Heat the remaining 1 teaspoon oil in the same skillet over medium-high heat. Cook the onion, garlic, and red-pepper flakes for 2 minutes, stirring occasionally, or until the onion starts to soften. Stir in the bell pepper and cook for 3 minutes. Add the tomatoes, tomato paste, and salt. Bring to a boil, reduce the heat to medium, and simmer for 5 minutes, or until slightly thickened. Add the penne and scallops, and cook for 1 minute, or until hot. Stir in the basil.

Per serving: 320 calories, 5 g fat, 1 g saturated fat, 22 g protein, 45 g carbohydrates, 4 g fiber, 264 mg sodium

Seafood Gumbo

This hearty Louisiana favorite gets its authentic flavor from okra, bell pepper, celery, and filé powder.

Prep time: 20 minutes ▶ **Cook time:** 30 minutes ▶ **Total time:** 50 minutes ▶ MAKES 4 SERVINGS

$2/3$ cup basmati rice
1 tablespoon olive oil
1 tablespoon whole wheat flour
1 medium onion, chopped
1 medium green bell pepper, chopped
1 rib celery, chopped
2 cans (14.5 ounces each) no-salt added diced tomatoes

1 cup fresh okra, sliced
$1/2$ pound haddock fillet, cut into 1" pieces
$1/4$ pound peeled and deveined medium shrimp
$1/4$ pound sea scallops
$1/4$ pound shucked oysters
1 teaspoon hot-pepper sauce
$1/2$ teaspoon filé powder (optional)

1. Prepare the rice according to package directions, omitting any salt or fat.

2. Combine the oil and flour in a large saucepan. Cook over medium heat for 4 minutes, stirring constantly, or until the mixture turns dark brown. Stir in the onion, bell pepper, and celery. Cook for 4 minutes, stirring, or until starting to soften. Add the tomatoes and okra. Bring to a boil, reduce the heat to medium-low, cover, and simmer for 5 minutes. Add the haddock, shrimp, scallops, and oysters. Return to a simmer and cook for 5 minutes, or until the shellfish are just opaque and the haddock flakes easily.

3. Remove from the heat and stir in the hot-pepper sauce and filé powder (if using). Serve over the rice.

Per serving: 318 calories, 6 g fat, 1 g saturated fat, 28 g protein, 36 g carbohydrates, 5 g fiber, 281 mg sodium

Seared Scallops with Quinoa Pilaf

Five-spice is a blend of cinnamon, star anise, cloves, Sichuan pepper, and fennel seeds.

Prep time: 15 minutes ⫶ **Cook time:** 45 minutes ⫶ **Total time:** 1 hour ⫶ MAKES 4 SERVINGS

SAUCE
- 1 cup pomegranate juice
- ³/₄ teaspoon less-sodium soy sauce
- ¹/₂ teaspoon Chinese five-spice powder
- 1 small shallot, finely chopped
- 1¹/₂ teaspoons grated fresh ginger
- 1 teaspoon cornstarch

PILAF
- 1 teaspoon olive oil
- 1 small onion, chopped

- ²/₃ cup quinoa
- 1¹/₃ cups low-sodium chicken broth
- ¹/₈ teaspoon ground cinnamon
- ¹/₄ cup dried cranberries
- 1 teaspoon fresh lemon juice

SCALLOPS
- 2 teaspoons olive oil
- ¹/₄ teaspoon toasted sesame oil
- 1 pound sea scallops
- ¹/₄ teaspoon ground black pepper

1. *To make the sauce:* Combine the pomegranate juice, soy sauce, five-spice powder, shallot, and ginger in a small saucepan over medium-low heat. Bring to a simmer and cook for 45 minutes, or until reduced to about ¹/₃ cup. Stir together the cornstarch and 1 tablespoon water in a small bowl until smooth and add to the saucepan. Cook for 2 minutes, stirring, or until thickened. Keep warm.

2. *Meanwhile, to make the pilaf:* Heat the oil in a medium saucepan over medium-high heat. Cook the onion for 5 minutes, stirring. Add the quinoa and cook for 5 minutes. Add the broth and cayenne. Bring to a boil, reduce the heat to low, cover, and simmer for 20 minutes, or until the quinoa is tender. Remove from the heat and stir in the cranberries and lemon juice.

3. Heat the olive and sesame oils in a large nonstick skillet over medium-high heat. Sprinkle the scallops with the black pepper. Cook for 5 minutes, turning once, or until just opaque. Divide the scallops and pilaf among 4 plates and drizzle with the sauce.

Per serving: 323 calories, 7 g fat, 1 g saturated fat, 25 g protein, 41 g carbohydrates, 3 g fiber, 251 mg sodium

Tuscan White Beans with Spinach, Shrimp, and Feta

Feta and shrimp is a classic combination in Greek cuisine. This dish uses only a small amount of the cheese, but because of its distinctive flavor, a little bit goes a long way.

Prep time: 15 minutes ⁖ **Cook time:** 10 minutes ⁖ **Total time:** 25 minutes ⁖ MAKES 4 SERVINGS

6 teaspoons extra-virgin olive oil
3/4 pound peeled and deveined medium shrimp
1 medium onion, chopped
4 cloves garlic, minced
2 teaspoons chopped fresh sage
2 tablespoons balsamic vinegar

1/2 cup low-sodium chicken broth
1 can (15 ounces) no-salt-added cannellini beans, rinsed and drained
4 cups baby spinach
1 1/2 ounces crumbled reduced-fat feta cheese

1. Heat 2 teaspoons of the oil in a large nonstick skillet over medium-high heat. Cook the shrimp for 2 minutes, or until just opaque. Transfer to a plate.

2. Heat the remaining 4 teaspoons oil in the same skillet over medium-high heat. Cook the onion, garlic, and sage for 4 minutes, stirring occasionally, or until the garlic starts to brown. Stir in the vinegar and cook for 30 seconds, or until nearly evaporated.

3. Add the broth, bring to a boil, and cook for 2 minutes. Stir in the beans and spinach and cook for 1 minute, stirring, or until the spinach is wilted. Remove from the heat and stir in the shrimp and feta cheese. Divide among 4 bowls.

Per serving: 286 calories, 10 g fat, 2 g saturated fat, 27 g protein, 22 g carbohydrates, 7 g fiber, 303 mg sodium

Garlic Shrimp and Kale Stir-Fry

Simple to throw together, this tasty stir-fry is sure to become part of your weeknight repertoire.

Prep time: 15 minutes ⁑ **Cook time:** 10 minutes ⁑ **Total time:** 25 minutes ⁑ MAKES 4 SERVINGS

1 cup quick-cooking brown rice
3 teaspoons toasted sesame oil
1 pound peeled and deveined medium shrimp
1 medium onion, chopped
4 cloves garlic, sliced

3 scallions, chopped
2 medium carrots, thinly sliced
6 cups chopped kale
½ cup low-sodium chicken broth
1 tablespoon hoisin sauce

1. Prepare the rice according to package directions, omitting any salt or fat.

2. Meanwhile, heat 1 teaspoon of the sesame oil in a large nonstick skillet over medium-high heat. Cook the shrimp for 3 minutes, turning once, or until just opaque. Transfer to a plate.

3. Heat the remaining 2 teaspoons sesame oil in the same skillet over medium heat. Cook the onion, garlic, scallions, and carrots for 2 minutes, or until just starting to soften. Add the kale and cook for 2 minutes. Add the broth and cook for 3 minutes, stirring occasionally, or until the kale has wilted. Stir in the reserved shrimp and the hoisin sauce. Cook for 1 minute, stirring, or until hot. Serve over the rice.

Per serving: 318 calories, 7 g fat, 1 g saturated fat, 30 g protein, 37 g carbohydrates, 5 g fiber, 311 mg sodium

WHITE BEANS
Chockful of potassium,
magnesium, and calcium

Vegetarian

Black Bean Tamale Pie

You can make the bean mixture a day ahead. Microwave on high power for 5 minutes to reheat.

Prep time: 25 minutes ⊪ **Cook time:** 50 minutes ⊪ **Total time:** 1 hour 15 minutes ⊪ MAKES 4 SERVINGS

1 onion, chopped

2 cloves garlic, minced

1 green bell pepper, chopped

1 rib celery, finely chopped

1 carrot, finely chopped

1 cup canned no-salt-added black beans, rinsed and drained

1 cup canned no-salt-added diced tomatoes

1 jalapeño chile pepper, seeded and minced (wear plastic gloves when handling)

1 teaspoon ground cumin

1 cup fresh cilantro leaves, chopped

¾ cup yellow cornmeal

¼ cup unbleached all-purpose flour

½ teaspoon baking powder

¼ teaspoon baking soda

½ cup fresh or thawed frozen corn kernels

¾ cup fat-free buttermilk

1 tablespoon maple syrup

2 teaspoons canola oil

1. Preheat the oven to 400°F. Coat a shallow 3-quart baking dish (about 8" round by 2" deep) with cooking spray.

2. Heat a large nonstick skillet coated with cooking spray over medium heat. Cook the onion, garlic, bell pepper, celery, and carrot for 7 minutes, stirring, or until the vegetables begin to soften. Add the beans, tomatoes, jalapeño, and cumin. Reduce the heat to low and simmer for 5 minutes, stirring occasionally, or until the flavors are blended. Remove from the heat, stir in the cilantro, and transfer to the baking dish.

3. Combine the cornmeal, flour, baking powder, and baking soda in a large bowl. Stir in the corn. Whisk the buttermilk, maple syrup, and oil in a small bowl. Add to the corn-meal mixture and stir just until blended. Spoon over the bean mixture. Bake for 30 to 35 minutes, or until a toothpick inserted in the center of the cornbread comes out clean.

Per serving: 304 calories, 4 g fat, 0 g saturated fat, 10 g protein, 59 g carbohydrates, 8 g fiber, 200 mg sodium

Bean and Vegetable Enchiladas

These gooey baked enchiladas packed with fiber-filled beans and nutrient-rich veggies are sure to satisfy a Mexican craving.

Prep time: 20 minutes ❧ **Cook time:** 40 minutes ❧ **Total time:** 1 hour ❧ MAKES 4 SERVINGS

1 yellow or red bell pepper, chopped
1 onion, chopped
2 cloves garlic, minced
1 teaspoon chili powder
1 can (15 ounces) no-salt-added pinto beans, rinsed and drained
1 can (14.5 ounces) no-salt-added diced tomatoes, drained, juice reserved

½ cup packed fresh cilantro leaves, chopped
¼ teaspoon red-pepper flakes
8 corn tortillas (6" diameter)
½ cup shredded reduced-fat pepper Jack cheese
2 cups shredded romaine lettuce
¼ cup fat-free sour cream

1. Preheat the oven to 350°F. Coat a 13" × 9" baking dish with cooking spray.

2. Heat a large nonstick skillet coated with cooking spray over medium heat. Cook the bell pepper, onion, garlic, and chili powder for 5 minutes, stirring occasionally, or until softened. Add the beans and the juice from the canned tomatoes. Bring to a simmer and cook for 5 minutes, or until hot. Mash some of the beans with the back of a spoon to thicken the mixture. Remove the skillet from the heat.

3. Combine the drained tomatoes, cilantro, and red-pepper flakes in a small bowl. Heat the tortillas according to the package directions. Lay the tortillas on a work surface. Divide the bean mixture among the tortillas and roll up. Place the enchiladas seam side down in the baking dish and top with the tomato mixture. Cover the dish tightly with foil.

4. Bake for 20 minutes. Remove the foil and sprinkle the cheese evenly over the enchiladas. Bake for 10 minutes, or until the cheese melts. Let stand for 5 minutes before serving. Serve 2 enchiladas, ½ cup lettuce, and 1 tablespoon sour cream per person.

Per serving: 307 calories, 5 g fat, 2 g saturated fat, 12 g protein, 52 g carbohydrates, 8 g fiber, 251 mg sodium

Chili with Beans, Corn, and Tofu

This chili is a good make-ahead choice, since it will taste even better the next day.

Prep time: 25 minutes ▷ **Cook time:** 40 minutes ▷ **Total time:** 1 hour 5 minutes ▷ MAKES 6 SERVINGS

1 onion, chopped

2 cloves garlic, minced

1$\frac{1}{2}$ tablespoons chili powder

2 teaspoons ground cumin

1 can (15 ounces) no-salt-added pinto beans, rinsed and drained

1 can (14.5 ounces) no-salt-added fire-roasted diced tomatoes

1$\frac{1}{2}$ cups reduced-sodium vegetable broth

1 large red bell pepper, coarsely chopped

2 carrots, shredded

6 ounces lite firm tofu, drained and cut into $\frac{1}{2}$" cubes

1$\frac{1}{2}$ cups fresh or thawed frozen corn kernels

$\frac{1}{3}$ cup shredded reduced-sodium Cheddar cheese

$\frac{1}{3}$ cup fat-free plain yogurt

2 tablespoons chopped fresh cilantro

1. Heat a large saucepan or Dutch oven coated with cooking spray over medium heat. Cook the onion for 4 minutes, stirring, or until softened. Stir in the garlic, chili powder, and cumin. Cook for 1 minute, stirring constantly, or until the spices are toasted.

2. Add the beans, tomatoes, broth, bell pepper, carrots, and tofu and bring to a boil. Reduce the heat to low, cover, and simmer for 25 minutes. Stir in the corn and cook for 5 minutes.

3. Divide the chili, cheese, yogurt, and cilantro among 6 bowls.

Per serving: 171 calories, 2 g fat, 0 g saturated fat, 10 g protein, 28 g carbohydrates, 7 g fiber, 200 mg sodium

 MAKE IT A SALT SOLUTION MEAL: Serve with 1 cup of sliced jicama and 1 cup of cubed cantaloupe (273 calories and 230 mg sodium total).

Indian Lentil Stew

You can substitute curry powder for the garam masala, and other greens for the spinach, such as Swiss chard or kale. Brown lentils can be substituted for the green lentils.

Prep time: 25 minutes ▷ **Cook time:** 45 minutes ▷ **Total time:** 1 hour 10 minutes ▷ MAKES 4 SERVINGS

½ cup brown basmati rice

1 onion, chopped

1 tablespoon minced fresh ginger

2 cloves garlic, minced

1 teaspoon garam masala

⅛ teaspoon salt

¾ cup French green lentils, rinsed and picked over

1 large sweet potato (12 ounces), peeled and cut into ¾" chunks

1¼ cups low-sodium vegetable broth

1 cup canned no-salt-added diced tomatoes in juice

1 bag (10 ounces) spinach, tough stems removed

¼ cup 0% plain Greek yogurt

½ cup fresh cilantro leaves, chopped

1. Prepare the rice according to package directions, omitting any salt or fat.

2. Heat a large saucepan coated with cooking spray over medium heat. Cook the onion for 6 minutes, stirring, or until softened and lightly browned. Stir in the ginger, garlic, garam masala, and salt. Cook for 1 minute, stirring constantly. Add the lentils, sweet potato, broth, tomatoes, and 1 cup of water. Bring to a boil. Reduce the heat to low, cover, and simmer for 30 minutes, stirring occasionally, or until the lentils and sweet potato are tender.

3. Add half of the spinach and increase the heat to medium. Cover and cook for 2 minutes, stirring, or until the spinach wilts. Repeat with the remaining spinach.

4. In a small bowl, combine the yogurt and cilantro.

5. Divide the rice and stew among 4 bowls. Dollop with the yogurt mixture.

Per serving: 305 calories, 2 g fat, 0 g saturated fat, 15 g protein, 60 g carbohydrates, 12 g fiber, 260 mg sodium

Meatless Sloppy Joes

You can make the sloppy Joe filling ahead of time. Just reheat and spoon onto the buns when you're ready to eat.

Prep time: 20 minutes ▸ **Cook time:** 15 minutes ▸ **Total time:** 35 minutes ▸ MAKES 4 SERVINGS

1 package (14 ounces) lite firm tofu
1 teaspoon canola oil
1 small onion, chopped
1 small zucchini, chopped
1 carrot, shredded
1 can (16 ounces) reduced-sodium tomato sauce

4 teaspoons cider vinegar
2 teaspoons packed brown sugar
2 teaspoons prepared mustard
½ teaspoon ground black pepper
4 whole wheat or multigrain hamburger buns

1. Place the tofu between 2 plates and place a heavy pot on top. Set aside for 10 minutes to release excess liquid. Pat dry. Coarsely crumble the tofu with a fork.

2. Heat the oil in a large nonstick skillet over medium heat. Cook the tofu, onion, zucchini, and carrot for 8 minutes, stirring frequently, or until the tofu is browned and the vegetables are tender.

3. Stir in the tomato sauce, vinegar, brown sugar, mustard, and pepper. Bring to a simmer and cook for 5 minutes, stirring frequently, or until the mixture thickens.

4. Place 1 bun on each of 4 plates and top with the tofu mixture.

Per serving: 239 calories, 6 g fat, 1 g saturated fat, 15 g protein, 38 g carbohydrates, 7 g fiber, 293 mg sodium

 MAKE IT A SALT SOLUTION MEAL: Serve with 1 medium apple (311 calories and 293 mg sodium total).

Veggie Meatloaf

Leftovers make a good sandwich the next day. Serve a slice in a whole wheat pita with lettuce, tomato, and a little fat-free mayonnaise.

Prep time: 15 minutes ▶ **Cook time:** 1 hour ▶ **Total time:** 1 hour 15 minutes ▶ MAKES 4 SERVINGS

  7 ounces firm tofu, cut into 1" cubes
  1 teaspoon olive oil
  1 small onion, finely chopped
  6 ounces baby spinach
  1 carrot, shredded
1½ teaspoons salt-free garlic-herb seasoning blend
  1 slice sprouted whole grain bread, torn into pieces

  1 can (15 ounces) no-salt-added chickpeas, rinsed and drained
  1 cup cooked brown rice
  1 large egg white
  ½ cup no-salt-added ketchup
  3 teaspoons Dijon mustard

1. Preheat the oven to 375°F. Line a rimmed baking sheet with foil and coat with cooking spray. Place the tofu between layers of paper towels and let drain while you cook the vegetables.

2. Heat the oil in a large nonstick skillet over medium-high heat. Cook the onion for 5 minutes, stirring, or until softened. Add the spinach, carrot, and seasoning. Cook for 2 minutes, stirring constantly, or until the spinach wilts. Transfer to a large bowl and let cool for 10 minutes.

3. Place the bread in a food processor and pulse to form crumbs. Add to the bowl with the vegetables. Add the tofu and chickpeas to the processor and pulse until mashed. Add to the bowl along with the brown rice, egg white, ¼ cup of the ketchup, and 2 teaspoons of the mustard. Stir until well blended and the mixture holds together. Let stand for 5 minutes.

4. Shape into a 7" × 3½" loaf on the center of the baking sheet. Combine the remaining ¼ cup ketchup and 1 teaspoon mustard in a small bowl. Spread over the top of the loaf.

5. Bake for 50 minutes, or until a thermometer inserted in the center registers 180°F. Let stand for 10 minutes. Cut into 8 slices with a serrated knife. Makes 2 slices per serving.

Per serving: 291 calories, 5 g fat, 1 g saturated fat, 15 g protein, 49 g carbohydrates, 9 g fiber, 215 mg sodium

 MAKE IT A SALT SOLUTION MEAL: Serve with 3 cups spinach, steamed, and a squeeze of lemon juice (311 calories and 286 mg sodium total).

Polenta Lasagna

To save time in the kitchen, you can cook the collard greens a day ahead.

Prep time: 20 minutes ⫸ **Cook time:** 1 hour 35 minutes ⫸ **Total time:** 1 hour 55 minutes
⫸ MAKES 4 SERVINGS

1 onion, chopped

1 carrot, shredded

2 cloves garlic, minced

1 bunch (1¼ pounds) collard greens, stems and ribs removed, coarsely chopped (about 10 cups)

1 cup part-skim ricotta cheese

½ teaspoon Italian seasoning blend

1½ cups unsweetened plain soymilk

¾ cup instant polenta

¼ cup grated Parmesan cheese

1½ cups reduced-sodium marinara sauce

1 cup shredded reduced-fat mozzarella cheese

2 plum tomatoes, sliced

1. Heat a large saucepot or Dutch oven coated with nonstick cooking spray over medium heat. Cook the onion for 6 minutes, stirring, or until softened and lightly browned. Add the carrot and garlic. Cook for 1 minute, stirring. Add the collard greens and ¼ cup of water. Reduce the heat to low, cover, and simmer for 15 minutes, stirring occasionally, or until the collards are tender. Set aside.

2. Preheat the oven to 375°F. Coat a shallow 11" × 7" baking dish (2-quart) with cooking spray. In a small bowl, combine the ricotta cheese and Italian seasoning.

3. Bring the soymilk and ¾ cup of water to a boil in a medium saucepan. Gradually whisk in the polenta. Reduce the heat to low and cook for 5 minutes, stirring constantly, or until thick. Remove from the heat and stir in 2 tablespoons of the Parmesan.

4. Spoon half of the polenta into the baking dish. Cover with a piece of plastic wrap and press to a thin, even layer. Discard the plastic wrap. Top with the ricotta mixture, spreading to cover. Evenly spread the marinara sauce over the ricotta. Top with the collard greens and sprinkle with ¾ cup of the mozzarella. Top with the remaining polenta in small spoonfuls. Spoon on the remaining marinara sauce, spreading evenly. Sprinkle with the remaining ¼ cup mozzarella, top with the tomato slices, and sprinkle with the remaining 2 tablespoons Parmesan. Spray a sheet of foil with nonstick spray and cover the dish.

5. Bake for 30 minutes. Uncover and bake for 25 minutes, or until bubbling at the edges. Let stand for 10 minutes before cutting into 4 rectangles, removing with a spatula.

Per serving: 307 calories, 8 g fat, 5 g saturated fat, 18 g protein, 43 g carbohydrates, 6 g fiber, 299 mg sodium

Sweet Potato Burgers

If you can't find canned no-salt-added black-eyed peas, try frozen ones.

Prep time: 30 minutes + 30 minutes chilling ⊱ **Cook time:** 40 minutes ⊱ **Total time:** 1 hour 40 minutes
⊱ MAKES 4 SERVINGS

1 onion, chopped

1 red bell pepper, chopped

1 rib celery, chopped

½ bunch kale, stems and ribs removed,
    coarsely chopped (about 5 cups)

3 cloves garlic, minced

1½ teaspoons salt free Cajun seasoning
    blend

¼ teaspoon salt

2 medium sweet potatoes (1 pound),
    peeled and shredded

1 can (15 ounces) no-salt-added
    black-eyed peas, rinsed and drained

4 ounces lite firm tofu, patted dry

2 tablespoons yellow cornmeal

3 teaspoons olive oil

1. Heat a large nonstick skillet coated with nonstick cooking spray over medium heat. Cook the onion, bell pepper, and celery for 8 minutes, stirring, or until the vegetables soften. Stir in the kale, garlic, seasoning, and salt. Cook for 4 minutes, stirring, or until the kale wilts. Add the sweet potatoes and cook for 10 minutes, stirring, or until the sweet potatoes soften. Set aside.

2. Combine the black-eyed peas and tofu in a large bowl. Mash with a potato masher until smooth. Stir in the sweet potato mixture until well blended. Refrigerate for 30 minutes.

3. Sprinkle 1 tablespoon of the cornmeal on a plate. Pack the burger mixture in a ½-cup measure and turn out onto the plate. Press to form 3" burgers, making 8 burgers total. Sprinkle the tops with the remaining 1 tablespoon cornmeal.

4. Wipe out the skillet. Add 1½ teaspoons of the oil to the skillet and heat over medium heat. Cook 4 burgers for 10 minutes, turning once, or until hot and browned. Repeat with the remaining 1½ teaspoons oil and burgers. Serve 2 burgers per person.

Per serving: 301 calories, 7 g fat, 1 g saturated fat, 13 g protein, 51 g carbohydrates, 10 g fiber, 273 mg sodium

 MAKE IT A SALT SOLUTION MEAL: Serve with 1 cup shredded romaine lettuce and ½ cup cherry tomatoes (323 calories and 281 mg sodium total).

Vegetable Stroganoff over Noodles

The sauce for this rich dish can be made ahead of time. A few hours in the refrigerator will only deepen and intensify the flavors!

Prep time: 30 minutes ▶ **Cook time:** 30 minutes ▶ **Total time:** 1 hour ▶ MAKES 4 SERVINGS

6 ounces whole wheat noodles

1 teaspoon olive oil

1 onion, halved and sliced

1 red bell pepper, thinly sliced

8 ounces sliced mushrooms

2 cloves garlic, minced

1 tablespoon tomato paste

1 teaspoon smoked paprika

1/4 teaspoon caraway seeds, crushed

1/4 teaspoon ground black pepper

2 cups broccoli florets

1/4 head Savoy cabbage, sliced

1 carrot, grated

1 cup reduced-sodium vegetable broth

2 teaspoons cornstarch

3/4 cup fat-free sour cream

1 tablespoon chopped fresh dill

1. Prepare the noodles according to package directions, omitting the salt. Drain and keep warm.

2. Meanwhile, heat the oil in a large deep nonstick skillet over medium heat. Cook the onion, bell pepper, and mushrooms for 10 minutes, stirring frequently, or until the mushrooms are tender. Stir in the garlic, tomato paste, paprika, caraway seeds, and black pepper. Add the broccoli, cabbage, carrot, and 1/2 cup of the broth. Bring to a boil. Reduce the heat, cover, and simmer for 10 minutes, or until the vegetables are tender.

3. While the vegetables cook, whisk the remaining 1/2 cup broth into the cornstarch in a small bowl. Stir into the vegetable mixture and simmer for 5 minutes, or until the sauce thickens. Remove the skillet from the heat and stir in the sour cream. Serve over the noodles and sprinkle with the dill.

Per serving: 290 calories, 3 g fat, 1 g saturated fat, 12 g protein, 55 g carbohydrates, 9 g fiber, 146 mg sodium

Eggplant Parmesan Lasagna

Eggplant bulks up the lasagna without adding a ton of salt or calories—and it provides a delicious, almost meatlike addition to this meal.

Prep time: 30 minutes ⠶ **Cook time:** 1 hour 5 minutes ⠶ **Total time:** 1 hour 35 minutes
⠶ MAKES 4 SERVINGS

1 eggplant (1 pound), cut lengthwise into ¼" slices

¾ cup fat-free ricotta cheese

3 ounces reduced-fat goat cheese

⅓ cup chopped fresh basil

¼ teaspoon red-pepper flakes

1 jar (26 ounces) low-sodium marinara sauce

6 uncooked whole wheat lasagna noodles

¼ cup shredded Parmesan cheese

1. Preheat the oven to 450°F. Line a baking sheet with foil and coat with cooking spray. Arrange the eggplant slices in a single layer on the baking sheet and coat with cooking spray. Roast for 15 minutes, or until tender.

2. Coat an 8" × 8" baking dish with cooking spray. Combine the ricotta, goat cheese, 3 tablespoons of the basil, and the red-pepper flakes in a medium bowl. Combine the marinara sauce and ½ cup of water in a bowl. Spread ½ cup of the sauce in the bottom of the baking dish. Place 2 noodles on top, breaking to fit. Spoon half of the ricotta mixture onto the noodles, spreading to cover. Top with half of the eggplant and spread the eggplant with ¾ cup of the sauce. Top with 2 noodles and the remaining ricotta mixture and eggplant. Top with the remaining 2 noodles and spread with the remaining sauce. Cover the dish with foil.

3. Bake for 45 minutes, or until the sauce is bubbling and the noodles are tender. Uncover and sprinkle with the Parmesan and remaining basil. Bake for 5 minutes, or until the Parmesan melts. Let stand for 10 minutes before serving.

Per serving: 311 calories, 5 g fat, 2 g saturated fat, 21 g protein, 49 g carbohydrates, 11 g fiber, 256 mg sodium

VEGETARIAN ⠶

Penne with Garlicky Greens and Beans

This Italian-inspired dish features two Salt Solution Stars—white beans and beet greens.

Prep time: 20 minutes ▷ **Cook time:** 25 minutes ▷ **Total time:** 45 minutes ▷ MAKES 4 SERVINGS

4 ounces whole wheat penne

1 tablespoon olive oil

1 onion, chopped

1 carrot, chopped

3 cloves garlic, minced

¼ teaspoon red-pepper flakes

1 bunch (1 pound) broccoli rabe, tough stem ends trimmed, cut into 1" pieces

1 bunch (½ pound) beet greens, stems trimmed, cut into 1" pieces

1 can (15 ounces) no-salt-added cannellini beans, rinsed and drained

3 tablespoons grated Parmesan cheese

1. Prepare the pasta according to package directions, omitting the salt. Reserve ¼ cup of the pasta cooking water and drain.

2. Meanwhile, heat the oil in a large deep skillet over medium heat. Cook the onion and carrot for 6 minutes, stirring, or until the onion softens and begins to brown. Stir in the garlic and red-pepper flakes. Cook for 1 minute, stirring, or until fragrant. Add half of the greens and ½ cup of water. Increase the heat to medium-high, cover, and cook for 2 minutes, or until the greens wilt. Stir in the remaining greens. Reduce the heat to medium, cover, and cook for 10 minutes, or until the greens are tender. Stir in the beans. Cover and cook for 2 minutes, or until the beans are hot.

3. Stir in the pasta and reserved pasta cooking water. Cook for 2 minutes, stirring, or until the pasta is hot. Remove the skillet from the heat and stir in 2 tablespoons of the cheese. Serve sprinkled with the remaining 1 tablespoon cheese.

Per serving: 300 calories, 7 g fat, 2 g saturated fat, 16 g protein, 47 g carbohydrates, 9 g fiber, 300 mg sodium

Skillet Mac and Cheese with Broccoli

Low-sodium mac and cheese? Yup—and ours is high in fiber, too, with the addition of the broccoli florets, tomatoes, and whole wheat panko bread crumbs.

Prep time: 10 minutes ❧ **Cook time:** 20 minutes ❧ **Total time:** 30 minutes ❧ MAKES 4 SERVINGS

2½ cups unsweetened plain soymilk
1 cup whole wheat elbow macaroni
4 cups small broccoli florets
1 teaspoon salt-free herb seasoning blend
1 teaspoon cornstarch
¾ teaspoon Dijon mustard
⅛ teaspoon cayenne pepper

⅓ cup part-skim ricotta cheese
3 tablespoons grated Romano cheese
8 tablespoons shredded reduced-fat Cheddar cheese
1 cup cherry tomatoes, halved
2 tablespoons whole wheat panko bread crumbs

1. Bring 2 cups of the soymilk and 1 cup of water to a boil in a large, deep ovenproof skillet. Stir in the pasta. Boil for 4 minutes, stirring frequently. Stir in the broccoli and boil for 4 minutes, stirring frequently, or until the pasta is al dente and the broccoli is tender-crisp.

2. Meanwhile, stir the seasoning, cornstarch, mustard, and cayenne into the remaining ½ cup soymilk in a measuring cup.

3. Preheat the broiler.

4. Reduce the heat under the skillet to medium and stir in the cornstarch mixture. Cook for 1 minute, stirring, or until the sauce thickens. Remove the skillet from the heat and stir in the ricotta, Romano, and 7 tablespoons of the Cheddar. Top with the tomatoes.

5. Mix the remaining 1 tablespoon Cheddar and the panko in a small bowl. Sprinkle over the pasta. Broil 5" to 6" from the heat for 4 to 5 minutes, or until browned.

Per serving: 270 calories, 9 g fat, 4 g saturated fat, 19 g protein, 32 g carbohydrates, 7 g fiber, 296 mg sodium

Spicy Coconut-Curried Vegetables

You can vary the vegetables you use here. Try broccoli instead of cauliflower, red potatoes instead of sweet, and wax beans instead of green beans.

Prep time: 30 minutes ▷ **Cook time:** 30 minutes ▷ **Total time:** 1 hour ▷ MAKES 4 SERVINGS

¾ cup brown basmati rice

1 teaspoon vegetable oil

1 onion, chopped

2 cloves garlic, minced

1 tablespoon minced fresh ginger

½ teaspoon red-pepper flakes

2 teaspoons curry powder

½ teaspoon ground cumin

½ teaspoon ground coriander

1 small cauliflower (1½ pounds), cut into 1½" florets

2 medium sweet potatoes, peeled and cut into ¾" cubes

½ pound green beans, halved crosswise

2 tomatoes, chopped

1½ cups reduced-sodium vegetable broth

½ cup lite coconut milk

½ cup low-fat plain yogurt

1. Prepare the rice according to package directions, omitting any salt or fat.

2. Heat the oil in a large, deep skillet over medium heat. Cook the onion, garlic, ginger, and red-pepper flakes for 3 minutes, stirring occasionally, or until the onion softens. Stir in the curry powder, cumin, and coriander and cook for 30 seconds. Add the cauliflower, potatoes, beans, tomatoes, and broth. Bring to a boil, reduce the heat to low, cover, and simmer for 20 minutes, stirring occasionally, or until the vegetables are tender.

3. Meanwhile, combine the coconut milk and yogurt in a small bowl. Remove the skillet from the heat and stir in the yogurt mixture. Serve over the rice.

Per serving: 292 calories, 5 g fat, 2 g saturated fat, 10 g protein, 56 g carbohydrates, 10 g fiber, 160 mg sodium

Cajun Rice and Beans

Like heat? Add a drop (or two, or ten) of your favorite hot-pepper sauce.

Prep time: 15 minutes ⁑ **Cook time:** 25 minutes ⁑ **Total time:** 40 minutes ⁑ MAKES 4 SERVINGS

1 teaspoon canola oil
1 onion, chopped
3 cloves garlic, minced
1 yellow bell pepper, thinly sliced
2 ribs celery, thinly sliced
½ teaspoon smoked paprika
½ teaspoon dried thyme
¼ teaspoon cayenne pepper

¼ teaspoon salt
¾ pound plum tomatoes, cut into large chunks
1 can (15 ounces) no-salt-added kidney beans, rinsed and drained
1 cup quick-cooking brown rice
1 tablespoon red wine vinegar

1. Heat the oil in a large saucepan or Dutch oven over medium heat. Cook the onion for 5 minutes, stirring, or until softened. Stir in the garlic. Transfer ¼ cup of the onion mixture to a medium saucepan and set aside.

2. Add the bell pepper and celery to the large saucepan and cook for 5 minutes, stirring, or until the vegetables soften. Add the paprika, thyme, cayenne, and salt and cook for 1 minute, stirring, or until fragrant. Add the tomatoes and ½ cup of water. Bring to a boil, reduce the heat to low, cover, and simmer for 10 minutes, or until the vegetables are tender, adding more water if necessary.

3. Meanwhile, add the beans, rice, and 1¼ cups of water to the reserved onion mixture in the medium saucepan. Bring to a boil, stir, reduce the heat to low, cover, and cook for 5 minutes, or until the rice is tender and the water is absorbed. Let stand for 5 minutes.

4. Divide the rice and bean mixture among 4 plates. Stir the vinegar into the vegetables and serve over the rice and beans.

Per serving: 240 calories, 3 g fat, 0 g saturated fat, 13 g protein, 43 g carbohydrates, 12 g fiber, 190 mg sodium

 MAKE IT A SALT SOLUTION MEAL: Serve with ¾ cup grapes (318 calories and 192 mg sodium total).

Egg Fried Rice

This fried rice dish is much faster—and healthier—than getting take-out Chinese food.

Prep time: 15 minutes ⁑ **Cook time:** 15 minutes ⁑ **Total time:** 30 minutes ⁑ MAKES 4 SERVINGS

3 teaspoons toasted sesame oil

3 large eggs, lightly beaten

1 onion, chopped

2 teaspoons grated fresh ginger

2 cloves garlic, minced

2 cups frozen stir-fry vegetables, thawed

$\frac{1}{2}$ cup frozen shelled edamame, thawed

2 cups cold cooked brown rice

1 tablespoon less-sodium soy sauce

2 scallions, chopped

1. Heat 1 teaspoon of the sesame oil in a large nonstick skillet over medium-high heat. Add the eggs and cook for 3 minutes without stirring, flipping over once, or until firm. Break into small pieces with a wooden spoon or spatula, transfer to a bowl, and set aside.

2. Add the remaining 2 teaspoons sesame oil to the skillet. Add the onion, ginger, and garlic. Cook for 2 minutes, stirring, or until soft. Add the vegetables and edamame. Cook for 2 minutes, stirring constantly, or until the vegetables are hot. Add the rice and soy sauce. Cook for 2 minutes, stirring, or until hot. Stir in the reserved eggs and the scallions. Cook for 30 seconds.

Per serving: 252 calories, 9 g fat, 2 g saturated fat, 11 g protein, 33 g carbohydrates, 5 g fiber, 301 mg sodium

Brown Rice Risotto with Butternut Squash

Brown rice kicks up the fiber in this risotto dish, and the butternut squash adds creaminess and flavor—and tons of nutrients.

Prep time: 20 minutes ❖ **Cook time:** 55 minutes ❖ **Total time:** 1 hour 15 minutes ❖ MAKES 4 SERVINGS

1 small onion, finely chopped
2 cloves garlic, minced
1 cup brown rice
¼ cup dry white wine
1½ cups low-sodium vegetable broth
⅛ teaspoon dried thyme
⅛ teaspoon salt

3 cups (1 pound) peeled and seeded butternut squash cubes (½")
5 ounces (half a 10-ounce package) frozen chopped kale, thawed
½ cup grated Parmesan cheese
¼ cup unsweetened plain soymilk
¼ teaspoon ground black pepper

1. Heat a large saucepot coated with cooking spray over medium heat. Cook the onion for 6 minutes, stirring, or until lightly browned. Add the garlic and cook for 1 minute, stirring. Add the rice and cook for 2 minutes, stirring. Add the wine and cook for 1 minute, stirring, or until the wine is absorbed.

2. Add 3 cups of water, the broth, thyme, and salt to the rice mixture. Bring to a boil, reduce the heat to medium-low, cover, and simmer for 10 minutes, stirring occasionally. Stir in the squash, cover, and simmer for 15 minutes, stirring occasionally. Stir in the kale, cover, and simmer for 20 minutes, stirring more towards the end of the cooking time to prevent sticking, or until the rice, squash, and kale are tender.

3. Remove from the heat. Stir in 6 tablespoons of the cheese, the soymilk, and pepper. Serve sprinkled with the remaining 2 tablespoons cheese.

Per serving: 304 calories, 5 g fat, 2 g saturated fat, 10 g protein, 54 g carbohydrates, 5 g fiber, 294 mg sodium

Quinoa Pilaf with White Beans and Almonds

You can substitute spinach or kale for the beet greens.

Prep time: 20 minutes ⊪ **Cook time:** 30 minutes ⊪ **Total time:** 50 minutes ⊪ MAKES 4 SERVINGS

2 teaspoons olive oil

1 small red onion, chopped

2 cloves garlic, minced

1 bunch (12 ounces) beet greens, chopped

¾ cup quinoa, rinsed

1 can (15 ounces) no-salt-added white beans, rinsed and drained

¼ cup dried apricots, chopped

¼ cup almonds, toasted and chopped

2 tablespoons crumbled feta cheese

1. Heat the oil in a large saucepan over medium heat. Add the onion and garlic. Cook for 5 minutes, stirring, or until softened. Stir in the beet greens and cook for 5 minutes, stirring, or until wilted. Add the quinoa and 1½ cups of water. Bring to a boil, reduce the heat, cover, and simmer for 20 minutes, or until the quinoa is tender and the liquid is absorbed.

2. Stir in the beans and apricots. Cover and cook for 5 minutes, stirring, or until the beans are hot. Stir in the almonds and cheese.

Per serving: 291 calories, 8 g fat, 1 g saturated fat, 13 g protein, 44 g carbohydrates, 11 g fiber, 273 mg sodium

Creamy Barley Risotto

Pearl barley is high in iron, and is a great substitute for rice or pasta.

Prep time: 15 minutes ⁂ **Cook time:** 1 hour 10 minutes ⁂ **Total time:** 1 hour 25 minutes
⁂ MAKES 4 SERVINGS

- 4 cups reduced-sodium vegetable broth
- 1 tablespoon extra-virgin olive oil
- 2 medium leeks, white and light green parts, halved lengthwise, rinsed, and thinly sliced crosswise, or 1 large onion, chopped
- 1 clove garlic, minced
- ¾ cup medium pearl barley

- ½ teaspoon dried basil, crumbled
- ¼ teaspoon ground black pepper
- ½ cup frozen peas, thawed
- 1 plum tomato, chopped
- ¼ cup (1 ounce) grated Parmesan cheese
- 1 tablespoon chopped fresh chives

1. Combine the broth and 2½ cups of water in a medium saucepan and bring to a boil over high heat. Reduce the heat to low, cover, and keep at a simmer.

2. Heat the oil in a large saucepan over medium heat. Cook the leeks or onion and garlic for 4 minutes, stirring, or until the leeks soften. Add the barley, basil, and pepper, stirring until the barley is coated.

3. Begin adding the hot broth mixture about ½ cup at a time, stirring frequently after each addition and cooking until the liquid is nearly evaporated. Continue adding the broth mixture, ½ cup at a time, for 55 minutes or until all has been added and the barley is very tender and creamy.

4. Stir in the peas, tomato, cheese, and chives. Cook, stirring, for 5 minutes, or until heated through.

Per serving: 260 calories, 6 g fat, 2 g saturated fat, 8 g protein, 42 g carbohydrates, 8 g fiber, 286 mg sodium

Stir-Fried Broccoli and Peppers with Ginger

This Asian-inspired dish is so filling and delicious, you'll never miss the meat (or the sodium!).

Prep time: 25 minutes ⁞▸ **Cook time:** 5 minutes ⁞▸ **Total time:** 30 minutes ⁞▸ MAKES 4 SERVINGS

½ cup reduced-sodium vegetable broth
1 tablespoon less-sodium soy sauce
1 tablespoon rice vinegar
2 teaspoons hoisin sauce
2 teaspoons cornstarch
1 teaspoon toasted sesame oil
¼ teaspoon red-pepper flakes
1 tablespoon peanut or vegetable oil
2 red bell peppers, cut into small strips

1 red onion, halved and thinly sliced
4 cups broccoli florets
1 cup frozen shelled edamame, thawed
4 ounces shiitake mushrooms, stems discarded and caps halved
2 cloves garlic, minced
2 teaspoons minced fresh ginger
2 cups hot cooked brown rice

1. Whisk together the broth, soy sauce, vinegar, hoisin sauce, cornstarch, sesame oil, and red-pepper flakes in a small bowl. Set aside.

2. Heat the peanut or vegetable oil in a wok or large nonstick skillet over high heat, tilting the pan to coat. Cook the bell peppers and onion for 1 minute, stirring constantly. Add the broccoli, edamame, mushrooms, garlic, ginger, and 3 tablespoons of water. Cook for 10 minutes, stirring constantly, or until the vegetables are tender-crisp. Quickly whisk the broth mixture and add it to the wok. Cook and stir for 20 seconds, or just until thickened.

3. Divide the rice and vegetable mixture among 4 bowls.

Per serving: 285 calories, 8 g fat, 1 g saturated fat, 10 g protein, 46 g carbohydrates, 8 g fiber, 295 mg sodium

Thai Tofu

This recipe has a long ingredient list, but once the ingredients are prepared, the cooking time is fast. You can cut up the vegetables a few hours ahead.

Prep time: 25 minutes ▷ **Cook time:** 25 minutes ▷ **Total time:** 50 minutes ▷ MAKES 4 SERVINGS

1 package (14 ounces) extra-firm tofu
1 teaspoon curry powder
1 teaspoon canola oil
3 shallots, thinly sliced
8 ounces sliced mushrooms
1 carrot, cut into matchsticks
1 tablespoon minced fresh ginger
2 cloves garlic, minced
1¼ cups reduced-sodium vegetable broth
2 teaspoons red curry paste

2 teaspoons packed brown sugar
1 teaspoon reduced-sodium fish sauce
½ pound green and/or wax beans, trimmed
3 cups shredded bok choy
1 tomato, cut into large chunks
¾ cup lite coconut milk
¼ cup chopped fresh basil leaves
1 lime, cut into wedges

1. Cut the tofu into 4 slices and press lightly between paper towels. Sprinkle the tofu on both sides with the curry powder and rub to coat.

2. Heat ½ teaspoon of the oil in a medium nonstick skillet over medium heat. Cook the tofu for 10 minutes, turning once, or until browned. Remove the skillet from the heat and cover to keep warm.

3. Heat the remaining ½ teaspoon oil in a large saucepot or Dutch oven over medium-high heat. Cook the shallots for 1 minute, stirring constantly, or until lightly browned. Add the mushrooms, carrot, ginger, and garlic. Cook for 3 minutes, stirring constantly, or until the mushrooms begin to brown and release some liquid.

4. Add the broth, curry paste, brown sugar, and fish sauce, stirring to dissolve the curry paste. Add the green beans, cover, and cook for 3 minutes, or until the beans are tender-crisp. Stir in the bok choy, tomato, and coconut milk. Cover and cook for 2 minutes, stirring a few times, or until the bok choy is tender. Divide the vegetable mixture among 4 shallow bowls, top each with a slice of tofu, and sprinkle with the basil. Serve with the lime wedges.

Per serving: 297 calories, 10 g fat, 3 g saturated fat, 19 g protein, 39 g carbohydrates, 6 g fiber, 282 mg sodium

Black Bean Tostadas with Tofu

To save time, the tortillas can be baked up to 2 days ahead and stored in a resealable food-storage bag. The vegetable mixture can be made 1 day ahead and reheated in the microwave.

Prep time: 25 minutes ⬝ **Cook time:** 30 minutes ⬝ **Total time:** 55 minutes ⬝ MAKES 4 SERVINGS

4 corn tortillas (6" diameter)
1 onion, halved and thinly sliced
4 ounces lite firm tofu, patted dry and cut into $1/2$" cubes
1 medium zucchini (7 ounces), quartered lengthwise and sliced crosswise
3 plum tomatoes, cut into $1/2$" chunks
1 cup canned no-salt-added black beans, rinsed and drained

$1^{1}/_{2}$ teaspoons salt-free chili-lime seasoning blend
$1/2$ cup shredded reduced-fat Cheddar cheese
1 cup shredded romaine lettuce (about 4 leaves)
$1/2$ Hass avocado, diced
$1/4$ cup 0% plain Greek yogurt
$1/2$ cup chopped fresh cilantro
4 lime wedges

1. Preheat the oven to 350°F. Lightly coat both sides of the tortillas with cooking spray. Place on a baking sheet. Bake for 15 minutes, or until crisp.

2. Heat a large nonstick skillet coated with cooking spray over medium-high heat. Cook the onion and tofu for 5 minutes, stirring, or until the onion and tofu brown lightly. Stir in the zucchini, tomatoes, beans, and seasoning. Cook for 6 minutes, stirring, or until the zucchini is tender.

3. To assemble the tostadas, top each tortilla with one-fourth of the zucchini mixture, 2 tablespoons cheese, $1/4$ cup lettuce, one-fourth of the avocado, 1 tablespoon yogurt, and 2 tablespoons cilantro. Serve with the lime wedges.

Per serving: 291 calories, 7 g fat, 1 g saturated fat, 16 g protein, 42 g carbohydrates, 10 g fiber, 187 mg sodium

Curried Tofu, Squash, and Lima Beans with Couscous

Whole wheat couscous cooks in minutes and adds tons of vitamins and fiber to any dish.

Prep time: 30 minutes ⁑ **Cook time:** 35 minutes ⁑ **Total time:** 1 hour 5 minutes ⁑ MAKES 4 SERVINGS

1 package (14 ounces) lite firm tofu
2 teaspoons canola oil
1 onion, coarsely chopped
1 tablespoon minced fresh ginger
2 cloves garlic, minced
2 teaspoons ground coriander
1 teaspoon cumin seeds
1 teaspoon turmeric

3 cups (1 pound) peeled and seeded butternut squash chunks (3/4")
1 1/2 cups reduced-sodium vegetable broth or water
10 ounces frozen lima beans, thawed
2 cups hot cooked whole wheat couscous
1/4 cup chopped fresh mint leaves

1. Set the tofu between two plates and place a heavy pot on top. Set aside for 10 minutes to release excess liquid. Cut into 3/4" cubes and pat dry. Set aside.

2. Heat the oil in a large saucepan over medium-high heat. Cook the onion, ginger, garlic, coriander, cumin seeds, and turmeric for 2 minutes, or until the onion begins to soften. Add the squash, broth or water, and tofu. Bring to a boil, reduce the heat to medium-low, cover, and cook for 15 minutes, stirring occasionally, or until the squash is tender. Stir in the lima beans. Cover and simmer for 5 minutes, or until the beans are tender.

3. Divide the couscous among 4 shallow bowls and top with the tofu mixture. Sprinkle with the mint.

Per serving: 283 calories, 5 g fat, 0 g saturated fat, 16 g protein, 46 g carbohydrates, 10 g fiber, 218 mg sodium

Stir-Fry with Tofu and Vegetables

Soba noodles can be found in most grocery stores in the Asian foods section—they're made from buckwheat flour.

Prep time: 10 minutes ᠅ **Cook time:** 25 minutes ᠅ **Total time:** 35 minutes ᠅ MAKES 4 SERVINGS

7 ounces firm tofu (half a 14-ounce package)

6 ounces buckwheat (soba) noodles

2 teaspoons canola oil

2 carrots, thinly sliced on the diagonal

8 ounces cremini mushrooms, sliced

1 yellow bell pepper, thinly sliced

6 scallions, cut on the diagonal into 1½" pieces

1 pound bok choy, coarsely chopped

4 ounces sugar snap peas, strings removed

2 tablespoons minced fresh ginger

1 tablespoon minced garlic

½ teaspoon red-pepper flakes

¼ cup ponzu sauce

1½ teaspoons toasted sesame oil

1. Set the tofu between 2 plates and place a heavy pot on top. Set aside for 10 minutes to release excess liquid. Cut into ½" cubes and pat dry.

2. Prepare the noodles according to package directions, omitting the salt. Drain and keep warm.

3. Heat 1 teaspoon of the oil in a large nonstick skillet over medium heat. Cook the tofu for 8 minutes, turning once, or until browned. Transfer to a plate.

4. Heat the remaining 1 teaspoon oil in the same skillet over medium-high heat. Cook the carrots, mushrooms, bell pepper, and scallions for 8 minutes, stirring constantly, or until tender-crisp. Add the bok choy, sugar snap peas, ginger, garlic, and red-pepper flakes. Cook for 4 minutes, stirring constantly, or until tender-crisp. Add the ponzu sauce, sesame oil, and tofu. Cook for 30 seconds to heat through.

5. Divide the noodles and vegetable mixture among 4 plates.

Per serving: 283 calories, 6 g fat, 1 g saturated fat, 14 g protein, 48 g carbohydrates, 7 g fiber, 175 mg sodium

White Pizza with Spinach and Tomatoes

Spinach, a Salt Solution Star, adds potassium, magnesium, calcium, vitamin C, beta-carotene, and folate to this pizza.

Prep time: 20 minutes ⊳ **Cook time:** 20 minutes ⊳ **Total time:** 40 minutes ⊳ MAKES 6 SERVINGS

- 1 thin whole wheat pizza crust (12" diameter)
- 1 bag (9 ounces) microwave-in-bag spinach
- 1/2 cup part-skim ricotta cheese
- 1/2 cup shredded reduced-sodium mozzarella cheese
- 1/2 cup packed fresh basil leaves, chopped
- 1 clove garlic, crushed through a press
- 1/8 teaspoon red-pepper flakes
- 2 plum tomatoes, thinly sliced
- 2 tablespoons grated Parmesan cheese

1. Preheat the oven to 450°F. Place the pizza crust on a large baking sheet.

2. Microwave the spinach according to package directions. Place in a colander and let cool for 10 minutes. Squeeze the spinach to remove any excess water.

3. Stir together the spinach, ricotta, mozzarella, basil, garlic, and red-pepper flakes in a medium bowl.

4. Bake the pizza crust for 5 minutes. Spread the crust with the spinach mixture, leaving a 1/2" border all around. Arrange the tomato slices on top. Sprinkle with the Parmesan. Bake for 8 to 10 minutes, or until the topping is hot and melted and the crust is crisp. Let stand for 5 minutes before cutting into 12 slices. Serve 2 slices per person.

Per serving: 200 calories, 7 g fat, 3 g saturated fat, 12 g protein, 26 g carbohydrates, 5 g fiber, 125 mg sodium

MAKE IT A SALT SOLUTION MEAL: Serve with a salad made from 2 cups arugula, 10 cherry tomatoes, 1 teaspoon olive oil, and 1 teaspoon lemon juice (281 calories and 144 mg sodium total).

Wild Mushroom and Red Onion Pizza

Wild mushrooms add a nutty, woodsy flavor to this pizza.

Prep time: 15 minutes ▸ **Cook time:** 25 minutes ▸ **Total time:** 40 minutes ▸ MAKES 6 SERVINGS

1 tablespoon yellow cornmeal

8 ounces whole wheat pizza dough

1 tablespoon olive oil

1 red onion, coarsely chopped

6 ounces portobello mushrooms, stems discarded, caps thinly sliced

4 ounces shiitake mushrooms, stems discarded, caps thinly sliced

2 cloves garlic, minced

3 ounces goat cheese, crumbled

2 teaspoons chopped fresh rosemary

1 ounce Parmesan cheese, in one piece

1. Preheat the oven to 475°F. Coat a baking sheet with cooking spray. Sprinkle with the cornmeal. On a lightly floured surface, with a floured rolling pin, roll the pizza dough to 1" smaller than the pan. Place on the baking sheet.

2. Heat the oil in a large nonstick skillet over medium heat. Add the onion, mushrooms, and garlic. Cook for 8 minutes, stirring frequently, or until browned. Spread the mixture over the dough, leaving a ½" border all around. Sprinkle with the goat cheese and rosemary.

3. Bake for 12 to 15 minutes, or until the crust is browned. Using a vegetable peeler, shave the Parmesan over the top of the pizza.

Per serving: 195 calories, 8 g fat, 3 g saturated fat, 9 g protein, 24 g carbohydrates, 4 g fiber, 295 mg sodium

 MAKE IT A SALT SOLUTION MEAL: Serve with 1 medium apple and 1 teaspoon unsalted peanut butter (298 calories and 297 mg sodium total).

Four-Veggie Pizza

Fresh vegetables add fiber and nutrients to this delicious, healthful pizza.

Prep time: 15 minutes ⊹ **Cook time:** 25 minutes ⊹ **Total time:** 40 minutes ⊹ MAKES 6 SERVINGS

1 tablespoon yellow cornmeal
8 ounces whole wheat pizza dough
2 teaspoons olive oil
1 small zucchini, sliced
1 red bell pepper, cut into thin strips
1 cup sliced cremini or button
   mushrooms

½ red onion, thinly sliced
2 ounces fresh mozzarella cheese,
   thinly sliced
2 tablespoons grated Parmesan cheese
¾ cup quartered grape or cherry
   tomatoes
¼ cup basil leaves

1. Preheat the oven to 475°F. Coat a baking sheet with cooking spray. Sprinkle with the cornmeal. On a lightly floured surface, with a floured rolling pin, roll the pizza dough to 1" smaller than the pan. Place on the baking sheet.

2. Heat the oil in a medium skillet over medium-high heat. Cook the zucchini, bell pepper, mushrooms, and onion for 8 minutes, stirring frequently, or until the vegetables are soft and the excess liquid has evaporated.

3. Top the crust evenly with the cheeses. Arrange the vegetables over the cheese and top with the tomatoes. Bake for 18 minutes, or until the crust is cooked through and slightly crisp. Sprinkle with the basil. Let stand a few minutes before cutting into quarters.

Per serving: 250 calories, 12 g fat, 3 g saturated fat, 10 g protein, 29 g carbohydrates, 5 g fiber, 330 mg sodium

 MAKE IT A SALT SOLUTION MEAL: Serve with 1 medium orange (319 calories and 332 mg sodium total).

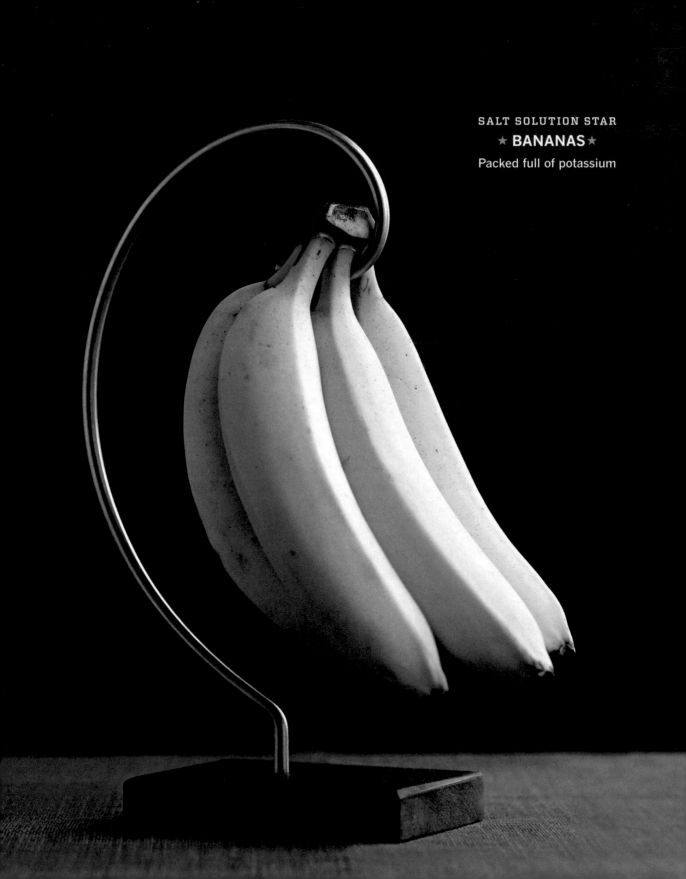

SALT SOLUTION STAR
★ **BANANAS** ★
Packed full of potassium

Sides and Snacks

Roasted Root Vegetables
with Edamame

For a quick dinner, toss half of these vegetables with cooked whole wheat pasta, chicken, and a splash of balsamic vinegar.

Prep time: 20 minutes ⫸ **Cook time:** 40 minutes ⫸ **Total time:** 1 hour ⫸ MAKES 6 SERVINGS

1 carrot, sliced on the diagonal	1½ teaspoons chopped fresh rosemary
½ turnip, cut into 1" pieces	1 teaspoon chopped fresh thyme
2 Yukon Gold potatoes, cut into 1" pieces	½ teaspoon salt
2 cloves garlic, sliced	½ teaspoon ground black pepper
2 teaspoons olive oil	¾ cup frozen shelled edamame

1. Preheat the oven to 400°F.

2. Combine the carrot, turnip, potatoes, and garlic in a rimmed baking sheet or roasting pan. Add the oil, rosemary, thyme, salt, and pepper. Toss to coat well.

3. Bake for 25 minutes, stirring occasionally. Stir in the edamame and bake for 15 minutes, or until the vegetables are tender and the potatoes are lightly browned.

Per serving: 123 calories, 4 g fat, 0 g saturated fat, 4 g protein, 15 g carbohydrates, 2 g fiber, 220 mg sodium

 MAKE IT A SALT SOLUTION MEAL: Mix the vegetables with ½ cup cooked whole wheat pasta and 2 ounces cooked boneless, skinless chicken breast, chopped (270 calories and 258 mg sodium total).

Braised Red Cabbage and Beet Greens

Beet greens are Salt Solution Stars—they're full of potassium, magnesium, calcium, vitamin K, and beta-carotene. You can use them in place of spinach or another leafy green.

Prep time: 10 minutes ⊳ **Cook time:** 25 minutes ⊳ **Total time:** 35 minutes ⊳ MAKES 4 SERVINGS

1 teaspoon olive oil
1 Granny Smith apple, cubed
1/2 bunch (8 ounces) beet greens, chopped
1 bag (10 ounces) shredded red cabbage

3 tablespoons turbinado or brown sugar
2 tablespoons white wine vinegar
1/4 teaspoon ground allspice

1. Heat the oil in a large skillet over medium-high heat. Cook the apple for 5 minutes, stirring occasionally. Add 1/2 cup of water, the beet greens, cabbage, sugar, vinegar, and allspice.

2. Reduce the heat to low and cook for 20 minutes, stirring occasionally, or until the vegetables are tender-crisp.

Per serving: 97 calories, 1 g fat, 0 g saturated fat, 2 g protein, 21 g carbohydrates, 4 g fiber, 151 mg sodium

MAKE IT A SALT SOLUTION MEAL: Serve with any Salt Solution recipe with 200 calories or less.

Baby Bok Choy and Shiitake Stir-Fry

If you cannot find baby bok choy at your supermarket, substitute an equal weight of regular bok choy, slicing the stems 1/4-inch thick and coarsely chopping the leaves.

Prep time: 15 minutes ▷ **Cook time:** 15 minutes ▷ **Total time:** 30 minutes ▷ MAKES 4 SERVINGS

1/2 teaspoon canola oil	1/2 cup frozen shelled edamame
6 baby bok choy (12 ounces), quartered lengthwise	4 scallions, diagonally sliced
6 ounces shiitake mushroom caps, halved	2 teaspoons grated fresh ginger
	2 teaspoons rice vinegar

1. Heat the oil in a large nonstick skillet over medium-high heat. Add the bok choy, cut sides down, and cook for 5 minutes, turning occasionally.

2. Push the bok choy to the outside of the pan and add the mushrooms. Cook for 2 minutes, stirring occasionally. Add the edamame, scallions, and ginger and cook for 3 minutes, or until the vegetables are just tender. Remove from the heat and stir in the vinegar.

Per serving: 56 calories, 2 g fat, 0 g saturated fat, 5 g protein, 7 g carbohydrates, 3 g fiber, 67 mg sodium

MAKE IT A SALT SOLUTION MEAL: Serve with any Salt Solution recipe with 250 calories or less.

Succotash

Think you don't like lima beans? Maybe you haven't had them since childhood? Try them again—you'll be surprised at their creamy, mild flavor.

Prep time: 15 minutes ⊱ **Cook time:** 25 minutes ⊱ **Total time:** 40 minutes ⊱ MAKES 6 SERVINGS

¾ cup frozen baby lima beans
1 teaspoon olive oil
1 zucchini, cut into small cubes
1½ cups frozen corn kernels
4 scallions, chopped

1 tomato, chopped
2 tablespoons chopped fresh flat-leaf parsley
⅛ teaspoon salt
⅛ teaspoon ground black pepper

1. Heat ¾ cup of water to a boil in a small saucepan. Add the beans and simmer for 10 minutes (do not cook until fully tender). Drain under cold running water.

2. Heat the oil in a nonstick skillet over medium heat. Cook the zucchini and corn for 5 minutes, stirring, or until the zucchini is almost tender. Add the lima beans and scallions. Cook for 3 minutes. Stir in the tomato, parsley, salt, and pepper. Cook for 2 minutes, or until heated through.

Per serving: 81 calories, 1 g fat, 0 g saturated fat, 4 g protein, 16 g carbohydrates, 3 g fiber, 72 mg sodium

 MAKE IT A SALT SOLUTION MEAL: Serve with any Salt Solution recipe with 200 calories or less.

Italian-Style Green Beans with Tomatoes

This dish can be made ahead of time and reheated—with a few hours in the fridge, the flavors will meld and intensify.

Prep time: 10 minutes ▷ **Cook time:** 10 minutes ▷ **Total time:** 20 minutes ▷ MAKES 4 SERVINGS

- 1 pound green beans, trimmed and cut into 2" pieces
- ½ teaspoon olive oil
- 1 cup canned no-salt-added diced tomatoes
- ½ cup canned no-salt-added kidney beans, rinsed and drained
- 2 tablespoons chopped fresh parsley
- ⅛ teaspoon salt
- ¼ teaspoon ground black pepper
- ¼ teaspoon Italian seasoning

1. Fill a large skillet with ¾" water and bring to a boil. Add the beans and cook for 6 minutes, or until just tender. Drain and return the beans to the skillet over medium heat.

2. Add the oil, tomatoes, kidney beans, parsley, salt, pepper, and seasoning. Cook for 3 minutes, stirring occasionally, or until flavored through.

Per serving: 79 calories, 1 g fat, 0 g saturated fat, 5 g protein, 15 g carbohydrates, 7 g fiber, 107 mg sodium

MAKE IT A SALT SOLUTION MEAL: Serve with any Salt Solution recipe with 200 calories or less.

Sautéed Cherry Tomatoes and White Beans

White beans—Salt Solution Stars—go perfectly with the other Italian flavors in this dish.

Prep time: 15 minutes ❊ **Cook time:** 5 minutes ❊ **Total time:** 20 minutes ❊ MAKES 4 SERVINGS

1 teaspoon olive oil
3 large scallions, chopped
2 teaspoons thinly sliced fresh sage
3 cups cherry tomatoes, halved

1 cup canned no-salt-added white beans, rinsed and drained
$1/_8$ teaspoon salt
$1/_8$ teaspoon ground black pepper

1. Heat the oil in a nonstick skillet over medium heat. Add the scallions and cook for 1 minute, stirring, or until softened. Stir in the sage.

2. Add the tomatoes and white beans. Cook for 2 minutes, stirring frequently, or until the tomatoes are softened. Stir in the salt and pepper.

Per serving: 90 calories, 2 g fat, 0 g saturated fat, 5 g protein, 15 g carbohydrates, 7 g fiber, 120 mg sodium

MAKE IT A SALT SOLUTION MEAL: Serve with any Salt Solution recipe with 200 calories or less.

Barley, Mushroom, and Edamame Pilaf

This rich dish brings to mind a cheesy risotto—but without all of the salt, fat, or calories.

Prep time: 5 minutes ⫶ **Cook time:** 45 minutes ⫶ **Total time:** 50 minutes ⫶ MAKES 4 SERVINGS

  1 teaspoon olive oil
  2 onions, chopped
  $\frac{1}{2}$ cup pearl barley
  $1\frac{1}{4}$ cups low-sodium chicken broth
  10 ounces cremini mushrooms, sliced
  4 carrots, coarsely chopped

  $\frac{1}{2}$ teaspoon dried rosemary
  $\frac{1}{4}$ teaspoon dried thyme
  $\frac{1}{4}$ teaspoon salt
  $\frac{1}{2}$ cup frozen shelled edamame
  $\frac{1}{8}$ teaspoon ground black pepper

1. Heat the oil in a medium saucepan over medium-high heat. Cook the onions for 5 minutes, or until softened. Stir in the barley and cook for 1 minute, stirring occasionally. Add the broth, mushrooms, carrots, rosemary, thyme, and salt. Bring to a boil. Reduce the heat to low, cover, and simmer for 30 minutes.

2. Stir in the edamame and cook for 10 minutes, or until the barley and edamame are tender. Stir in the pepper.

Per serving: 129 calories, 2 g fat, 0 g saturated fat, 6 g protein, 23 g carbohydrates, 5 g fiber, 243 mg sodium

 MAKE IT A SALT SOLUTION MEAL: Pair the pilaf with 3 ounces grilled chicken breast and 2 cups steamed green beans (287 calories and 312 mg sodium total).

Mashed Sweet Potatoes with Chives

Sweet potatoes are Salt Solution Stars—they're incredibly high in potassium. If you don't mind a little texture in your mashed potatoes, leave the skin on, and you'll get an extra dose of fiber.

Prep time: 10 minutes ▷ **Cook time:** 15 minutes ▷ **Total time:** 25 minutes ▷ MAKES 4 SERVINGS

1 sweet potato (8 ounces), cut into 1" chunks

4 carrots, thinly sliced

1 large apple, peeled and cut into 1" chunks

¼ teaspoon apple pie spice

2 teaspoons honey

1 teaspoon fresh lemon juice

1 tablespoon chopped fresh chives

1. Bring ¾ cup of water to a boil in a medium saucepan over medium-high heat. Add the sweet potato, carrots, and apple. Reduce the heat to low, cover, and simmer for 12 minutes, or until the carrots are soft.

2. Drain off the liquid and reserve. Add the pie spice, honey, lemon juice, and chives. Mash with a potato masher, adding enough of the reserved liquid to make a fluffy mixture.

Per serving: 112 calories, 0 g fat, 0 g saturated fat, 2 g protein, 27 g carbohydrates, 5 g fiber, 73 mg sodium

 MAKE IT A SALT SOLUTION MEAL: Serve with any Salt Solution recipe with 200 calories or less.

Quinoa Pilaf with Poblanos

Fresh cabbage, onions, and carrots not only add flavor, but bulk up this side dish, making a generous portion.

Prep time: 10 minutes ▷ **Cook time:** 30 minutes ▷ **Total time:** 40 minutes ▷ MAKES 6 SERVINGS

¼ teaspoon olive oil
1 onion, chopped
½ cup quinoa, rinsed
1 cup low-sodium chicken broth
3 cups chopped cabbage (7 ounces)
1 poblano or green bell pepper, chopped

1 carrot, shredded
½ teaspoon dried marjoram
¼ teaspoon salt
2 tablespoons chopped fresh parsley
1 teaspoon red wine vinegar

1. Heat the oil in a nonstick saucepan over medium-high heat. Cook the onion for 6 minutes, or until softened. Add the quinoa and cook for 1 minute, stirring.

2. Stir in the broth, cabbage, pepper, carrot, marjoram, and salt. Bring to a boil. Reduce the heat to low, cover, and simmer for 20 minutes, or until the quinoa and vegetables are tender. Stir in the parsley and vinegar.

Per serving: 84 calories, 1 g fat, 0 g saturated fat, 4 g protein, 15 g carbohydrates, 3 g fiber, 126 mg sodium

 MAKE IT A SALT SOLUTION MEAL: Serve with any Salt Solution recipe with 200 calories or less.

Garlicky Kale and Beet Greens

Shredded potato adds creaminess and lightens up this tasty side dish.

Prep time: 10 minutes ⁂ **Cook time:** 20 minutes ⁂ **Total time:** 30 minutes ⁂ MAKES 4 SERVINGS

1 teaspoon olive oil
1 small red onion, cut into thin slivers
2 cloves garlic, cut into thin slivers
¼ teaspoon red-pepper flakes
½ bunch (8 ounces) kale, rinsed and chopped

½ bunch (8 ounces) beet greens, rinsed and chopped
1 red-skinned potato
2 teaspoons sherry vinegar
½ teaspoon grated orange zest

1. Heat the oil in a large skillet over medium-high heat. Cook the onion for 5 minutes, stirring occasionally, or until softened. Stir in the garlic and red-pepper flakes. Cook for 1 minute, stirring.

2. Add the kale and beet greens with the water clinging to them and cook for 1 minute, stirring, or until wilted. Reduce the heat to low, cover, and cook for 5 minutes.

3. Grate the potato and stir into the greens. Cook for 8 minutes, or until the vegetables are tender. Remove from the heat and stir in the vinegar and orange zest.

Per serving: 87 calories, 2 g fat, 0 g saturated fat, 4 g protein, 17 g carbohydrates, 5 g fiber, 146 mg sodium

MAKE IT A SALT SOLUTION MEAL: Serve with any Salt Solution recipe with 200 calories or less.

Spinach and Cheese Poppers

The poppers can be made and baked up to 2 days ahead. Reheat in a microwave for about 20 seconds, or until hot.

Prep time: 20 minutes ⁘ **Cook time:** 25 minutes ⁘ **Total time:** 45 minutes ⁘ MAKES 4 SERVINGS

1 teaspoon olive oil

1 onion, finely chopped

2 cloves garlic, minced

1 package (10 ounces) frozen chopped spinach, thawed and squeezed dry

$\frac{1}{2}$ cup shredded reduced-fat mozzarella cheese

$\frac{1}{3}$ cup whole wheat panko bread crumbs

$\frac{1}{4}$ cup grated Parmesan cheese

$\frac{1}{4}$ cup part-skim ricotta cheese

1 large egg white

1 cup cherry or grape tomatoes

1. Preheat the oven to 350°F. Coat a large baking sheet with cooking spray.

2. Heat the oil in a large nonstick skillet over medium-high heat. Cook the onion for 6 minutes, stirring, or until lightly browned. Stir in the garlic and cook for 1 minute. Let cool.

3. Combine the spinach, mozzarella, panko, Parmesan, ricotta, egg white, and onion mixture in a food processor. Process until well blended and the mixture holds together easily. Shape the spinach mixture by level 1-tablespoon measuring spoon into twenty-four $1\frac{1}{4}$" balls. Place $1\frac{1}{2}$" apart on the baking sheet.

4. Bake for 13 minutes, or until firm. Remove from the baking sheet with a spatula and serve warm. Serve 6 poppers per person, with the tomatoes.

Per serving: 152 calories, 6 g fat, 3 g saturated fat, 13 g protein, 14 g carbohydrates, 4 g fiber, 275 mg sodium

 MAKE IT A SALT SOLUTION MEAL: Serve with 3 ounces baked salmon (276 calories and 314 mg sodium total).

Mushroom-Cheddar Quesadillas

The quesadillas can also be made with frozen chopped spinach, which should be squeezed dry before using. Monterey Jack cheese is a nice alternative to the Cheddar.

Prep time: 15 minutes ▷ **Cook time:** 30 minutes ▷ **Total time:** 45 minutes ▷ MAKES 4 SERVINGS

1 red onion, halved and thinly sliced
8 ounces sliced white mushrooms
5 ounces frozen chopped kale, thawed
1 teaspoon ground cumin
½ teaspoon ground chipotle pepper

4 whole wheat tortillas (8" diameter)
½ cup shredded reduced-fat sharp
  Cheddar cheese
3 tablespoons part-skim ricotta cheese
4 apples, thinly sliced

1. Heat a large nonstick skillet coated with cooking spray over medium-high heat. Cook the onion for 6 minutes, stirring, or until softened. Add the mushrooms and cook for 8 minutes, stirring, or until tender. Stir in the kale, cumin, and chipotle pepper. Cook for 5 minutes, stirring, or until the kale is tender.

2. Place the tortillas on a work surface and spoon the filling over half of each tortilla. Sprinkle the filling with the Cheddar. Spread the uncovered half of the tortillas with the ricotta. Fold the ricotta-spread half over the filling to make half-moons. Press lightly to adhere.

3. Wipe the skillet with a paper towel. Coat with cooking spray and heat over medium-high heat. Add 2 quesadillas and cook for 5 minutes, turning once, or until browned and the cheese melts. Repeat with more cooking spray and the remaining 2 quesadillas. To serve, cut each into 3 wedges. Serve with the apples.

Per serving: 252 calories, 5 g fat, 1 g saturated fat, 10 g protein, 46 g carbohydrates, 8 g fiber, 298 mg sodium

 MAKE IT A SALT SOLUTION MEAL: Serve with a salad made from 2 cups mixed greens, 5 cherry tomatoes, 1 teaspoon olive oil, and 1 teaspoon fresh lemon juice (322 calories and 313 mg sodium total).

Herbed Cheese Spread

Here's something that only tastes bad for you—a rich and creamy cheese spread that's low in sodium and calories.

Prep time: 10 minutes ⁛ **Total time:** 10 minutes + chilling time ⁛ MAKES 4 SERVINGS

1 cup fat-free sour cream

1 cup shredded reduced-fat Cheddar cheese

1 scallion, minced

2 tablespoons chopped fresh parsley

½ teaspoon dried thyme

½ teaspoon dried rosemary, crushed

½ teaspoon ground black pepper

Stir together the sour cream, cheese, scallion, parsley, thyme, rosemary, and pepper in a small bowl until well blended. Cover and refrigerate overnight to allow the flavors to develop.

Per serving: 143 calories, 7 g fat, 4 g saturated fat, 10 g protein, 12 g carbohydrates, 0 g fiber, 278 mg sodium

MAKE IT A SALT SOLUTION MEAL: Serve with ½ cup cucumber slices, 1 cup red bell pepper strips, and 2 tablespoons unsalted almonds (282 calories and 281 mg sodium total).

Creamy White Bean Dip with Lemon and Garlic

Serve the dip with vegetables such as broccoli, red bell pepper strips, zucchini sticks, baby carrots, and cherry tomatoes.

Prep time: 20 minutes ▷ **Cook time:** 5 minutes ▷ **Total time:** 25 minutes ▷ MAKES 4 SERVINGS

1 tablespoon olive oil
3 cloves garlic, thinly sliced
1 can (15 ounces) no-salt-added cannellini beans, rinsed and drained
½ cup part-skim ricotta cheese
¼ cup grated Parmesan cheese

1 teaspoon grated lemon zest
2 tablespoons fresh lemon juice
⅛ teaspoon salt
⅛ teaspoon ground black pepper
½ cup fresh basil leaves
8 cups assorted cut-up raw vegetables

1. Cook the oil and garlic in a small skillet over low heat for 3 minutes, stirring frequently, or until the garlic is golden. Pour into a small bowl and let cool for 5 minutes.

2. Process the beans, ricotta, Parmesan, the lemon zest, lemon juice, salt, pepper, the garlic and oil mixture, and 2 tablespoons water in a food processor until smooth. Add the basil and process until chopped. Serve the dip with the vegetables.

Per serving: 243 calories, 8 g fat, 3 g saturated fat, 13 g protein, 30 g carbohydrates, 8 g fiber, 266 mg sodium

MAKE IT A SALT SOLUTION MEAL: Serve with 1 apple (315 calories and 266 mg sodium total).

Homemade Hummus

Tahini, a paste made from ground sesame seeds, is the secret ingredient in hummus, and it adds a rich, roasted flavor.

Prep time: 15 minutes ⫸ **Total time:** 15 minutes ⫸ MAKES 6 SERVINGS

1 can (15 ounces) no-salt-added chickpeas, rinsed and drained
1/3 cup fat-free plain yogurt
3 scallions, finely chopped
1/4 cup finely chopped fresh parsley
1/4 cup fresh lemon juice

3 tablespoons tahini
1 tablespoon extra-virgin olive oil
3 cloves garlic, minced
1/8 teaspoon ground black pepper
Pinch of cayenne pepper

1. Process the chickpeas in a food processor or blender until smooth.

2. Add the yogurt, scallions, parsley, lemon juice, tahini, oil, garlic, black pepper, and cayenne. Process until smooth and creamy. (If necessary, add a small amount of water to achieve the desired consistency.)

3. Transfer to a serving bowl. Serve at room temperature.

Per serving: 146 calories, 7 g fat, 1 g saturated fat, 6 g protein, 17 g carbohydrates, 3 g fiber, 29 mg sodium

 MAKE IT A SALT SOLUTION MEAL: Serve with 20 baby carrots and a 4" whole wheat pita (290 calories and 335 mg sodium total).

Spicy Peanut Dipping Sauce

The sauce can be refrigerated and stored in a covered container up to 5 days.

Prep time: 10 minutes ⁝▷ **Total time:** 10 minutes ⁝▷ MAKES 6 SERVINGS

⅓ cup unsalted natural peanut butter
2 small fresh chile peppers (¾–1 ounce each), seeded and chopped (wear plastic gloves when handling)
2 small cloves garlic, minced

¼ cup fresh lime juice
3 tablespoons mango nectar or apple juice
2 tablespoons less-sodium soy sauce

Process the peanut butter, chile peppers, garlic, lime juice, nectar or apple juice, and soy sauce in a blender until a thick and smooth sauce forms, adding a little more nectar or apple juice as needed.

Per serving: 142 calories, 7 g fat, 1 g saturated fat, 6 g protein, 15 g carbohydrates, 4 g fiber, 235 mg sodium

MAKE IT A SALT SOLUTION MEAL: Serve with 20 snow peas, 1 cup red bell pepper slices, and ½ avocado, sliced. Dip the snow peas and bell pepper into the sauce, and, instead of dipping the avocado, drizzle some of the sauce over the slices (301 calories and 244 mg sodium total).

Pita with Hummus and Veggies

Edamame—fresh soybeans—are Salt Solution Stars, packed with calcium, potassium, and magnesium.

Prep time: 10 minutes ▷ **Cook time:** 5 minutes ▷ **Total time:** 15 minutes ▷ MAKES 4 SERVINGS

¾ cup frozen shelled edamame
1 tablespoon fresh lemon juice
2 teaspoons olive oil
½ teaspoon ground cumin
½ bag (6 ounces) baby spinach, coarsely chopped
½ English (seedless) cucumber, diced
2 tomatoes, coarsely chopped

¼ cup chopped red onion
2 whole wheat pitas (6" diameter), toasted
¼ cup prepared red pepper hummus
4 teaspoons finely crumbled feta cheese
½ pound green or red seedless grapes

1. Cover the edamame with water in a small microwaveable bowl. Microwave on high power for 3 minutes, or until cooked. Drain off the water and let cool.

2. Combine the lemon juice, oil, and cumin in a large bowl. Add the edamame, spinach, cucumber, tomatoes, and red onion. Toss to coat well.

3. Spread the pitas with the hummus and cut in half. Spoon the vegetable mixture onto plates and sprinkle with the cheese. Serve with the pitas and grapes.

Per serving: 212 calories, 6 g fat, 1 g saturated fat, 9 g protein, 35 g carbohydrates, 9 g fiber, 301 mg sodium

MAKE IT A SALT SOLUTION MEAL: Serve with 1 medium orange (274 calories and 301 mg sodium total).

Spinach Squares

Think of these as mini spinach quiches, but without the hassle (and calories) of making pie crust.

Prep time: 10 minutes ⁛ **Cook time:** 35 minutes ⁛ **Total time:** 45 minutes + cooling
⁛ MAKES 8 SERVINGS

2 tablespoons butter

3 large eggs

1 cup unbleached all-purpose flour

1 cup 1% milk

1 teaspoon baking powder

2 packages (10 ounces each) frozen cut-leaf spinach, thawed and squeezed dry

1 cup shredded reduced-fat sharp Cheddar cheese

3 scallions, finely chopped

1. Preheat the oven to 350°F. Put the butter in a 13" × 9" baking dish. Place the dish in the oven for 3 minutes, or until the butter melts. Remove the dish from the oven.

2. Beat the eggs in a large bowl. Whisk in the flour, milk, and baking powder until well blended. Whisk in the spinach, cheese, and scallions. Spread evenly into the baking dish.

3. Bake for 35 minutes, or until set and the top is lightly browned. Cool on a rack for 45 minutes before cutting into squares.

Per serving: 184 calories, 9 g fat, 4 g saturated fat, 11 g protein, 17 g carbohydrates, 3 g fiber, 280 mg sodium

 MAKE IT A SALT SOLUTION MEAL: Serve with 3 ounces roasted boneless, skinless chicken breast (274 calories and 336 mg sodium total).

Pita Pizzas

Pizza gets a healthy upgrade with the addition of spinach and reduced-fat cheese. Trust us, it'll still taste delicious!

Prep time: 10 minutes ▷ **Cook time:** 10 minutes ▷ **Total time:** 20 minutes ▷ MAKES 6 SERVINGS

2 whole wheat pitas (6" diameter)

1 package (10 ounces) frozen chopped spinach, thawed and squeezed dry

½ cup shredded reduced-fat mozzarella cheese

3 tablespoons crumbled feta cheese

1 tomato, diced

¼ cup thinly sliced red onion

1. Preheat the oven to 400°F.

2. Prick the pitas several times with a fork. Divide the spinach, mozzarella, feta, tomato, and onion between the pitas and place them on a baking sheet. Bake for 10 minutes. To serve, cut each pizza into 6 wedges.

Per serving: 113 calories, 3 g fat, 2 g saturated fat, 7 g protein, 16 g carbohydrates, 3 g fiber, 269 mg sodium

 MAKE IT A SALT SOLUTION MEAL: Serve with a salad made from 2 cups arugula, ¼ cup cubed avocado, 1 tablespoon pine nuts, 1 teaspoon olive oil, and 1 teaspoon fresh lemon juice (280 calories and 283 mg sodium total).

Tomato and Black Soybean Salsa

Prepared salsa is normally super high in salt, so make your own for a tastier, low-salt dip.

Prep time: 15 minutes ❖ **Total time:** 15 minutes + chilling time ❖ MAKES 4 SERVINGS

1½ cups coarsely chopped tomatoes

1 cup canned no-salt-added black soybeans, rinsed and drained

¼ cup chopped fresh cilantro

¼ cup chopped scallions

1 small jalapeño chile pepper, minced (wear plastic gloves when handling)

2 tablespoons red wine vinegar

1 small clove garlic, minced

¼ teaspoon dried oregano

¼ teaspoon salt

4 ounces unsalted low-fat tortilla chips

Combine the tomatoes, soybeans, cilantro, scallions, jalapeño, vinegar, garlic, oregano, and salt in a large bowl. Cover and refrigerate for at least 15 minutes to allow the flavors to blend. Serve with the tortilla chips.

Per serving: 197 calories, 5 g fat, 1 g saturated fat, 9 g protein, 30 g carbohydrates, 6 g fiber, 172 mg sodium

 MAKE IT A SALT SOLUTION MEAL: Serve the salsa on top of 3 ounces baked halibut and have the chips on the side (274 calories and 242 mg sodium total).

Nachos for One

Our nachos taste delicious, but they have an unexpected ingredient—the Salt Solution Star edamame.

Prep time: 15 minutes ▷ **Cook time:** 15 minutes ▷ **Total time:** 30 minutes ▷ MAKES 1 SERVING

1 tablespoon fat-free plain yogurt

1 teaspoon fresh lime juice

¼ cup frozen shelled edamame

1 ounce baked tortilla chips

3 tablespoons shredded reduced-fat Cheddar cheese

1 small plum tomato, seeded and chopped

⅛ teaspoon ground cumin

1 teaspoon minced jalapeño chile pepper (wear plastic gloves when handling)

1 tablespoon chopped fresh cilantro

1. Preheat the oven to 375°F. Combine the yogurt and lime juice in a small bowl. Combine the edamame and 2 tablespoons of water in a small microwaveable bowl. Microwave on high power for 2 minutes, or until cooked. Drain.

2. In a 9" pie plate, arrange the tortilla chips in a 5" circle, overlapping and stacking the chips. Top with half of the cheese and the tomato. Sprinkle with the cumin and top with the edamame, the remaining cheese, and the jalapeño.

3. Bake for 10 minutes, or until hot and the cheese melts. Dollop with the yogurt mixture and sprinkle with the cilantro. Serve hot.

Per serving: 189 calories, 7 g fat, 3 g saturated fat, 13 g protein, 20 g carbohydrates, 4 g fiber, 268 mg sodium

 MAKE IT A SALT SOLUTION MEAL: Serve with 1 medium grapefruit (271 calories and 268 mg sodium total).

Spicy Roast Pumpkin Seed Snack Mix

Serve this crunchy, spicy mix with a banana for a satisfying snack.

Prep time: 5 minutes ❖ **Cook time:** 15 minutes ❖ **Total time:** 20 minutes ❖ MAKES 6 SERVINGS

½ teaspoon packed brown sugar

½ teaspoon chili powder

½ teaspoon ground cumin

½ teaspoon smoked paprika

¼ teaspoon cayenne pepper

⅛ teaspoon salt

⅓ cup almonds

⅓ cup unsalted hulled raw pumpkin seeds

1 teaspoon hot-pepper sauce

½ teaspoon Worcestershire sauce

⅓ cup unsalted dry-roasted soybeans

1. Preheat the oven to 325°F. Line a rimmed baking sheet with parchment paper.

2. Stir together the brown sugar, chili powder, cumin, paprika, cayenne, and salt in a large bowl. Stir in the almonds, pumpkin seeds, hot-pepper sauce, and Worcestershire sauce. Spread onto the baking sheet.

3. Bake for 15 minutes, stirring once, or until dry and toasted. Stir in the soybeans. Let cool on the baking sheet. Store in an airtight container.

Per serving: 128 calories, 10 g fat, 1 g saturated fat, 6 g protein, 5 g carbohydrates, 2 g fiber, 76 mg sodium

 MAKE IT A SALT SOLUTION MEAL: Serve with 1 small banana and 20 bite-size unsalted pretzels (310 calories and 147 mg sodium total).

Spiced Tropical Fruit Salad

Spices in fruit salad? Trust us, it brings a new dimension of flavor to the salad.

Prep time: 15 minutes ▸ **Total time:** 15 minutes + chilling time ▸ MAKES 4 SERVINGS

2 tangerines, peeled and sectioned

2 medium bananas, sliced

1 Golden Delicious apple, cubed

1 cup red seedless grapes

1 kiwifruit, peeled and cut into bite-size chunks

1 cup fresh pineapple chunks

2 tablespoons unsweetened shredded coconut

1 tablespoon orange or pineapple juice

½ teaspoon grated lemon zest

⅛ teaspoon ground cinnamon

⅛ teaspoon ground nutmeg

Cut the tangerine sections in half and remove the seeds. Combine the tangerines, bananas, apple, grapes, kiwi, pineapple, coconut, and orange or pineapple juice in a large bowl. Sprinkle with the lemon zest, cinnamon, and nutmeg, tossing gently to coat. Cover and refrigerate for at least 20 minutes to allow the flavors to blend.

Per serving: 171 calories, 2 g fat, 1 g saturated fat, 2 g protein, 40 g carbohydrates, 5 g fiber, 5 mg sodium

 MAKE IT A SALT SOLUTION MEAL: Serve with 4 ounces grilled shrimp (291 calories and 173 mg sodium total).

SALT SOLUTION STAR
★ **MILK** ★
Chockful of calcium

Desserts

Chocolate Bundt Cake

Ground almonds and a small amount of semisweet chocolate give this cake a decadent flavor.

Prep time: 25 minutes ⁍ **Cook time:** 35 minutes ⁍ **Total time:** 1 hour + cooling time
⁍ MAKES 12 SERVINGS

1 cup sliced almonds

2 ounces semisweet chocolate, coarsely chopped

$1\frac{1}{2}$ cups granulated sugar

$2\frac{1}{3}$ cups whole grain pastry flour

$\frac{2}{3}$ cup unsweetened Dutch process cocoa powder

2 teaspoons baking powder

$\frac{3}{4}$ teaspoon baking soda

1 cup fat-free milk

$\frac{3}{4}$ cups fat-free egg substitute

$\frac{2}{3}$ cup fat-free plain yogurt

2 teaspoons vanilla extract

$1\frac{1}{2}$ teaspoons confectioners' sugar

1. Preheat the oven to 350°F. Coat a 12-cup Bundt pan with cooking spray and lightly dust with flour. Set aside.

2. Process the almonds, chocolate, and $\frac{1}{2}$ cup of the granulated sugar in a food processor until finely ground. Place in a large bowl. Whisk in the flour, cocoa, baking powder, baking soda, and remaining 1 cup granulated sugar. Whisk in the milk, egg substitute, yogurt, and vanilla until well blended.

3. Pour the batter into the pan. Bake for 35 minutes, or until a toothpick inserted halfway between the tube and the edge of the pan comes out clean.

4. Cool in the pan on a rack for 10 minutes. Turn out of the pan and cool completely on the rack. Dust with the confectioners' sugar before cutting into 12 slices.

Per serving: 269 calories, 9 g fat, 1 g saturated fat, 8 g protein, 47 g carbohydrates, 4 g fiber, 208 mg sodium

Molasses Cake with Cream Cheese Frosting

Don't worry that the batter is very liquid-y when you make it. It bakes up incredibly light and moist!

Prep time: 15 minutes ▷ **Cook time:** 30 minutes ▷ **Total time:** 45 minutes + cooling time
▷ MAKES 12 SERVINGS

2 cups whole grain pastry flour
3/4 teaspoon baking soda
1/2 teaspoon baking powder
1/2 teaspoon ground ginger
1/2 teaspoon ground allspice
1/2 teaspoon ground cinnamon
1 cup 1% milk
2/3 cup molasses
2/3 cup granulated sugar

4 tablespoons unsalted butter, melted
3 large egg whites, lightly beaten
4 ounces Neufchâtel cheese, at room temperature
4 ounces fat-free cream cheese, at room temperature
1/2 cup confectioners' sugar
1 teaspoon vanilla extract

1. Preheat the oven to 350°F. Coat a 9" × 9" baking pan with cooking spray, line the bottom with parchment, coat again with cooking spray, and lightly dust with flour.

2. Whisk together the flour, baking soda, baking powder, ginger, allspice, and cinnamon in a large bowl. Whisk together the milk, molasses, granulated sugar, butter, and egg whites in a separate bowl until well blended. Add the milk mixture to the flour mixture and stir just until combined. Pour the batter into the baking pan.

3. Bake for 30 minutes, or until a toothpick inserted in the center comes out clean. Cool in the pan on a rack for 15 minutes. Remove the cake from the pan, remove the parchment from the bottom, and cool on the rack for 1 hour.

4. Meanwhile, combine the Neufchâtel, fat-free cream cheese, confectioners' sugar, and vanilla in a medium bowl. Beat with an electric mixer on medium speed until smooth. Spread over the cooled cake. Cut into 12 squares.

Per serving: 252 calories, 7 g fat, 4 g saturated fat, 6 g protein, 43 g carbohydrates, 2 g fiber, 218 mg sodium

Lemon Pound Cake

Leftover pound cake makes for a special breakfast treat. Toast a slice and spread with 1 tablespoon of your favorite jam and a glass of fat-free milk.

Prep time: 15 minutes ⁑ **Cook time:** 55 minutes ⁑ **Total time:** 1 hour 10 minutes + cooling time
⁑ MAKES 12 SERVINGS

2¼ cups whole grain pastry flour

1¼ cups granulated sugar

2 teaspoons baking powder

¼ teaspoon baking soda

¼ teaspoon salt

5 tablespoons unsalted butter, at room temperature

3 tablespoons trans-free margarine, at room temperature

1 cup fat-free sour cream

¼ cup fat-free milk

2 large egg whites

1 teaspoon grated lemon zest

1 teaspoon lemon extract

1 teaspoon vanilla extract

¾ cup confectioners' sugar

4 teaspoons fresh lemon juice

1. Preheat the oven to 350°F. Coat a 9" × 5" nonstick loaf pan with cooking spray and lightly dust with flour.

2. Combine the flour, granulated sugar, baking powder, baking soda, and salt in a large bowl and mix well. Add the butter, margarine, sour cream, milk, egg whites, lemon zest, lemon extract, and vanilla. Beat with an electric mixer on low speed for 1 minute, scraping the sides of the bowl often. Increase the speed to medium and beat for 2 minutes, or until the batter is light and fluffy. Pour into the pan.

3. Bake for 55 minutes, or until a toothpick inserted in the center comes out clean. Cool in the pan for 10 minutes. Remove from the pan and cool completely on a rack.

4. Stir together the confectioners' sugar and lemon juice in a bowl. Drizzle over the cake and let set for 20 minutes before cutting into 12 slices.

Per serving: 257 calories, 7 g fat, 3 g saturated fat, 4 g protein, 45 g carbohydrates, 2 g fiber, 216 mg sodium

Raspberry-Swirl Cheesecake

Raspberries add sweet-tart flavors to this rich and creamy classic dessert.

Prep time: 15 minutes ⊪ **Cook time:** 55 minutes ⊪ **Total time:** 1 hour 10 minutes + cooling and chillling times ⊪ MAKES 12 SERVINGS

CRUST

10 whole low-fat graham crackers

2 tablespoons sugar

1 tablespoon trans-free margarine, melted

FILLING

12 ounces fat-free cream cheese, at room temperature

8 ounces Neufchâtel cheese, at room temperature

1¼ cups fat-free ricotta cheese

3 large eggs

1 cup sugar

1 tablespoon + 2 teaspoons cornstarch

1 teaspoon grated lemon zest

1 teaspoon fresh lemon juice

1 package (10 ounces) frozen raspberries in light syrup, thawed

3 cups fresh raspberries

1. To make the crust: Preheat the oven to 350°F. Coat a 9" springform pan with cooking spray.

2. Process the graham crackers and sugar in a food processor until fine crumbs form. Add the margarine and pulse just until blended. Press the mixture into the bottom of the pan. Bake for 8 minutes, or until lightly browned. Remove from the oven and let cool for 10 minutes. Leave the oven on.

3. To make the filling: Combine the fat-free cream cheese, Neufchâtel, ricotta, eggs, sugar, 1 tablespoon of the cornstarch, the lemon zest, and lemon juice in a large bowl. Beat with an electric mixer on medium speed until smooth. Measure out 2 cups of the mixture and place in a medium bowl.

4. Press the thawed raspberries through a fine-mesh sieve to remove the seeds. Add the strained raspberries and the remaining 2 teaspoons cornstarch to the 2 cups of filling and mix well. Pour half of the plain filling over the crust. Spoon the raspberry mixture alternately with the remaining plain filling into the pan. Swirl the raspberry filling through the plain filling with a knife.

5. Place the springform pan on a baking sheet. Bake for 45 minutes, or until the center is almost set. Remove from the oven and cool in the pan on a rack for 1 hour. Refrigerate for 3 hours or overnight. Cut into 12 slices and garnish each serving with ¼ cup fresh raspberries.

Per serving: 249 calories, 7 g fat, 3 g saturated fat, 11 g protein, 37 g carbohydrates, 3 g fiber, 303 mg sodium

Light Orange Cupcakes with Orange Yogurt Glaze

Yogurt and confectioners' sugar make for an easy and delicious tangy-sweet glaze. Serve with a cold glass of milk.

Prep time: 20 minutes ⊪ **Cook time:** 25 minutes ⊪ **Total time:** 45 minutes + cooling time
⊪ MAKES 12 CUPCAKES

1 cup unbleached all-purpose flour
$^{1}/_{2}$ cup granulated sugar
$^{3}/_{4}$ cup instant nonfat dry milk
1 teaspoon baking powder
$^{1}/_{4}$ teaspoon baking soda
$^{1}/_{4}$ teaspoon salt
4 tablespoons unsalted butter, at room temperature

$^{1}/_{2}$ cup + 2 tablespoons fat-free vanilla yogurt
1 large egg
$^{1}/_{4}$ teaspoon orange extract
1 cup dried apricots, chopped
1 cup confectioners' sugar
2 teaspoons grated orange zest

1. Preheat the oven to 350°F. Line a 12-cup muffin pan with paper liners.

2. Combine the flour, granulated sugar, dry milk, baking powder, baking soda, and salt in a large bowl. Add the butter, $^{1}/_{2}$ cup of the yogurt, the egg, orange extract, and $^{1}/_{4}$ cup of water. Beat with an electric mixer on low speed for 1 minute, or until combined. Increase the speed to medium and beat for 2 minutes, or until smooth. Stir in the apricots. Spoon the batter into the muffin cups.

3. Bake for 25 minutes, or until the cupcakes are lightly browned and spring back when lightly touched in the center. Cool in the pan on a rack for 10 minutes. Remove from the pan and cool completely on a rack.

4. Combine the confectioners' sugar, remaining 2 tablespoons yogurt, and orange zest in a small bowl. Evenly drizzle the mixture over the cupcakes and let set for 10 minutes.

Per cupcake: 205 calories, 5 g fat, 3 g saturated fat, 5 g protein, 37 g carbohydrates, 2 g fiber, 172 mg sodium

Apple-Walnut Chocolate Chip Snack Bars

These bars can be stored up to 3 days at room temperature or frozen up to 3 months.

Prep time: 10 minutes ⊳ **Cook time:** 25 minutes ⊳ **Total time:** 35 minutes + cooling time
⊳ MAKES 12 SERVINGS

1 cup unsweetened applesauce
3/4 cup packed brown sugar
1/2 cup fat-free egg substitute
2 cups whole wheat flour
1 1/2 cups quick-cooking oats
1 teaspoon baking soda

1/2 teaspoon ground cinnamon
1/4 teaspoon salt
1 apple, peeled, cored, and chopped
3/4 cup semisweet chocolate chips
1/2 cup walnuts, chopped
1/3 cup dried cranberries

1. Preheat the oven to 350°F. Line a 13" × 9" baking pan with foil, leaving overhang on the two short ends to use as handles for lifting the cake out after it's baked. Coat with cooking spray.

2. Stir together the applesauce, brown sugar, and egg substitute in a large bowl. Stir in the flour, oats, baking soda, cinnamon, and salt just until blended. Stir in the apple, chocolate chips, walnuts, and cranberries. Scrape the batter into the baking pan.

3. Bake for 25 minutes, or until a toothpick inserted in the center comes out clean. Cool completely in the pan on a wire rack. To serve, use the foil to remove the cake from the pan and cut into 24 bars. Store in an airtight container. Serve 2 bars per person.

Per serving: 292 calories, 8 g fat, 3 g saturated fat, 7 g protein, 52 g carbohydrates, 6 g fiber, 180 mg sodium

Brazil Nut Brownies

These rich-tasting brownies are guaranteed to satisfy the cravings of any sweet tooth.

Prep time: 15 minutes ⁖ **Cook time:** 30 minutes ⁖ **Total time:** 45 minutes + cooling time
⁖ MAKES 12 SERVINGS

4 tablespoons trans-free margarine
1 ounce unsweetened chocolate
1 cup whole grain pastry flour
⅔ cup unsweetened cocoa powder
1 teaspoon baking powder
¼ teaspoon salt
1¼ cups granulated sugar

2 large eggs
1 large egg white
1 medium banana, mashed
½ cup Brazil nuts, chopped
½ cup dried tart cherries
1 tablespoon confectioners' sugar
   (optional)

1. Preheat the oven to 350°F. Coat an 8" × 8" baking pan with cooking spray and dust lightly with flour. Melt the margarine and chocolate in a microwaveable bowl on high power for 30 seconds. Set aside.

2. Whisk together the flour, cocoa, baking powder, and salt in a large bowl. Whisk together the granulated sugar, whole eggs, egg white, banana, and chocolate-margarine mixture in a medium bowl. Stir the banana-chocolate mixture into the flour mixture until well combined. Fold in the Brazil nuts and cherries. Place in the baking pan.

3. Bake for 30 minutes, or until a toothpick inserted in the center comes out with a few moist crumbs clinging to it. Cool in the pan on a rack for 30 minutes. Turn out onto a cutting board and cut into 12 brownies. Sprinkle with confectioners' sugar (if using).

Per serving: 241 calories, 9 g fat, 3 g saturated fat, 5 g protein, 38 g carbohydrates, 5 g fiber, 145 mg sodium

Zucchini-Chocolate Chip Snack Cake

Zucchini makes this cake super moist, without adding significant calories, fat, or sodium.

Prep time: 15 minutes ⁛ **Cook time:** 40 minutes ⁛ **Total time:** 55 minutes + cooling time ⁛ MAKES 16 SERVINGS

1³⁄₄ cups whole grain pastry flour
1¹⁄₂ teaspoons baking powder
1¹⁄₂ teaspoons ground cinnamon
¹⁄₂ teaspoon baking soda
¹⁄₂ teaspoon ground ginger
¹⁄₄ teaspoon salt
2 large eggs

¹⁄₃ cup packed brown sugar
¹⁄₂ cup low-fat plain yogurt
¹⁄₃ cup canola oil
2 teaspoons vanilla extract
1¹⁄₂ cups shredded zucchini
³⁄₄ cup mini semisweet chocolate chips

1. Preheat the oven to 350°F. Line an 8" × 8" baking pan with foil, leaving overhang on two opposite sides to use as handles for lifting the cake out after it's baked. Coat the foil with cooking spray.

2. Combine the flour, baking powder, cinnamon, baking soda, ginger, and salt in a large bowl.

3. Whisk together the eggs, brown sugar, yogurt, oil, and vanilla in a medium bowl until smooth. Stir in the zucchini and chocolate chips. Stir the zucchini mixture into the flour mixture just until blended. Scrape the batter into the pan.

4. Bake for 40 minutes, or until a toothpick inserted in the center comes out clean. Let the cake cool completely in the pan on a rack. Use the foil to remove the cake from the pan and cut into 16 squares.

Per serving: 151 calories, 8 g fat, 2 g saturated fat, 3 g protein, 19 g carbohydrates, 2 g fiber, 139 mg sodium

 MAKE IT A SALT SOLUTION MEAL: Serve with ¹⁄₂ cup soymilk and 2 tablespoons unsalted pecan halves (287 calories and 199 mg sodium total).

Roasted-Fruit Wraps
with Ginger Dipping Sauce

Roasting fruit brings out its sweetness by caramelizing the fruits' natural sugars.

Prep time: 25 minutes ▷ **Cook time:** 25 minutes ▷ **Total time:** 50 minutes ▷ MAKES 4 SERVINGS

1 cup low-fat vanilla yogurt
¼ cup orange juice
2 teaspoons finely chopped crystallized ginger
2 Golden Delicious apples, peeled, cored, and sliced
1 mango or 2 peaches, peeled, seeded, and thinly sliced

4 rings juice-packed canned pineapple, halved
4 teaspoons sugar
½ teaspoon pumpkin pie spice
4 whole wheat omega-3 tortillas (8" diameter)

1. Stir together the yogurt, 2 tablespoons of the orange juice, and the crystallized ginger in a small bowl. Cover and refrigerate.

2. Preheat the oven to 425°F. Coat a large rimmed baking sheet with cooking spray.

3. Place the apples, mango or peaches, pineapple, sugar, pumpkin pie spice, and the remaining 2 tablespoons orange juice on the baking sheet with sides. Toss to coat and spread in a single layer. Roast for 10 minutes, or until the fruit is tender.

4. Place the warm fruit down the center of each tortilla. Roll up like an envelope and place, seam side down, on a nonstick baking sheet. Bake for 8 minutes, or until crisp and golden. Cut each wrap in half diagonally. Serve warm with the ginger dipping sauce.

Per serving: 272 calories, 3 g fat, 1 g saturated fat, 6 g protein, 58 g carbohydrates, 6 g fiber, 233 mg sodium

Chocolate-Hazelnut Paninis

Think of this as a grilled chocolate sandwich! You can assemble the sandwiches ahead of time, and grill them just before serving.

Prep time: 15 minutes ⊱ **Cook time:** 5 minutes ⊱ **Total time:** 20 minutes ⊱ MAKES 2 SERVINGS

2 slices sprouted whole grain bread
1 tablespoon chocolate-hazelnut spread
2 tablespoons part-skim ricotta cheese

$\frac{1}{2}$ ounce bittersweet or semisweet chocolate, finely chopped
2 pears

1. Spread one slice of bread with the hazelnut spread and then the ricotta. Sprinkle with the chocolate and top with the remaining slice of bread, pressing lightly.

2. Heat a nonstick skillet coated with cooking spray over medium heat. Cook the sandwich for 5 minutes, turning once, or until the bread is lightly browned and the chocolate melts. Remove the panini from the skillet and let stand for 5 minutes. Cut in half with a serrated knife. Serve with the pears.

Per serving: 284 calories, 8 g fat, 3 g saturated fat, 7 g protein, 52 g carbohydrates, 9 g fiber, 98 mg sodium

Sweet Potato Pie

A family favorite around holiday time, this pie can be made and refrigerated up to 3 days ahead.

Prep time: 15 minutes ⁑ **Cook time:** 55 minutes ⁑ **Total time:** 1 hour 10 minutes + cooling time
⁑ MAKES 8 SERVINGS

 4 sweet potatoes (about 2 pounds)
10 whole low-fat graham crackers
 2 tablespoons + $\frac{2}{3}$ cup sugar
 3 tablespoons unsalted butter, melted
 3 large eggs

$\frac{3}{4}$ cup fat-free milk
 2 teaspoons pumpkin pie spice
 2 teaspoons vanilla extract
$\frac{1}{4}$ teaspoon salt

1. Preheat the oven to 350°F.

2. Prick the sweet potatoes with a fork in several places. Microwave on high for 10 minutes, or until tender. Cool for 5 minutes. Peel the potatoes, transfer to a bowl, and mash.

3. Meanwhile, process the graham crackers and 2 tablespoons of the sugar in a food processor until fine crumbs form. Add the butter and pulse just until blended. Press the mixture into the bottom and up the sides of a 9" pie plate. Bake for 8 minutes, or until lightly browned. Leave the oven on.

4. Add the eggs, milk, pumpkin pie spice, vanilla, salt, and remaining $\frac{2}{3}$ cup sugar to the sweet potatoes. Beat with an electric mixer on medium-high for 3 minutes, or until well blended. Pour the mixture into the crust. Bake for 45 minutes, or until a knife inserted in the center comes out clean. Cool on a wire rack for 1 hour before cutting into 8 slices.

Per serving: 260 calories, 6 g fat, 3 g saturated fat, 5 g protein, 46 g carbohydrates, 4 g fiber, 200 mg sodium

Pumpkin Pie

Substituting a reduced-fat graham cracker crust for the usual butter-laden crust saves both fat and calories without sacrificing flavor.

Prep time: 5 minutes ▸ **Cook time:** 45 minutes ▸ **Total time:** 50 minutes + cooling time
▸ MAKES 8 SERVINGS

1 can (15 ounces) unsweetened pumpkin puree
1 cup packed dark brown sugar
1 tablespoon molasses
1¼ teaspoons ground cinnamon
¾ teaspoon ground ginger

⅛ teaspoon ground allspice
⅛ teaspoon salt
¾ cup egg substitute
1 cup fat-free evaporated milk
1 store-bought 9" reduced-fat graham cracker pie crust

1. Preheat the oven to 425°F.

2. Whisk together the pumpkin puree, brown sugar, molasses, cinnamon, ginger, allspice, and salt in a large bowl. Stir in the egg substitute and evaporated milk, mixing well. Pour the batter into the prepared crust.

3. Bake for 45 minutes, or until a knife inserted in the center comes out clean. Cool on a wire rack for at least 30 minutes before cutting into 8 slices.

Per serving: 325 calories, 7 g fat, 1 g saturated fat, 7 g protein, 59 g carbohydrates, 2 g fiber, 280 mg sodium

Chocolate Cream Pie

Fancy food trends abound, but nothing is more comforting than the tried and true we all grew up with. What could be more satisfying and delicious than a slice of rich chocolate cream pie?

Prep time: 15 minutes ⁚⊳ **Cook time:** 20 minutes ⁚⊳ **Total time:** 35 minutes + cooling and chilling times ⁚⊳ MAKES 8 SERVINGS

CRUST
- 10 whole low-fat graham crackers
- ¼ cup walnuts
- 3 tablespoons sugar
- 2 tablespoons unsalted butter, melted

FILLING
- 2¾ cups fat-free milk
- 1 cup sugar
- 1 large egg
- ¼ cup unsweetened cocoa powder
- ¼ cup cornstarch
- 1 teaspoon unsalted butter
- ¼ teaspoon salt

1. Preheat the oven to 350°F. Coat a 9" pie plate with cooking spray.

2. To make the crust: Process the graham crackers, walnuts, and sugar in a food processor until fine crumbs form. Add the butter and pulse just until blended. Press the mixture into the bottom and up the sides of the pie plate. Bake for 10 minutes, or until lightly browned. Cool on a wire rack for 10 minutes.

3. Meanwhile, to make the filling: Whisk together the milk, sugar, egg, cocoa, cornstarch, and salt in a large saucepan until well combined. Constantly whisk over medium heat until the mixture comes to a boil. Cook for 5 minutes, whisking frequently, until thickened. Remove from the heat and whisk in the butter until melted.

4. Press a piece of plastic wrap directly onto the surface of the filling and let cool for 20 minutes. Chill in the refrigerator for 1 hour, or until completely cooled. Remove the plastic wrap and spread the filling into the crust. Refrigerate for at least 2 hours before cutting into 8 slices.

Per serving: 251 calories, 7 g fat, 3 g saturated fat, 5 g protein, 44 g carbohydrates, 1 g fiber, 160 mg sodium

Apple Strudel

Granny Smith apples have a nice tart flavor, which helps to balance the sugar in this dessert.

Prep time: 20 minutes ⫶ **Cook time:** 35 minutes ⫶ **Total time:** 55 minutes + cooling time
⫶ MAKES 6 SERVINGS

Butter-flavored cooking spray
¾ cup sliced almonds
3 Granny Smith apples, peeled and coarsely chopped
¼ cup dried apricots, chopped

⅓ cup sugar
¼ teaspoon ground cinnamon
10 sheets (14" ⨯ 9") frozen whole wheat phyllo dough, thawed
1 teaspoon canola oil

1. Preheat the oven to 350°F. Coat a large baking sheet with the cooking spray.

2. Heat a small nonstick skillet over medium heat. Add the almonds and cook for 4 minutes, shaking often, or until lightly toasted. Transfer to a plate to cool, then finely chop.

3. Combine the apples, apricots, sugar, cinnamon, and 3 tablespoons of the almonds in a bowl. Place 1 sheet of the phyllo dough on a work surface with the long edge toward you. Coat lightly with the cooking spray. Repeat with 2 more sheets of phyllo and cooking spray. Sprinkle with 2 tablespoons of the almonds. Top with another phyllo sheet and coat with cooking spray. Repeat the layering with 1 sheet of phyllo, cooking spray, and almonds 5 more times. Top with the last sheet of phyllo and brush with the oil.

4. Spread the phyllo stack with the apple filling, leaving a 2" border on all sides. Starting at the long side closest to you, roll up jelly-roll style, tucking in the sides as you go. Place seam side down on the baking sheet and coat the strudel lightly with cooking spray.

5. Bake for 30 minutes, or until browned and crisp. Cool on a rack for 15 minutes before cutting into 6 slices.

Per serving: 256 calories, 7 g fat, 1 g saturated fat, 5 g protein, 46 g carbohydrates, 5 g fiber, 113 mg sodium

Apricot and Plum Slump

A slump, sometimes called a grunt, is an old New England dessert of baked or stewed fruit topped with biscuitlike dough.

Prep time: 10 minutes ⟩ **Cook time:** 25 minutes ⟩ **Total time:** 35 minutes + cooling time ⟩ MAKES 8 SERVINGS

$2\frac{1}{4}$ pounds plums, cut into wedges

$1\frac{1}{4}$ cups dried apricots

$\frac{1}{3}$ cup white grape juice

$\frac{1}{4}$ cup + 3 tablespoons sugar

2 tablespoons honey

1 tablespoon fresh lemon juice

$1\frac{3}{4}$ cups whole grain pastry flour

1 teaspoon baking powder

$\frac{1}{2}$ teaspoon baking soda

$\frac{1}{8}$ teaspoon salt

3 tablespoons chilled unsalted butter, cut into small pieces

$\frac{3}{4}$ cup low-fat buttermilk

$\frac{1}{8}$ teaspoon ground cinnamon

1. Combine the plums, apricots, grape juice, $\frac{1}{4}$ cup of the sugar, the honey, and lemon juice in a large, deep skillet over medium-high heat. Bring to a boil, reduce the heat to medium-low, cover, and simmer for 8 minutes, or until the fruit is tender but not mushy.

2. Meanwhile, process the flour, baking powder, baking soda, salt, and 2 tablespoons of the sugar in a food processor until blended. Add the butter and pulse until the mixture resembles fine crumbs. Add the buttermilk and pulse until a soft dough forms.

3. Drop the dough by heaping tablespoons onto the hot fruit mixture. Combine the remaining 1 tablespoon sugar and cinnamon in a bowl. Sprinkle over the dough. Increase the heat to medium-high and bring the fruit mixture to a boil. Reduce the heat to medium-low, cover, and simmer for 12 minutes, or until the dumplings are firm to the touch. Let cool, uncovered, for 10 minutes before serving.

Per serving: 294 calories, 5 g fat, 3 g saturated fat, 5 g protein, 61 g carbohydrates, 5 g fiber, 203 mg sodium

Fresh and Dried Fruit Crisp

Peaches and blueberries are one of nature's perfect combinations. The addition of dried apricots adds both texture and a bit of tangy contrast to this already perfect summer dessert.

Prep time: 20 minutes ⫸ **Cook time:** 40 minutes ⫸ **Total time:** 1 hour ⫸ MAKES 8 SERVINGS

1½ pounds peaches, sliced
3 cups blueberries
1 cup dried apricots, sliced
1 cup packed light brown sugar
1 tablespoon cornstarch
1 teaspoon vanilla extract

¾ teaspoon ground ginger
½ cup quick-cooking oats
½ cup whole grain pastry flour
½ cup sliced almonds
3 tablespoons trans-free margarine

1. Preheat the oven to 375°F. Coat a 2-quart baking dish with cooking spray.

2. Toss together the peaches, blueberries, apricots, ½ cup of the brown sugar, the cornstarch, vanilla, and ginger in a large bowl. Pour into the baking dish.

3. Combine the oats, flour, almonds, margarine, and remaining ½ cup brown sugar in a separate bowl. Rub the mixture together with your fingers until it resembles coarse crumbs and begins to form clumps when squeezed. Sprinkle over the peach mixture to cover. Bake for 35 minutes, or until the filling is thick and bubbling and the top is lightly golden.

Per serving: 307 calories, 7 g fat, 1 g saturated fat, 5 g protein, 61 g carbohydrates, 5 g fiber, 34 mg sodium

Dried Fruit Bites

For a berry version, replace the prunes, dates, and apricots with the same amounts of dried blueberries, cranberries, and strawberries. Use brown sugar instead of granulated sugar, and replace the rice cereal with 1 cup reduced-fat vanilla wafer crumbs.

Prep time: 25 minutes ⫶ **Cook time:** 5 minutes ⫶ **Total time:** 30 minutes + cooling and drying times ⫶ MAKES 6 SERVINGS

½ cup pitted dried plums (prunes)
½ cup pitted dates
½ cup dried apricots
1 tablespoon grated lemon zest
½ cup sugar
2 tablespoons frozen orange juice concentrate

2 tablespoons butter
1 tablespoon honey
1 teaspoon ground cinnamon
1½ cups crispy rice cereal
2 tablespoons confectioners' sugar

1. Process the prunes, dates, apricots, and lemon zest in a food processor until finely chopped.

2. Combine the sugar, orange juice concentrate, butter, honey, and cinnamon in a heavy saucepan. Cook over medium-low heat, stirring occasionally, until the sugar is dissolved. Stir in the fruit mixture and cereal until well blended. Remove from the heat and set aside to cool.

3. When cooled, pinch off small pieces of the mixture and roll into 1" balls to make a total of 36. Place the confectioners' sugar in a shallow bowl or pie plate. Roll the balls in the sugar and set on wax paper to dry. Serve 6 per person.

Per serving: 256 calories, 4 g fat, 2 g saturated fat, 2 g protein, 57 g carbohydrates, 3 g fiber, 85 mg sodium

 MAKE IT A SALT SOLUTION MEAL: Serve with 3 ounces of fat-free plain Greek yogurt (301 calories and 118 mg sodium total).

Bananas Canadienne

Hazelnuts and maple syrup give baked bananas a fun, mouthwateringly good twist.

Prep time: 5 minutes ⁑ **Cook time:** 15 minutes ⁑ **Total time:** 20 minutes ⁑ MAKES 4 SERVINGS

4 large bananas, halved lengthwise
2 tablespoons fresh lemon juice
$1/2$ cup maple syrup
$1/3$ cup chopped hazelnuts

1. Preheat the oven to 325°F. Coat a 13" × 9" baking dish with cooking spray.

2. Place the bananas cut side up in a single layer in the baking dish. Drizzle with the lemon juice and maple syrup. Sprinkle with the hazelnuts.

3. Bake for 12 minutes, or until the bananas are lightly browned and glazed.

Per serving: 298 calories, 7 g fat, 1 g saturated fat, 3 g protein, 60 g carbohydrates, 5 g fiber, 5 mg sodium

Fruit Kebabs with Raspberry-Mango Dip

The dip can be made and refrigerated up to 3 days ahead. You can use frozen raspberries instead of fresh. To save time, purchase precut cantaloupe, pineapple, and watermelon from the grocery store.

Prep time: 20 minutes ▶ **Total time:** 20 minutes ▶ MAKES 4 SERVINGS

1 mango, cut into chunks
$\frac{1}{2}$ cup raspberries
$\frac{1}{4}$ cup 2% plain Greek yogurt
2 tablespoons honey
$1\frac{1}{2}$ cups strawberries, halved if large
1 banana, cut into 1" chunks

1 cup cubed cantaloupe
1 cup cubed pineapple
1 cup cubed watermelon
$\frac{1}{2}$ cup green or red grapes
$\frac{1}{4}$ cup almonds

1. Process the mango in a food processor until pureed. Add the raspberries, yogurt, and honey. Process until blended and the raspberries are pureed. Pour into a small bowl. Cover and refrigerate while assembling the kebabs.

2. Thread the strawberries, banana, cantaloupe, pineapple, watermelon, and grapes onto eight 8" wooden skewers. Serve 2 kebabs per person, with the dip and almonds.

Per serving: 233 calories, 5 g fat, 1 g saturated fat, 5 g protein, 47 g carbohydrates, 6 g fiber, 16 mg sodium

Yogurt and Fresh Fruit Ambrosia

Refreshing and satisfying, this quick-to-throw-together dessert also doubles as a great breakfast dish when sprinkled with a little bit of granola or your favorite cereal.

Prep time: 15 minutes ▷ **Total time:** 15 minutes ▷ MAKES 4 SERVINGS

2 cups fat-free plain yogurt

2 tablespoons honey

2 medium bananas, sliced

¼ fresh pineapple, chopped

1 cup blueberries

1 cup raspberries

1 cup seedless red grapes, halved

¼ cup sliced almonds, toasted

Combine the yogurt and honey in a large bowl until well blended. Stir in the bananas, pineapple, blueberries, raspberries, and grapes. Divide among 4 bowls and sprinkle with the almonds.

Per serving: 278 calories, 4 g fat, 0 g saturated fat, 10 g protein, 56 g carbohydrates, 6 g fiber, 97 mg sodium

Strawberry Yogurt Cup

Agave nectar is a sweetener produced from the juice of several species of agave plants. Agave is sweeter than honey but not as thick. If you don't have it on hand, honey will work as a substitute.

Prep time: 5 minutes ⁖ **Total time:** 5 minutes ⁖ MAKES 1 SERVING

1 cup fat-free strawberry yogurt
2 teaspoons agave nectar
1 teaspoon vanilla extract

1 teaspoon grated orange zest
½ cup strawberries, sliced
2 tablespoons low-fat granola

1. Combine the yogurt, agave nectar, vanilla, and orange zest in a small bowl.

2. Place all but 3 strawberry slices in the bottom of a large parfait glass. Sprinkle with 1 tablespoon of the granola and top with the yogurt mixture. Sprinkle with the remaining 1 tablespoon granola. Garnish with the reserved strawberry slices.

Per serving: 254 calories, 1 g fat, 0 g saturated fat, 10 g protein, 51 g carbohydrates, 2 g fiber, 146 mg sodium

Mexican-Style Flan

Cinnamon and chocolate are a traditional Mexican combination that works wonderfully well in this silky smooth baked custard.

Prep time: 10 minutes ⊳ **Cook time:** 45 minutes ⊳ **Total time:** 55 minutes + cooling and chilling times
⊳ MAKES 8 SERVINGS

¾ cup sugar

3½ cups fat-free milk

1 cup fat-free sweetened condensed milk

½ cup unsweetened cocoa powder

¾ teaspoon ground cinnamon

5 large eggs

2 teaspoons vanilla extract

1. Preheat the oven to 350°F with a rack in the center position.

2. Combine the sugar and ⅓ cup of water in a medium heavy-bottomed saucepan over medium-high heat and cook for 15 minutes, shaking the pan occasionally, until the sugar turns golden brown. Pour into a 9" deep-dish glass pie plate. Tilt the pan to evenly coat the bottom. Set aside to cool for 10 minutes.

3. Meanwhile, combine the fat-free milk, sweetened condensed milk, cocoa, and cinnamon in a medium saucepan. Bring to a simmer over medium heat. While the milk heats, combine the eggs and vanilla in a large bowl. Whisk the hot milk mixture, a little at a time, into the egg mixture until completely combined. Pour the custard mixture into the pie plate.

4. Place the pie plate in a roasting pan and pour enough hot water in to come halfway up the sides of the pie plate. Bake for 40 minutes, or until the custard is set. Remove the pie plate from the roasting pan and cool on a rack for 1 hour. Cover with plastic wrap and chill for 3 hours or overnight.

5. Run the tip of a knife around the edge of the pie plate to loosen. Invert a plate larger than the pie plate and quickly flip over so that the flan and sauce fall onto the plate. Cut into 8 wedges to serve.

Per serving: 270 calories, 4 g fat, 1 g saturated fat, 11 g protein, 50 g carbohydrates, 2 g fiber, 117 mg sodium

Chocolate-Almond Pudding with Amaretti

Amaretti are almond-flavored cookies available in Italian specialty shops and some high-end supermarkets. If you can't find them, substitute almond biscotti.

Prep time: 5 minutes ⁑ **Cook time:** 5 minutes ⁑ **Total time:** 10 minutes ⁑ MAKES 4 SERVINGS

$\frac{1}{2}$ cup sugar

$\frac{1}{3}$ cup unsweetened cocoa powder

2 tablespoons + 2 teaspoons cornstarch

2 cups 1% milk

1 teaspoon vanilla extract

$\frac{1}{4}$ teaspoon almond extract

8 amaretti cookies, crushed (about $\frac{1}{3}$ cup)

1. Combine the sugar, cocoa, and cornstarch in a medium saucepan. Gradually whisk in the milk until the cornstarch dissolves. Bring to a boil over medium-low heat. Cook, stirring, for 6 minutes, or until thickened and smooth. Remove from the heat and stir in the vanilla and almond extracts.

2. Spoon half of the pudding into four 4-ounce ramekins or parfait glasses. Sprinkle with half of the cookies. Top with the remaining pudding and cookies. Serve warm.

Per serving: 293 calories, 8 g fat, 2 g saturated fat, 7 g protein, 51 g carbohydrates, 3 g fiber, 103 mg sodium

Butterscotch Pudding with Bananas

For a twist, melt 1 teaspoon margarine in a medium nonstick skillet over medium heat. Add the sliced banana and 1 teaspoon of sugar and cook for 5 minutes, or until the banana is softened and warm. Then spoon over the puddings just before serving.

Prep time: 5 minutes ⁂ **Cook time:** 10 minutes ⁂ **Total time:** 15 minutes + chilling time
⁂ MAKES 4 SERVINGS

2¼ cups fat-free milk
 2 large egg yolks
½ cup packed light brown sugar
 1 tablespoon honey
 3 tablespoons cornstarch

 1 tablespoon vanilla extract
 1 tablespoon trans-free margarine
 1 banana, cut into 20 slices
12 raspberries

1. Whisk together ¼ cup of the milk, the egg yolks, brown sugar, honey, cornstarch, and vanilla in a large bowl.

2. Heat the remaining 2 cups milk in a small saucepan over medium heat for 4 minutes, or until it just starts to simmer. Whisking constantly, slowly pour the hot milk into the yolk mixture until well combined. Pour the warmed milk mixture back into the saucepan and bring to a boil, whisking constantly. Boil for 1 minute, or until thickened. Remove from the heat and whisk in the margarine until melted. Immediately pour into 4 dessert dishes. Press a small piece of plastic wrap directly onto the puddings to prevent skins from forming. Refrigerate for at least 3 hours.

3. Top with the banana slices and raspberries just before serving.

Per serving: 281 calories, 5 g fat, 1 g saturated fat, 7 g protein, 53 g carbohydrates, 1 g fiber, 99 mg sodium

Arborio Rice Pudding with Soymilk and Toasted Coconut

Arborio rice takes rice pudding to the next level. This pudding is extra creamy from the long, slow cooking process, but the rice maintains a slight toothy quality to give a pleasant contrast in textures.

Prep time: 5 minutes ▷ **Cook time:** 35 minutes ▷ **Total time:** 40 minutes + cooling time
▷ MAKES 4 SERVINGS

3 cups unsweetened plain soymilk

$\frac{1}{2}$ cup sugar

$\frac{1}{8}$ teaspoon ground cinnamon

$\frac{1}{8}$ teaspoon salt

$\frac{1}{2}$ cup Arborio rice

$\frac{1}{2}$ teaspoon coconut extract

$\frac{1}{4}$ cup sweetened flaked coconut, toasted

1. Bring the soymilk, sugar, cinnamon, and salt to a simmer in a medium saucepan over medium heat, stirring occasionally. Stir in the rice, return to a simmer, and cook for 35 minutes, stirring every 2 minutes, until the rice is tender but still slightly al dente. Remove from the heat and stir in the coconut extract.

2. Divide among 4 bowls and cover each with plastic wrap pressed onto the surface. Cool for at least 20 minutes. Remove the plastic wrap and sprinkle with the toasted coconut before serving.

Per serving: 303 calories, 5 g fat, 2 g saturated fat, 8 g protein, 58 g carbohydrates, 3 g fiber, 180 mg sodium

Peanut Butter Pudding

Chilling helps give the pudding a silky smooth texture and allows time for the flavors to develop.

Prep time: 5 minutes ▷ **Cook time:** 10 minutes ▷ **Total time:** 15 minutes + chilling time
▷ MAKES 6 SERVINGS

1 envelope unflavored gelatin	¾ cup packed light brown sugar
1⅓ cups fat-free evaporated milk	⅓ cup creamy peanut butter
1 cup fat-free milk	1 tablespoon vanilla extract

1. Sprinkle the gelatin over 3 tablespoons of water in a small bowl. Let stand for 5 minutes to soften.

2. Meanwhile, combine the evaporated milk, fat-free milk, brown sugar, and peanut butter in a medium saucepan. Cook over medium heat, whisking constantly, until the mixture just starts to simmer. Stir in the gelatin mixture and vanilla. Remove from the heat and let cool to room temperature. Pour into 6 dessert dishes and refrigerate for 4 hours or overnight.

Per serving: 258 calories, 7 g fat, 2 g saturated fat, 10 g protein, 39 g carbohydrates, 1 g fiber, 195 mg sodium

Nutty Oatmeal Cookies

Simple to make and surprisingly crisp, these delicious cookies get extra crunch from chopped almonds.

Prep time: 15 minutes ⫶ **Cook time:** 15 minutes ⫶ **Total time:** 30 minutes
⫶ MAKES 8 SERVINGS (24 COOKIES)

$^3/_4$ cup packed light brown sugar

3 tablespoons trans-free margarine

1 large egg

$1^1/_2$ teaspoons vanilla extract

1 cup old-fashioned rolled oats

$^3/_4$ cup unbleached all-purpose flour

$^1/_2$ teaspoon ground cinnamon

$^1/_4$ teaspoon baking soda

$^1/_8$ teaspoon ground nutmeg

$^1/_8$ teaspoon salt

$^1/_2$ cup whole almonds, coarsely chopped

1. Preheat the oven to 350°F. Line 2 large baking sheets with parchment paper or coat with cooking spray.

2. Combine the brown sugar, margarine, egg, and vanilla in a mixing bowl. Beat with an electric mixer on medium-high until well blended. Add the oats, flour, cinnamon, baking soda, nutmeg, and salt and beat on medium speed for 1 minute, or until well combined. Add the almonds and beat on low for 1 minute.

3. Drop by level tablespoons about 2" apart onto the prepared baking sheets. Bake for 14 minutes, or until the cookies are lightly browned. Cool on the baking sheets for 5 minutes. Remove to a rack to cool completely. Serve 3 cookies per person.

Per serving: 254 calories, 9 g fat, 1 g saturated fat, 6 g protein, 38 g carbohydrates, 2 g fiber, 123 mg sodium

Almond-and-Anise Biscotti

Biscotti means "twice baked" and refers to the method that gives these cookies their crunchy texture.

Prep time: 25 minutes ⊪ **Cook time:** 50 minutes ⊪ **Total time:** 1 hour 15 minutes + chilling and cooling times ⊪ MAKES 16 SERVINGS (3 BISCOTTI EACH)

½ cup sugar

2 tablespoons unsalted butter, at room temperature

¼ cup honey, warmed

2 large egg whites

1 teaspoon vanilla extract

1½ cups whole grain pastry flour

½ cup coarsely ground almonds

1 teaspoon aniseeds

1 teaspoon baking powder

½ teaspoon salt

1. Preheat the oven to 350°F. Line a large baking sheet with parchment paper.

2. Combine the sugar, butter, honey, egg whites, and vanilla in a medium bowl. Beat with an electric mixer on medium speed until smooth. Add the flour, almonds, aniseeds, baking powder, and salt. Beat on low speed until the dough is smooth and thick. Divide the dough into 2 equal pieces. Refrigerate for 30 minutes, or until firm.

3. Shape each piece into a 12"-long log and place both on the baking sheet. Bake for 20 minutes, or until golden. Transfer the logs to a rack to cool for 15 minutes. Reduce the oven temperature to 300°F.

4. Transfer the cooled logs to a cutting board and slice into 48 ($\frac{1}{3}$"-thick) slices. Return to the baking sheet. Bake for 30 minutes, turning once, or until dry. Transfer the cookies to a rack to cool completely.

Per serving: 105 calories, 3 g fat, 1 g saturated fat, 2 g protein, 18 g carbohydrates, 1 g fiber, 84 mg sodium

 MAKE IT A SALT SOLUTION MEAL: Serve with 1 banana and 1 cup 1% milk.

Orange Cheesecake Bars

For a rich-tasting indulgence, these bars are remarkably light. Be sure that the cream cheeses are at room temperature before beating.

Prep time: 15 minutes ▷ **Cook time:** 50 minutes ▷ **Total time:** 1 hour 5 minutes ▷ MAKES 8 SERVINGS

6 whole low-fat graham crackers
2 tablespoons + ¾ cup sugar
1 tablespoon trans-free margarine, melted
6 ounces Neufchâtel cheese, at room temperature
6 ounces fat-free cream cheese, at room temperature

2 large eggs
2 large egg whites
¾ cup fat-free plain yogurt
¼ cup orange juice
1 tablespoon grated orange zest
1 teaspoon orange extract
½ cup whole grain pastry flour

1. Preheat the oven to 350°F. Line an 8" × 8" baking pan with foil, leaving a 2" overhang on two opposite sides to use as handles for lifting the cake out after it's baked. Coat the foil with cooking spray.

2. Process the graham crackers and 2 tablespoons of the sugar in a food processor until fine crumbs form. Add the margarine and pulse just until blended. Press the mixture into the bottom of the baking pan and bake for 8 minutes, or until lightly browned. Cool on a rack for 10 minutes. Leave the oven on.

3. Meanwhile, beat the Neufchâtel and fat-free cream cheese in a bowl with an electric mixer on medium-high for 2 minutes, or until well combined. Add the remaining ¾ cup sugar, the whole eggs, egg whites, yogurt, orange juice, orange zest, and orange extract. Beat on medium-high for 3 minutes, or until the mixture is smooth. Add the flour and beat on low speed until combined. Pour into the crust.

4. Bake for 40 minutes, or until the mixture is set and a toothpick inserted in the center comes out clean. Cool on a wire rack for 1 hour. Chill for 2 hours or overnight. Remove from the baking pan with the foil and cut into 16 bars. Serve 2 bars per person.

Per serving: 242 calories, 8 g fat, 4 g saturated fat, 10 g protein, 36 g carbohydrates, 1 g fiber, 279 mg sodium

Oreo Delight

Simple but satisfying, this dessert gets lots of flavor from dried cherries and Oreo crisps.

Prep time: 5 minutes ⁛ **Total time:** 5 minutes ⁛ MAKES 1 SERVING

¾ cup low-fat vanilla ice cream

1 pack (100 calories) Oreo Thin Crisps, crumbled

1 tablespoon chopped dried cherries

2 teaspoons sliced almonds

Place the ice cream in a shallow bowl. Sprinkle with the crumbled cookies and dried cherries. Top with the almonds.

Per serving: 317 calories, 7 g fat, 2 g saturated fat, 7 g protein, 55 g carbohydrates, 3 g fiber, 69 mg sodium

Roasted Soybean and Nut Brittle

This crunchy treat is satisfying and delicious, and it's chockful of healthy soynuts and peanuts, too.

Prep time: 5 minutes ⊳ **Cook time:** 10 minutes ⊳ **Total time:** 15 minutes + cooling time
⊳ MAKES 8 SERVINGS

1 cup sugar

½ cup light corn syrup

1 tablespoon fresh lemon juice

¼ teaspoon salt

1½ cups unsalted soynuts

½ cup unsalted peanuts

1 tablespoon trans-free margarine

1½ teaspoons vanilla extract

½ teaspoon baking soda

1. Coat a large baking sheet with cooking spray.

2. Bring the sugar, corn syrup, lemon juice, and salt to a boil in a medium saucepan over medium-high heat. Cook, stirring occasionally to help the sugar dissolve, until the mixture turns golden and has reached 325°F on a candy thermometer.

3. Remove from the heat and stir in the soynuts, peanuts, margarine, vanilla, and baking soda. Mix well. Pour onto the baking sheet and, working as quickly as possible, spread the mixture into a thin layer with a heatproof spatula. Let cool for 1 hour to harden. Break into smaller pieces to serve.

Per serving: 305 calories, 10 g fat, 1 g saturated fat, 8 g protein, 49 g carbohydrates, 1 g fiber, 176 mg sodium

Banana, Almond, and Coconut Angel Food Parfaits

Similar to Bananas Foster, this dessert has a tropical flavor thanks to the toasted coconut and orange.

Prep time: 10 minutes ❧ **Cook time:** 5 minutes ❧ **Total time:** 15 minutes ❧ MAKES 4 SERVINGS

1 teaspoon unsalted butter
2 medium bananas, sliced
½ cup strawberries, sliced
1 tablespoon sugar
¼ teaspoon almond extract
3 tablespoons orange juice

3 slices angel food cake (from a 9"
   cake), cut into cubes
2 cups low-fat vanilla ice cream
¼ cup sliced almonds, toasted
3 tablespoons sweetened flaked
   coconut, toasted

1. Melt the butter in a large skillet over medium-high heat. Add the bananas, strawberries, sugar, and almond extract. Cook for 3 minutes, tossing occasionally, or until the bananas and strawberries are softened. Stir in the orange juice and cook for 30 seconds, stirring. Remove from the heat and keep warm.

2. Fill the bottoms of 4 tall glasses with the angel food cake cubes. Scoop ½ cup ice cream into each and top with one-fourth of the banana mixture. Sprinkle with the almonds and coconut and serve immediately.

Per serving: 306 calories, 8 g fat, 2 g saturated fat, 6 g protein, 53 g carbohydrates, 4 g fiber, 213 mg sodium

Classic Vanilla Malt

For an extra-thick malt, place the milk in the freezer for about 1 hour before using so that it partially freezes.

Prep time: 5 minutes ⁖ **Total time:** 5 minutes ⁖ MAKES 2 SERVINGS

1½ cups low-fat vanilla ice cream

1 cup fat-free milk

2 tablespoons malted milk powder

1 tablespoon vanilla syrup

Blend the ice cream, milk, malted milk powder, and syrup in a blender until smooth. Pour into 2 glasses and serve immediately.

Per serving: 279 calories, 3 g fat, 2 g saturated fat, 10 g protein, 51 g carbohydrates, 2 g fiber, 156 mg sodium

Homemade Fruity Yogurt Pops

Tangy and sweet, these easy-to-make treats are better and less expensive than their store-bought counterparts. If you don't have popsicle molds, just use 4-ounce paper cups and then peel them off when ready to eat.

Prep time: 10 minutes ⁖ **Total time:** 10 minutes + freezing time ⁖ MAKES 8 SERVINGS

1½ large mangoes, cut into chunks
  2 cups fat-free plain yogurt

½ cup sugar
½ cup fat-free milk

Pulse the mangoes, yogurt, sugar, and milk in a blender until smooth. Pour the mixture into eight 4-ounce popsicle molds. Insert a wooden stick into each and freeze for 6 hours. Unmold before serving.

Per serving: 113 calories, 0 g fat, 0 g saturated fat, 4 g protein, 25 g carbohydrates, 1 g fiber, 54 mg sodium

Vanilla Egg Cream Float

This New York City classic gets a decadent boost with a scoop of chocolate ice cream. If chocolate is not your favorite, just sub in the flavor of your choice.

Prep time: 5 minutes ⊳ **Total time:** 5 minutes ⊳ MAKES 2 SERVINGS

4 tablespoons vanilla syrup

1 cup very cold fat-free milk

1 cup very cold seltzer or sparkling water

1 cup low-fat chocolate ice cream

Place 2 tablespoons of the vanilla syrup in the bottom of a tall glass. Pour in ½ cup of the milk. While vigorously stirring with a spoon, pour in ½ cup of the seltzer or sparkling water. Scoop ½ cup of the ice cream into the glass. Repeat with the remaining ingredients for the second serving. Serve with straws and long spoons.

Per serving: 273 calories, 2 g fat, 1 g saturated fat, 7 g protein, 46 g carbohydrates, 4 g fiber, 105 mg sodium

Banana Ice Cream Sundaes

For a more intense banana flavor, be sure to use bananas that are very ripe. Make sure to peel them before freezing.

Prep time: 10 minutes ⁝▸ **Total time:** 10 minutes + freezing time ⁝▸ MAKES 4 SERVINGS

2 large frozen bananas, sliced
1½ cups fat-free milk
2 tablespoons sugar
½ teaspoon ground cinnamon
½ teaspoon vanilla extract

Scant ⅛ teaspoon ground nutmeg
¼ cup semisweet chocolate chips
1 cup raspberries
4 tablespoons chocolate syrup

1. Process the bananas, milk, sugar, cinnamon, vanilla, and nutmeg in a blender for 3 minutes, or until smooth.

2. Transfer to a metal or plastic container and stir in the chocolate chips. Cover and freeze for 4 hours or overnight. Remove from the freezer and break the mixture into smaller pieces with a knife. Transfer to a food processor or blender. Process briefly. Return to the container and freeze for 30 minutes.

3. Divide the ice cream among 4 bowls. Top each with ¼ cup raspberries and 1 tablespoon chocolate syrup.

Per serving: 268 calories, 4 g fat, 2 g saturated fat, 5 g protein, 57 g carbohydrates, 6 g fiber, 64 mg sodium

APPENDIX A

THE SALT SOLUTION WEIGHT-LOSS WORKOUT

On its own, the Salt Solution eating plan has the power to slim and transform your body. However, if you pair it with a regular fitness regimen, you'll get results faster, sculpt calorie-burning muscle, and boost your protection against high blood pressure, heart disease, diabetes, and all the other diseases associated with a high-sodium diet.

We've specifically created the ultimate way to burn off a few extra pounds—and boost your overall health simultaneously—that works for anyone, regardless of your schedule, fitness level, or lack of access to exercise equipment. With the help of fitness expert Myatt Murphy (author of *The Body You Want in the Time You Have, The Men's Health Gym Bible,* and *Men's Health Ultimate Dumbbell Guide*), we devised a Salt Solution workout that works *with* you, letting you decide how hard, or even how long, you want to exercise, so you're more likely to stick with the program—and harness all the benefits.

Included in this appendix you'll find everything you need to start the walking and strength-training workouts, including easy-to-read charts, clear descriptions of all the exercises, and smart tricks to help you maximize your workouts!

Equipment

To ensure that you'll target as many muscles as possible within the shortest period of time, we've designed a routine that systematically works all of your muscles from head to toe using just seven simple moves. All you need to perform this routine are a few exercise tools you probably already have in your closet:

1 pair of good walking shoes
2 pairs of dumbbells (or 1 pair of adjustable dumbbells)

If you find that you want to raise the intensity of this workout at any time, there are a few additional pieces of fitness equipment you may need—such as a stability ball or exercise bench—but to do the workout and get fast results, dumbbells are all you need. (See page 366 for guidance on how much weight you need.)

The next few pages explain the walking workouts. To jump to the strength-training workouts, flip to page 364.

THE WALKING WORKOUTS

To get the best results from each walking workout, you'll need to push yourself as much as required each day. That's not always easy to do—especially for a beginner—which is why the best way to gauge exactly how hard you're exercising is to use the Rate of Perceived Exertion (RPE) Scale.

How the RPE Scale Works: As you exercise, rate how hard you're exercising on a scale of 1 to 10 (one being "as little as possible" and 10 being "as hard as possible") by judging how well you can carry on a conversation as you go. The faster you walk, the less you'll be able to talk, so higher tempos mean you're working harder. Here's how to tell what level of exertion you're at as you exercise:

The Tempos You Need to Know

RPE 1–2 (VERY EASY):

A very slow pace that allows you to carry on a conversation with no effort.

RPE 3–4 (EASY TO MODERATELY EASY)

A very easy pace that lets you carry on a conversation comfortably with minimum effort.

RPE 5–6 (MODERATE TO MODERATELY HARD)

A brisk pace that lets you talk, but it would be impossible to sing.

RPE 7–8 (DIFFICULT TO VERY DIFFICULT)

A high-intensity pace that lets you blurt out short phrases, but anything beyond that is impossible.

RPE 9–10 (MAX EFFORT)

An extremely high-intensity pace that makes carrying on a conversation virtually impossible.

The Four Walking Styles

There are four unique styles of walking that you'll be utilizing in the walking portion of the Salt Solution Workout. They are as follows: Interval Walks, Steady-State Walks, Power Walks, and Recuperative Walks. Each of these routines allows you to exercise at different intensities, which help elevate your metabolism and burn stored fat in different ways—and stall your body from reaching a weight-loss plateau.

1. Interval Walks

After a 3- to 5-minute, low-intensity warmup, you'll begin your first interval set by walking briskly for 3 minutes at a pace that's around 5–6 on the Rate of Perceived Exertion (RPE) Scale.

Next, you'll speed up to a pace that's about a 7–8 on the RPE Scale and walk for 1 minute. You'll repeat this pattern—3 minutes moderate intensity/1 minute high intensity—for the length of the workout. Afterwards, finish with a 3- to 5-minute cooldown walk.

2. Steady-State Walks

After a 3- to 5-minute, low-intensity warmup, you'll walk at a tempo that's about a 5 on the RPE Scale. You'll walk at this pace for the length of the workout, then finish with a 3- to 5-minute cooldown walk.

3. Power Walks

After a 3- to 5-minute, low-intensity warmup, you'll begin walking at a pace that's roughly 6–7 on the RPE Scale. You'll walk at this pace for the length of the workout, then finish with a 3- to 5-minute cooldown walk.

4. Recuperative Walks

After a 3- to 5-minute, low-intensity warmup, you'll pick a comfortable moderate pace that you can easily walk for the prescribed amount of time. If you're tired from the week, stick with a tempo that's around a 4 on the RPE Scale; if you have the energy, up the tempo to a 5 instead. You'll walk at this pace for the length of the workout, then finish with a 3- to 5-minute cooldown walk.

ADJUSTING THE PROGRAM TO YOUR FITNESS LEVEL

WITH EVERY WALKING WORKOUT

• Instead of doing the number of minutes suggested for each day, you can divide that number by half. (For example, if the program asks you to walk for 30 minutes, try walking for 15 minutes instead.) As the weeks progress and you gradually become more fit, you can begin adding a few extra minutes back into your workouts until you eventually feel comfortable exercising for the recommended time limit.

• If the length of any walking workout is too long for you to complete timewise because of your schedule, simply split the workout up into two segments. (For example, if you can't walk for the recommended 40 minutes one day, try breaking your workout up into two 20-minute walks instead.)

Week	Day 1	Day 2	Day 3
1	Interval Walk (35 minutes)	Steady-State Walk (40 minutes)	Interval Walk (35 minutes)
	OFF	Strength Training (2 sets; 15 reps; 45–60 seconds rest)	OFF
2	Interval Walk (35 minutes)	Steady-State Walk (40 minutes)	Interval Walk (35 minutes)
	OFF	Strength Training (2 sets; 12 reps; 30–45 seconds rest)	OFF
3	Interval Walk (40 minutes)	Steady-State Walk (55 minutes)	Interval Walk (40 minutes)
	Weight Training (2 sets; 15 reps; 45–60 seconds rest)	OFF	Strength Training (2 sets; 12 reps; 30–45 seconds rest)
4	Interval Walk (40 minutes)	Steady-State Walk (55 minutes)	Interval Walk (40 minutes)
	Strength Training (2 sets; 15 reps; 45–60 seconds rest)	OFF	Strength Training (2 sets; 12 reps; 30–45 seconds rest)
5	Interval Walk (45 minutes)	Steady-State Walk (1 hour 10 minutes)	Interval Walk (45 minutes)
	Strength Training (3 sets; 15 reps; 45–60 seconds rest)	OFF	Strength Training (3 sets; 12 reps; 30–45 seconds rest)
6	Interval Walk (45 minutes)	Steady-State Walk (1 hour)	Interval Walk (45 minutes)
	Strength Training (3 sets; 15 reps; 45–60 seconds rest)	OFF	Strength Training (3 sets; 12 reps; 30–45 seconds rest)

Day 4	Day 5	Day 6	Day 7
Power Walk (30 minutes)	Interval Walk (35 minutes)	Recuperative Walk (50 minutes)	Rest
OFF	Strength Training (2 sets; 15 reps; 45–60 seconds rest)	OFF	
Power Walk (30 minutes)	Interval Walk (35 minutes)	Recuperative Walk (1 hour)	Rest
OFF	Strength Training (2 sets; 12 reps; 30–45 seconds rest)	OFF	
Power Walk (40 minutes)	Interval Walk (40 minutes)	Recuperative Walk (1 hour 10 minutes)	Rest
OFF	Strength Training (2 sets; 10 reps; 15–30 seconds rest)	OFF	
Power Walk (40 minutes)	Interval Walk (40 minutes)	Recuperative Walk (1 hour 20 minutes)	Rest
OFF	Strength Training (2 sets; 10 reps; 15–30 seconds rest)	OFF	
Power Walk (50 minutes)	Interval Walk (45 minutes)	Recuperative Walk (1 hour 30 minutes)	Rest
OFF	Strength Training (3 sets; 10 reps; 15–30 seconds rest)	OFF	
Power Walk (50 minutes)	Interval Walk (45 minutes)	Recuperative Walk (1 hour 40 minutes)	Rest
OFF	Strength Training (3 sets; 10 reps; 15–30 seconds rest)	OFF	

Week One

DAY 1 — INTERVAL WALK

Total Workout Time	The Routine	Intensity
35 minutes	3- to 5-minute warmup	3–4
(25 minutes + 6–10 minutes warmup and cooldown)	3 minutes (brisk pace)	5–6
	1 minute (fast pace)	7–8
	Continue to do 3-minute brisk/1-minute fast intervals 5 more times (for a total of 6 intervals)	
	1 minute (brisk pace)	5–6
	3- to 5-minute cooldown	3–4

DAY 2 — STEADY-STATE WALK

Total Workout Time	The Routine	Intensity
40 minutes	3- to 5-minute warmup	3–4
(30 minutes + 6–10 minutes warmup and cooldown)	30 minutes (moderate pace)	5
	3- to 5-minute cooldown	3–4

DAY 3 — INTERVAL WALK

Total Workout Time	The Routine	Intensity
35 minutes	3- to 5-minute warmup	3–4
(25 minutes + 6–10 minutes warmup and cooldown)	3 minutes (brisk pace)	5–6
	1 minute (fast pace)	7–8
	Continue to do 3-minute brisk/1-minute fast intervals 5 more times (for a total of 6 intervals)	
	1 minute (brisk pace)	5–6
	3- to 5-minute cooldown	3–4

DAY 4 — POWER WALK

Total Workout Time	The Routine	Intensity
30 minutes	3- to 5-minute warmup	3–4
(20 minutes + 6–10 minutes warmup and cooldown)	20 minutes (brisk/fast pace)	6–7
	3- to 5-minute cooldown	3–4

DAY 5 — INTERVAL WALK

Total Workout Time	The Routine	Intensity
35 minutes	3- to 5-minute warmup	3–4
(25 minutes + 6–10 minutes warmup and cooldown)	3 minutes (brisk pace)	5–6
	1 minute (fast pace)	7–8
	Continue to do 3-minute brisk/1-minute fast intervals 5 more times (for a total of 6 intervals)	
	1 minute (brisk pace)	5–6
	3- to 5-minute cooldown	3–4

DAY 6 — RECUPERATIVE WALK

Total Workout Time	The Routine	Intensity
50 minutes	3- to 5-minute warmup	3–4
(40 minutes + 6–10 minutes warmup and cooldown)	40 minutes (easy pace)	4
	3- to 5-minute cooldown	3–4

DAY 7 — REST

Week Two

DAY

1

INTERVAL WALK

Total Workout Time	The Routine	Intensity
35 minutes	3- to 5-minute warmup	3–4
(25 minutes + 6–10 minutes warmup and cooldown)	3 minutes (brisk pace)	5–6
	1 minute (fast pace)	7–8
	Continue to do 3-minute brisk/1-minute fast intervals 5 more times (for a total of 6 intervals)	
	1 minute (brisk pace)	5–6
	3- to 5-minute cooldown	3–4

DAY

2

STEADY-STATE WALK

Total Workout Time	The Routine	Intensity
40 minutes	3- to 5-minute warmup	3–4
(30 minutes + 6–10 minutes warmup and cooldown)	30 minutes (moderate pace)	5
	3- to 5-minute cooldown	3–4

DAY

3

INTERVAL WALK

Total Workout Time	The Routine	Intensity
35 minutes	3- to 5-minute warmup	3–4
(25 minutes + 6–10 minutes warmup and cooldown)	3 minutes (brisk pace)	5–6
	1 minute (fast pace)	7–8
	Continue to do 3-minute brisk/1-minute fast intervals 5 more times (for a total of 6 intervals)	
	1 minute (brisk pace)	5–6
	3- to 5-minute cooldown	3–4

DAY 4 — POWER WALK

Total Workout Time	The Routine	Intensity
30 minutes	3- to 5-minute warmup	3–4
(20 minutes + 6–10 minutes warmup and cooldown)	20 minutes (brisk/fast pace)	6–7
	3- to 5-minute cooldown	3–4

DAY 5 — INTERVAL WALK

Total Workout Time	The Routine	Intensity
35 minutes	3- to 5-minute warmup	3–4
(25 minutes + 6–10 minutes warmup and cooldown)	3 minutes (brisk pace)	5–6
	1 minute (fast pace)	7–8
	Continue to do 3-minute brisk/1-minute fast intervals 5 more times (for a total of 6 intervals)	
	1 minute (brisk pace)	5–6
	3- to 5-minute cooldown	3–4

DAY 6 — RECUPERATIVE WALK

Total Workout Time	The Routine	Intensity
60 minutes	3- to 5-minute warmup	3–4
(50 minutes + 6–10 minutes warmup and cooldown)	50 minutes (easy pace)	4
	3- to 5-minute cooldown	3–4

DAY 7 — REST

Week Three

DAY 1 — INTERVAL WALK

Total Workout Time	The Routine	Intensity
40 minutes	3- to 5-minute warmup	3–4
(30 minutes + 6–10 minutes warmup and cooldown)	3 minutes (brisk pace)	5–6
	1 minute (fast pace)	7–8
	Continue to do 3-minute brisk/1-minute fast intervals 6 more times (for a total of 7 intervals)	
	2 minutes (brisk pace)	5–6
	3- to 5-minute cooldown	3–4

DAY 2 — STEADY-STATE WALK

Total Workout Time	The Routine	Intensity
55 minutes	3- to 5-minute warmup	3–4
(45 minutes + 6–10 minutes warmup and cooldown)	45 minutes (moderate pace)	5
	3- to 5-minute cooldown	3–4

DAY 3 — INTERVAL WALK

Total Workout Time	The Routine	Intensity
40 minutes	3- to 5-minute warmup	3–4
(30 minutes + 6–10 minutes warmup and cooldown)	3 minutes (brisk pace)	5–6
	1 minute (fast pace)	7–8
	Continue to do 3-minute brisk/1-minute fast intervals 6 more times (for a total of 7 intervals)	
	2 minutes (brisk pace)	5–6
	3- to 5-minute cooldown	3–4

DAY 4

POWER WALK

Total Workout Time	The Routine	Intensity
40 minutes	3- to 5-minute warmup	3–4
(30 minutes + 6–10 minutes warmup and cooldown)	30 minutes (brisk/fast pace)	6–7
	3- to 5-minute cooldown	3–4

DAY 5

INTERVAL WALK

Total Workout Time	The Routine	Intensity
40 minutes	3- to 5-minute warmup	3–4
(30 minutes + 6–10 minutes warmup and cooldown)	3 minutes (brisk pace)	5–6
	1 minute (fast pace)	7–8
	Continue to do 3-minute brisk/1-minute fast intervals 6 more times (for a total of 7 intervals)	
	2 minutes (brisk pace)	5–6
	3- to 5-minute cooldown	3–4

DAY 6

RECUPERATIVE WALK

Total Workout Time	The Routine	Intensity
70 minutes	3- to 5-minute warmup	3–4
(60 minutes + 6–10 minutes warmup and cooldown)	60 minutes (easy pace)	4
	3- to 5-minute cooldown	3–4

DAY 7

REST

Week Four

INTERVAL WALK

1

Total Workout Time	The Routine	Intensity
40 minutes	3- to 5-minute warmup	3–4
(30 minutes + 6–10 minutes warmup and cooldown)	3 minutes (brisk pace)	5–6
	1 minute (fast pace)	7–8
	Continue to do 3-minute brisk/1-minute fast intervals 6 more times (for a total of 7 intervals)	
	2 minutes (brisk pace)	5–6
	3- to 5-minute cooldown	3–4

DAY

2

STEADY-STATE WALK

Total Workout Time	The Routine	Intensity
55 minutes	3- to 5-minute warmup	3–4
(45 minutes + 6–10 minutes warmup and cooldown)	45 minutes (moderate pace)	5
	3- to 5-minute cooldown	3–4

DAY

3

INTERVAL WALK

Total Workout Time	The Routine	Intensity
40 minutes	3- to 5-minute warmup	3–4
(30 minutes + 6–10 minutes warmup and cooldown)	3 minutes (brisk pace)	5–6
	1 minute (fast pace)	7–8
	Continue to do 3-minute brisk/1-minute fast intervals 6 more times (for a total of 7 intervals)	
	2 minutes (brisk pace)	5–6
	3- to 5-minute cooldown	3–4

DAY 4 — POWER WALK

Total Workout Time	The Routine	Intensity
40 minutes	3- to 5-minute warmup	3–4
(30 minutes + 6–10 minutes warmup and cooldown)	30 minutes (brisk/fast pace)	6–7
	3- to 5-minute cooldown	3–4

DAY 5 — INTERVAL WALK

Total Workout Time	The Routine	Intensity
40 minutes	3- to 5-minute warmup	3–4
(30 minutes + 6–10 minutes warmup and cooldown)	3 minutes (brisk pace)	5–6
	1 minute (fast pace)	7–8
	Continue to do 3-minute brisk/1-minute fast intervals 6 more times (for a total of 7 intervals)	
	2 minutes (brisk pace)	5–6
	3- to 5-minute cooldown	3–4

DAY 6 — RECUPERATIVE WALK

Total Workout Time	The Routine	Intensity
80 minutes	3- to 5-minute warmup	3–4
(70 minutes + 6–10 minutes warmup and cooldown)	70 minutes (easy pace)	4
	3- to 5-minute cooldown	3–4

DAY 7 — REST

Week Five

INTERVAL WALK

1

Total Workout Time	The Routine	Intensity
45 minutes	3- to 5-minute warmup	3–4
(35 minutes + 6–10 minutes warmup and cooldown)	3 minutes (brisk pace)	5–6
	1 minute (fast pace)	7–8
	Continue to do 3-minute brisk/1-minute fast intervals 7 more times (for a total of 8 intervals)	
	3 minutes (brisk pace)	5–6
	3- to 5-minute cooldown	3–4

DAY

STEADY-STATE WALK

2

Total Workout Time	The Routine	Intensity
70 minutes	3- to 5-minute warmup	3–4
(60 minutes + 6–10 minutes warmup and cooldown)	60 minutes (moderate pace)	5
	3- to 5-minute cooldown	3–4

DAY

INTERVAL WALK

3

Total Workout Time	The Routine	Intensity
45 minutes	3- to 5-minute warmup	3–4
(35 minutes + 6–10 minutes warmup and cooldown)	3 minutes (brisk pace)	5–6
	1 minute (fast pace)	7–8
	Continue to do 3-minute brisk/1-minute fast intervals 7 more times (for a total of 8 intervals)	
	3 minutes (brisk pace)	5–6
	3- to 5-minute cooldown	3–4

POWER WALK

4

Total Workout Time	The Routine	Intensity
50 minutes	3- to 5-minute warmup	3–4
(40 minutes + 6–10 minutes warmup and cooldown)	40 minutes (brisk/fast pace)	6–7
	3- to 5-minute cooldown	3–4

DAY

INTERVAL WALK

5

Total Workout Time	The Routine	Intensity
45 minutes	3- to 5-minute warmup	3–4
(35 minutes + 6–10 minutes warmup and cooldown)	3 minutes (brisk pace)	5–6
	1 minute (fast pace)	7–8
	Continue to do 3-minute brisk/1-minute fast intervals 7 more times (for a total of 8 intervals)	
	3 minutes (brisk pace)	5–6
	3- to 5-minute cooldown	3–4

DAY

RECUPERATIVE WALK

6

Total Workout Time	The Routine	Intensity
90 minutes	3- to 5-minute warmup	3–4
(80 minutes + 6–10 minutes warmup and cooldown)	80 minutes (easy pace)	4
	3- to 5-minute cooldown	3–4

DAY   ## REST

7

Week Six

DAY 1 — INTERVAL WALK

Total Workout Time	The Routine	Intensity
45 minutes	3- to 5-minute warmup	3–4
(35 minutes + 6–10 minutes warmup and cooldown)	3 minutes (brisk pace)	5–6
	1 minute (fast pace)	7–8
	Continue to do 3-minute brisk/1-minute fast intervals 7 more times (for a total of 8 intervals)	
	3 minutes (brisk pace)	5–6
	3- to 5-minute cooldown	3–4

DAY 2 — STEADY-STATE WALK

Total Workout Time	The Routine	Intensity
70 minutes	3- to 5-minute warmup	3–4
(60 minutes + 6–10 minutes warmup and cooldown)	60 minutes (moderate pace)	5
	3- to 5-minute cooldown	3–4

DAY 3 — INTERVAL WALK

Total Workout Time	The Routine	Intensity
45 minutes	3- to 5-minute warmup	3–4
(35 minutes + 6–10 minutes warmup and cooldown)	3 minutes (brisk pace)	5–6
	1 minute (fast pace)	7–8
	Continue to do 3-minute brisk/1-minute fast intervals 7 more times (for a total of 8 intervals)	
	3 minutes (brisk pace)	5–6
	3- to 5-minute cooldown	3–4

DAY 4 — POWER WALK

Total Workout Time	The Routine	Intensity
50 minutes	3- to 5-minute warmup	3–4
(40 minutes + 6–10 minutes warmup and cooldown)	40 minutes (brisk/fast pace)	6–7
	3- to 5-minute cooldown	3–4

DAY 5 — INTERVAL WALK

Total Workout Time	The Routine	Intensity
45 minutes	3- to 5-minute warmup	3–4
(35 minutes + 6–10 minutes warmup and cooldown)	3 minutes (brisk pace)	5–6
	1 minute (fast pace)	7–8
	Continue to do 3-minute brisk/1-minute fast intervals 7 more times (for a total of 8 intervals)	
	3 minutes (brisk pace)	5–6
	3- to 5-minute cooldown	3–4

DAY 6 — RECUPERATIVE WALK

Total Workout Time	The Routine	Intensity
100 minutes	3- to 5-minute warmup	3–4
(90 minutes + 6–10 minutes warmup and cooldown)	90 minutes (easy pace)	4
	3- to 5-minute cooldown	3–4

DAY 7 — REST

THE STRENGTH-TRAINING WORKOUT

The strength-training portion of the Salt Solution Weight-Loss Workout is specifically crafted to work all of your muscles from head to toe in the shortest amount of time. Lift weights only 2 to 3 days a week in order to develop lean muscle, build core strength, and elevate your metabolism. Increasing your overall lean muscle mass raises your resting metabolic rate—the amount of calories your body burns all day long. Targeting your larger muscles—your quadriceps, hamstrings, gluteal muscles, back, and chest—plays a big part in helping you burn the most calories. This routine does just that, so you build more muscle—and burn more calories, even when you're at rest, at work, or fast asleep in bed.

Strength-Training Basics

If you've never used dumbbells before—or it's been a while since you've performed any strength-training exercises—you'll need to know a few weight-lifting basics to start.

ADJUSTING THE PROGRAM TO YOUR FITNESS LEVEL

WITH EVERY STRENGTH-TRAINING EXERCISE

• As you follow all 6 weeks of the Salt Solution Weight-Loss Workout, you'll gradually begin to do more and more sets of the exercises. However, if the number of sets is too much for you—either because of time or intensity—then simply do one less set per exercise. (For example, if you're asked to do two sets of an exercise, try doing one set instead.)

• In between each exercise, the Salt Solution Weight-Loss Workout instructs you to rest for a certain number of seconds to allow your muscles to recover. However, if the pace of the workout feels too intense, try resting an additional 15 to 30 seconds between each set to catch your breath.

WEIGHT-LIFTING GLOSSARY

Rep is short for repetition, which means performing an exercise once.

Set is a specific number of reps (8, 10, 12, or 15, for example).

So, if you're asked to perform two sets of 15 reps of an exercise, that means you'll do that exercise 15 times (that's one set), then perform the exercise 15 times again, for a second set. (You'll be instructed how long to rest in between each set in each workout.)

A few other rules to keep in mind:

- If you have never done any strength-training exercises, haven't exercised in more than 6 months, or have any preexisting knee problems, start with the Make It Easier option. You can also perform the Make It Easier option if the original exercise is too difficult. (Similarly, if the original exercise is not challenging enough, perform the Make It Harder option.)

- Before you start the program, always warm up your muscles first by walking at an easy pace (3–4 RPE) for 4 to 5 minutes.

- Do each exercise in the exact numerical order listed in the program.

- For each exercise, try to maintain a comfortable pace that allows you to raise the weight in 2 seconds and lower it in 2 seconds. Rushing through each exercise any faster will only increase your risk of injury.

- Each day, you'll follow the instructions in the chart on page 366 for how many sets/reps to do of each exercise (as well as how many seconds to rest between each set). Do the required number of sets for each exercise *before* moving on to the next exercise.

HOW MUCH WEIGHT SHOULD YOU USE?

For each exercise, you want to start with a moderate weight that lets you perform the required amount of repetitions. If you can easily do more reps than recommended, you need to increase the amount of weight you're lifting. If you can't do at least eight reps, then the weight is too heavy; either choose a lighter weight or try the easier version of the exercise. *Note:* Because some muscles are bigger than others, you'll need to use heavier dumbbells for exercises that target your chest, back, legs, and butt. For smaller muscles, like your arms and shoulders, you'll probably want to choose lighter dumbbells.

Our recommendation for maximum results: A few days before you plan to start the program, try giving each exercise a test run and do a sample set of each move. If you're a

THE 6-WEEK STRENGTH-TRAINING WORKOUT SCHEDULES

Week	Day 1	Day 2	Day 3
1	OFF	2 sets; 15 reps; 45–60 seconds rest	OFF
2	OFF	2 sets; 12 reps; 30–45 seconds rest	OFF
3	2 sets; 15 reps; 45–60 seconds rest	OFF	2 sets; 12 reps; 30–45 seconds rest
4	2 sets; 15 reps; 45–60 seconds rest	OFF	2 sets; 12 reps; 30–45 seconds rest
5	3 sets; 15 reps; 45–60 seconds rest	OFF	3 sets; 12 reps; 30–45 seconds rest
6	3 sets; 15 reps; 45–60 seconds rest	OFF	3 sets; 12 reps; 30–45 seconds rest

beginner, start by using 3- to 5 pound dumbbells, just to be safe. Advanced exercisers can start with 5- to 8-pound dumbbells. Use the tips above to gauge if the weight you're using is too light or too heavy, and assess whether you need to adjust the exercise by either using the Make It Easier or Make It Harder variations. This way, you'll be more likely to start the program on Day One using the right amount of weight—and the variation of each exercise—that works best for you.

Final safety note: If you think that using the heaviest weight you can handle will yield even more results, please don't take that risk. Choosing weights that are too heavy for you to handle will only increase your risk of injury, which could cause you to quit the program midway before it has a chance to work with the diet. Instead, be smart and pick a weight that follows the above recommendations.

Day 4	Day 5	Day 6	Day 7
OFF	2 sets; 15 reps; 45–60 seconds rest	OFF	OFF
OFF	2 sets; 12 reps; 30–45 seconds rest	OFF	OFF
OFF	2 sets; 10 reps; 15–30 seconds rest	OFF	OFF
OFF	2 sets; 10 reps; 15–30 seconds rest	OFF	OFF
OFF	3 sets; 10 reps; 15–30 seconds rest	OFF	OFF
OFF	3 sets; 10 reps; 15–30 seconds rest	OFF	OFF

1. Squat Sweep

Works the quadriceps, hamstrings, inner thighs, and glutes

START POSITION: Stand with your feet shoulder-width apart holding a dumbbell in each hand. Curl the weights up until the ends rest on the front of your shoulders.

A. Keeping your back straight, slowly bend your hips and sit back until your thighs are almost parallel to the floor.

B. As you stand back up, lift your left leg straight out to your side as if you were going to step out—shoot for raising your foot about 6 inches off the floor, but avoid raising your leg any higher than hip height. Pause for 1 second, then return your foot to the floor so you're back in the start position. Pause for 1 second.

C. Repeat the exercise, this time by lifting your right leg out to the side.

D. Alternate legs between every squat for the entire set.

MAKE IT EASIER:
Perform the exercise without weights, or try squatting down about half the distance during each repetition.

MAKE IT HARDER:
Instead of pausing for 1 second in each position, pause for 2, so that you are doing the entire exercise twice as slowly.

2. Double Chest Press + Fly

Works the chest, shoulders, and triceps

START POSITION: Lie face up on the floor (or a bench) holding a light dumbbell in each hand, knees bent, feet flat on the floor. Raise your arms straight above your chest, with your palms facing each other.

A. Bend your elbows out to your sides and slowly lower the weights until your upper arms touch the floor (Your palms should stay facing each other as you go.)

B. Press the weights back up into the start position, then repeat the move once more. This is the chest press.

C. Next, slowly sweep your arms out to your sides and down as far as you can. Reverse the motion by sweeping your arms back up in front of you (as if you're hugging someone) until they're back in the start position. This is the fly. Alternate between presses and fly for the recommended amount of repetitions.

MAKE IT EASIER: Once your upper arms touch the floor, rest for 1 second before pushing the weights back into the start position.

MAKE IT HARDER: Lie on a stability ball with your head, shoulders, and upper back supported by the ball; your knees should be bent and your feet flat on the floor. Your body should be one straight line from your head to your knees.

3. Lunge

Works the quadriceps, hamstrings, and glutes

START POSITION: Stand straight with a dumbbell in each hand and your arms hanging straight down at your sides, palms facing in.

A. Take a big step forward with your left foot and lower your body until your left thigh is almost parallel to the floor. (Your right leg should be extended behind you with only the ball of your right foot on the floor.)

B. Reverse the motion by pressing yourself back into the start position, then repeat the exercise by stepping forward with your right foot. Alternate between stepping forward with your left and right feet throughout the set.

MAKE IT EASIER: Do the exercise without any weights (hands on hips), or try a reverse lunge instead. Stand with your feet together, then step back about 2 to 3 feet with your right foot. Bend your left knee and slowly lower yourself down. (Your left knee should stay directly over your ankle.) Stop right before your right knee touches the floor, then push off with your right foot to get back into the start position. Repeat the move with your left leg.

MAKE IT HARDER: Try turning the movement into a traveling lunge. Instead of stepping back into the start position, keep your front foot planted, then bring the leg that's behind you forward and raise your knee up in front of you. (You'll be balancing on just your front leg.) Plant your foot back down so your feet are even once more.

4. Unilateral Bent-Over Row

Works the latissimus dorsi, the rhomboids, lower back, and core

START POSITION: Stand holding a light dumbbell in each hand with an overhand grip, knees slightly bent. Bend forward at the hips until your torso is almost parallel to the floor—your arms should be hanging straight beneath you, palms facing in towards each other.

A. Keeping your elbows close to your body, pull the weight in your left hand up to the side of your chest. (Your right arm will stay straight.)

B. Lower the weight in your left hand back down as you simultaneously pull the weight in your right hand up to your side. Continue alternating back and forth for the entire set.

MAKE IT EASIER: Try doing the exercise one arm at a time. To support your lower back, place one hand on a sturdy chair, then bend forward until your torso is at a 45-degree angle to the floor. Do the required repetitions for one arm, then switch positions to work your other arm.

MAKE IT HARDER: Every 1 or 2 repetitions, pull both weights up along your sides, then push your heels into the floor and straighten back up into a standing position—keeping the weights locked into your sides as you go. Immediately reverse the motion—bending forward at the waist first, then lowering the weights back down by straightening your arms.

5. Deadlift Curl Press

Works the trapezius, lower back, glutes, hamstrings, shoulders, triceps, and biceps

START POSITION:
Stand with your feet spaced 6 to 8 inches apart with a dumbbell placed along the outside of each foot. Bend your knees and grab the dumbbells so that your palms face in towards each other. Before you begin the exercise, make sure that your back and shoulders are straight (not rounded), and your head is up.

A. Keeping your head and back straight, slowly stand up until your legs are straight—knees unlocked—keeping the dumbbells close to your body as you lift.

B. Without moving your upper arms, bend your elbows and curl the weights up to the front of your shoulders, palms facing each other.

C. Press the weights up over your head until your arms are straight, elbows unlocked, palms facing each other. Reverse the entire exercise until you're back in the start position.

MAKE IT EASIER: Instead of starting the exercise with the weights on the floor, place them on a pair of sturdy boxes to start. This will prevent you from having to lower yourself down as far, which makes the move much simpler to perform.

MAKE IT HARDER: Try pausing a few times during the exercise—this will keep your muscles under a longer duration of tension, so you utilize even more muscle fibers. During each repetition:

- Pause for 1 second during the deadlift portion (when your thighs are at a 45-degree angle as you rise up).
- Pause for 1 second during the curl portion (when your forearms are parallel to the floor).
- Pause for 1 second during the pressing portion (when your arms are bent at 90-degree angles).

6. Bicycle Crunch

Works the abdominal muscles

START POSITION: Lie face-up on the floor with your knees bent, feet flat on the floor. Lightly cup your hands over your ears, letting your elbows point out to the sides.

A. Draw your left knee toward your chest while simultaneously extending your right leg. Simultaneously curl your torso up and twist to the left, so that your right elbow and left knee touch (or at least come close).

B. Repeat the exercise, this time pulling your right knee in as you curl and twist your torso to the right—touching your left elbow to your right knee. Alternate back and forth from side to side for the entire exercise, keeping your feet off the floor the entire time.

MAKE IT EASIER: Keep your knees bent and feet on the floor, then only raise one knee at a time, leaving the opposite foot on the floor.

MAKE IT HARDER: Try pausing for 1 to 2 seconds each time your elbow meets your knee—or better yet, pulse by doing 1 or 2 mini-reps (bringing your knee and elbow together, then apart by an inch or so, then back together again). Either way will keep your abs contracted for a longer period of time.

7. Plank

Works the core muscles

START POSITION: Get in a pushup position—legs extended behind you, feet shoulder-width apart, with your weight on your toes. Rest yourself on your forearms so that your arms are at 90-degree angles.

A. Keeping your head and back straight, hold this position for the prescribed amount of time. (For Week One, hold for 30 seconds; for each additional week, add between 5 to 10 seconds, depending on your strength level.)

MAKE IT EASIER: Bend your legs so that you're resting on one knee (your other leg stays extended) or both knees.

MAKE IT HARDER: Instead of staying in place, keep your arms and feet in place, then slowly twist and lower your left hip towards the floor. Repeat by twisting the opposite way and lowering your right hip. Alternate back and forth for the entire duration.

APPENDIX B

SAMPLE SHAKE THE SALT MENUS

During the 4-Week Shake the Salt Meal Plan you will eat four 300-calorie meals per day plus a daily Mineral Boost Juice. You can choose from any of the recipes in this cookbook or in *The Salt Solution*, or any of the meals from the 2-Week Salt Solution Cleanse. They all have the right number of calories and the right amount of sodium. (Dessert and sweet snack recipes and meals should be limited to no more than one per day as they're not as nutritious as the breakfast, lunch, dinner, and savory snack options.)

All of the Salt Solution meals provide around the same number of calories and have a balanced nutritional profile, so you can mix and match them as you please. Just be sure to have a meal or juice every 4 to 5 hours in order to keep your body fueled and your blood sugar levels in check, and to prevent overeating. While you may repeat meals that you find most enjoyable, variety is strongly encouraged.

We've given you plenty of options, so that you can pick just the meals that suit your tastes and your lifestyle. Vegetarian? Cooking for a family (including picky children)? Like to entertain? On the run and don't have time to prepare elaborate meals? We've provided you with the following 4 sample weeks of Shake the Salt menus so that you can see different ways in which you might pull the recipes together into a daily eating plan that works for you.

While the Cleanse meals are all single servings, most of the Salt Solution recipes yield more than one portion. If you are also cooking for someone who is not on the diet, you can just increase the size of their portions. If you have any leftovers, you can repeat a meal the next day, or simply freeze them for later use.

VEGETARIAN 1-WEEK MENU

Reminder: While the Cleanse meals (marked with an asterisk) are all single servings, most of the Salt Solution recipes yield more than one portion. If you are also cooking for someone who is not on the diet, you can just increase the size of their portions. If you have any leftovers, you can repeat a meal the next day, or simply freeze them for later use.

DAY
1

MINERAL BOOST JUICE (6:30 A.M.)

Mango-Avocado Smoothie (page 40)

Per serving: 304 calories, 145 mg sodium

MEAL 1: BREAKFAST (8:30 A.M.)

Arugula Omelet (page 76)

Per serving: 274 calories, 327 mg sodium

Note: Feel free to substitute spinach (a Salt Solution Star) for the arugula in this omelet!

MEAL 2: LUNCH (12:00 P.M.)

Creamy Tomato and Tofu Soup (page 111)

Served with 1 medium apple and ½ tablespoon unsalted peanut butter

Per serving: 285 calories, 291 mg sodium

MEAL 3: DINNER (5:30 P.M.)

Quinoa Pilaf with White Beans and Almonds (page 256)

Per serving: 291 calories, 273 mg sodium

Note: High in protein and fiber, quinoa is a great grain choice for vegetarian meals.

MEAL 4: DESSERT (7:30 P.M.)

Orange-Yogurt Pops* (page 48)

Per serving: 293 calories, 97 mg sodium

DAY 2

MEAL 1: BREAKFAST (8:00 A.M.)

Three-Grain Ricotta Pancakes
(page 83)

Per serving: 292 calories, 277 mg sodium

MINERAL BOOST JUICE (10:00 A.M.)

Almond, Blueberry, and Banana
Smoothie (page 40)

Per serving: 323 calories, 300 mg sodium

MEAL 2: LUNCH (1:00 P.M.)

Sweet Potato Burgers (page 245)

Per serving: 301 calories, 273 mg sodium

MEAL 3: SNACK (4:00 P.M.)

Berry Kebabs* (page 46)

Per serving: 305 calories, 134 mg sodium

Note: You can mix and match your kebabs, as long as you end up with about 3 cups of berries. Can't find blackberries at the grocery store? Just use extra strawberries or raspberries. Crazy for strawberries? Use more of these.

MEAL 4: DINNER (7:00 P.M.)

Eggplant Parmesan* (page 42)

Per serving: 290 calories, 104 mg sodium

DAY 3

MEAL 1: BREAKFAST (9:00 A.M.)

Soy Oatmeal* (page 48)

Per serving: 299 calories, 92 mg sodium

MEAL 2: LUNCH (12:00 P.M.)

Cucumber, Cantaloupe, and Tomato
Salad (page 128)

Per serving: 289 calories, 305 mg sodium

MINERAL BOOST JUICE (3:00 P.M.)

Banana-Spinach Smoothie (page 40)

Per serving: 319 calories, 174 mg sodium

MEAL 3: DINNER (6:30 P.M.)

Cajun Rice and Beans (page 253)

Served with ¾ cup grapes

Per serving: 318 calories, 192 mg sodium

Note: You can substitute black beans or white beans for the kidney beans; beans are loaded with fiber and protein.

MEAL 4: DESSERT (8:00 P.M.)

Brazil Nut Brownies (page 309)

Served with ½ cup soymilk

Per serving: 291 calories, 205 mg sodium

DAY

4

MINERAL BOOST JUICE (6:30 A.M.)

Orange-Banana Cream Smoothie
(page 41)

Per serving: 293 calories, 65 mg sodium

MEAL 1: BREAKFAST (9:30 A.M.)

Baked Apples with Cranberries and
Yogurt (page 98)

Per serving: 282 calories, 24 mg sodium

MEAL 2: LUNCH (1:30 P.M.)

Edamame Salad* (page 46)

Per serving: 283 calories, 223 mg sodium

*Note: Edamame (young soybeans), a Salt Solution
Star, are loaded with protein, fiber, and nutrients,
and are a stellar vegetarian choice.*

MEAL 3: SNACK (4:00 P.M.)

White Bean Hummus* (page 44)

Per serving: 298 calories, 317 mg sodium

MEAL 4: DINNER (7:00 P.M.)

Thai Tofu (page 259)

Per serving: 297 calories, 282 mg sodium

*Note: Can't find bok choy at the supermarket?
Substitute napa or savoy cabbage instead.*

DAY

5

MEAL 1: BREAKFAST (8:30 A.M.)

Good Morning Muffins (page 100)

Served with 1 cup soymilk

Per serving: 287 calories, 347 mg sodium

MEAL 2: LUNCH (12:00 P.M.)

Mushroom and Zucchini Pizzas
(page 141)

Per serving: 294 calories, 321 mg sodium

*Note: Load up your pizza with additional veggies, if
desired. Try red bell peppers, spinach, or fresh basil.*

MINERAL BOOST JUICE (3:00 P.M.)

Berry-Mango Smoothie (page 40)

Per serving: 321 calories, 191 mg sodium

MEAL 3: DINNER (6:00 P.M.)

Meatless Sloppy Joes (page 239)

Served with 1 medium apple

Per serving: 311 calories, 293 mg sodium

*Note: The tofu in these meatless sandwiches is an
excellent source of vegetarian protein.*

MEAL 4: DESSERT (8:00 P.M.)

Chocolate Fondue* (page 45)

Per serving: 295 calories, 36 mg sodium

DAY 6

MINERAL BOOST JUICE (6:30 A.M.)

Almond, Blueberry, and Banana
Smoothie (page 40)

Per serving: 323 calories, 300 mg sodium

MEAL 1: BREAKFAST (9:30 A.M.)

Easy Veggie Omelet (page 73)

Per serving: 261 calories, 303 mg sodium

MEAL 2: LUNCH (2:30 P.M.)

Greens and Couscous Salad* (page 48)

Per serving: 301 calories, 319 mg sodium

MEAL 3: DINNER (6:30 P.M.)

Veggie Gazpacho with Red Lentils
(page 114)

Per serving: 290 calories, 264 mg sodium

*Note: Go color crazy—try yellow or orange lentils
instead of the red.*

MEAL 4: SNACK (8:30 P.M.)

Spicy Roast Pumpkin Seed Snack
Mix (page 296)

Served with 1 small banana and 20 bite-size
unsalted pretzels

Per serving: 310 calories, 147 mg sodium

DAY 7

MEAL 1: BREAKFAST (8:00 A.M.)

Hot Couscous Bowl* (page 47)

Per serving: 304 calories, 276 mg sodium

MEAL 2: LUNCH (12:00 P.M.)

Stir-Fried Broccoli and Peppers with
Ginger and Sesame (page 258)

Per serving: 285 calories, 295 mg sodium

MEAL 3: SNACK (3:00 P.M.)

Berry Kebabs* (page 46)

Per serving: 305 calories, 134 mg sodium

MINERAL BOOST JUICE (5:30 P.M.)

Peanut Butter Smoothie (page 41)

Per serving: 325 calories, 210 mg sodium

MEAL 4: DINNER (7:30 P.M.)

Polenta Lasagna (page 242)

Per serving: 307 calories, 299 mg sodium

*Note: Feel free to substitute kale for the collard
greens.*

FAMILY STYLE 1-WEEK MENU

Reminder: While the Cleanse meals (marked with an asterisk) are all single servings, most of the Salt Solution recipes yield more than one portion. If you are cooking for family members who are not on the diet, you can just increase the size of their portions.

DAY

1

MEAL 1: BREAKFAST (7:00 A.M.)

French Toast with Raspberries and Almonds (page 85)

Per serving: 282 calories, 307 mg sodium

Note: You can substitute any fruit and nuts for the raspberries and almonds—ask your spouse or the kids what they prefer.

MINERAL BOOST JUICE (10:00 A.M.)

Almond, Blueberry, and Banana Smoothie (page 40)

Per serving: 323 calories, 300 mg sodium

Note: Double the smoothie recipe and encourage your family to taste and share your Mineral Boost Juice. The Miracle Minerals are good for them, too!

MEAL 2: LUNCH (1:00 P.M.)

Turkey Sloppy Joes (page 134)

Per serving: 268 calories, 276 mg sodium

Note: Children and adults alike will love these comforting sandwiches. Serve with lots of kid-friendly freebie raw veggies (see page 37), like carrots and celery.

MEAL 3: SNACK (4:00 P.M.)

Berry Kebabs* (page 46)

Per serving: 305 calories, 134 mg sodium

Note: Involving the family with food preparation is a surefire way to get them excited about trying new foods and recipes, and these fun-to-make snacks are bound to be a hit. The family can skewer not just berries, but any of their favorite fruits cut into bite-size pieces.

MEAL 4: DINNER (7:00 P.M.)

Shepherd's Pie (page 159)

Per serving: 278 calories, 246 mg sodium

Note: The kids will never guess there are nutritious turnips hiding in the potato topping! Serve this family-style with a large salad.

DAY
2

MEAL 1: BREAKFAST (8:30 A.M.)

Banana-Bran Muffins (page 99)

Served with 1 cup fat-free milk

Per serving: 258 calories, 309 mg sodium

MEAL 2: LUNCH (1:00 P.M.)

Curried Tuna and Apple Salad Sandwich (page 136)

Per serving: 298 calories, 228 mg sodium

Note: Whip up a side of plain tuna salad for the kids, but encourage them to taste your curried tuna salad as well. Encouraging children to taste new flavors (like the curry tuna dish) helps them develop their palates.

MINERAL BOOST JUICE (3:00 P.M.)

Berry-Mango Smoothie (page 40)

Per serving: 321 calories, 191 mg sodium

MEAL 3: DINNER (6:00 P.M.)

Mushroom and Zucchini Pizzas (page 141)

Per serving: 294 calories, 321 mg sodium

Note: Throw a pizza party in your kitchen! Offer a variety of good-for-you toppings buffet-style on the counter. Let each family member customize his own pie, then just pop the pizzas in the oven!

MEAL 4: DESSERT (8:00 P.M.)

Nutty Oatmeal Cookies (page 334)

Per serving: 254 calories, 123 mg sodium

Note: The kids can have these immediately following dinner.

MINERAL BOOST JUICE (6:30 A.M.)

Banana-Spinach Smoothie (page 40)

Per serving: 319 calories, 174 mg sodium

Note: Children (of a certain age!) will love the look of these green smoothies. They will also be surprised at how yummy they taste! Prepare a larger portion and encourage them to give these "green monster" (as named by my sister's niece) smoothies a whirl.

MEAL 1: BREAKFAST (8:30 A.M.)

Yogurt Parfait with Berries* (page 43)

Per serving: 282 calories, 191 mg sodium

MEAL 2: LUNCH (1:30 P.M.)

Chicken Chili Verde (page 197)

Per serving: 300 calories, 281 mg sodium

Note: To reduce the heat, substitute a green bell pepper and half of a seeded chopped jalapeño pepper for the poblano.

MEAL 3: SNACK (4:00 P.M.)

PB&J Graham* (page 42)

Per serving: 283 calories, 195 mg sodium

Note: Nothing says kid-friendly like peanut butter and jelly (or in this case jam)!

MEAL 4: DINNER (7:00 P.M.)

Fish and Chips (page 220)

Per serving: 302 calories, 319 mg sodium

Note: Chips (a.k.a. fries) are sure to be a crowd pleaser.

DAY
4

MEAL 1: BREAKFAST (7:30 A.M.)

Waffle Sandwich with Banana and Strawberries (page 86)

Per serving: 270 calories, 260 mg sodium

MINERAL BOOST JUICE (10:30 A.M.)

Peanut Butter Smoothie (page 41)

Per serving: 325 calories, 210 mg sodium

MEAL 2: LUNCH (12:00 P.M.)

Quinoa and Chicken Salad (page 119)

Per serving: 318 calories, 270 mg sodium

Note: To make this salad more family-friendly, deconstruct the dish and serve the chicken, lima beans, peppers, and oranges separately for the kids or picky eaters.

MEAL 3: SNACK (3:30 P.M.)

Orange-Yogurt Pops* (page 48)

Per serving: 293 calories, 97 mg sodium

MEAL 4: DINNER (6:30 P.M.)

Spaghetti and Meatballs (page 156)

Per serving: 306 calories, 280 mg sodium

Note: Serve this family favorite with a side of steamed freebie veggies (see page 37).

DAY
5

MEAL 1: BREAKFAST (8:00 A.M.)

Cranberries-on-a-Banana* (page 44)

Per serving: 289 calories, 6 mg sodium

Note: Place the ingredients (bananas, peanut butter, and cranberries) of this simple morning meal in the middle of the table, and let the kids have fun creating their own breakfasts.

MEAL 2: LUNCH (11:30 P.M.)

Mushroom-Cheddar Quesadillas (page 284)

Served with a salad made from 2 cups mixed greens, 5 cherry tomatoes, 1 teaspoon olive oil, and 1 teaspoon fresh lemon juice

Per serving: 322 calories, 313 mg sodium

Note: You can customize each quesadilla to suit individual tastes.

MINERAL BOOST JUICE (3:00 P.M.)

Berry-Mango Smoothie (page 40)

Per serving: 321 calories, 191 mg sodium

MEAL 3: DINNER (6:00 P.M.)

Halibut en Papillote with Asparagus, Onions, and Lemon (page 215)

Per serving: 255 calories, 240 mg sodium

Note: The straightforward flavors of this simple dish make this a family-friendly go-to dish.

MEAL 4: DESSERT (8:00 P.M.)

Chocolate Fondue* (page 45)

Per serving: 295 calories, 36 mg sodium

Note: Dipping fruit into chocolate is a fun way to get your nutrients. Any bite-size fruit works, so serve this family-style with lots of fruits for people to pick and dip.

DAY

6

MEAL 1: BREAKFAST (7:00 A.M.)

Easy Veggie Omelet (page 73)

Per serving: 261 calories, 303 mg sodium

Note: You can customize each omelet to suit individual tastes.

MINERAL BOOST JUICE (10:30 A.M.)

Orange-Banana Cream Smoothie (page 41)

Per serving: 293 calories, 65 mg sodium

MEAL 2: LUNCH (12:30 P.M.)

Chicken Tacos with Cilantro Cream (page 198)

Per serving: 290 calories, 260 mg sodium

Note: Serve the tacos with the cilantro cream sauce on the side, and with mounds of lettuce and tomatoes.

MEAL 3: SNACK (4:00 P.M.)

Mini Pizza* (page 43)

Per serving: 286 calories, 228 mg sodium

MEAL 4: DINNER (7:00 P.M.)

Meatloaf with Mushroom Gravy (page 152)

Served with a salad made from 2 cups spinach, 1 teaspoon olive oil, and 1 teaspoon fresh lemon juice

Per serving: 294 calories, 333 mg sodium

Note: Serve the meatloaf family-style with the gravy on the side.

391

DAY
7

MINERAL BOOST JUICE (7:00 A.M.)

Mango-Avocado Smoothie (page 40)

Per serving: 304 calories, 145 mg sodium

MEAL 1: BREAKFAST (9:00 A.M.)

Fruit Bowls with Ricotta Cream
(page 95)

Served with 1 hard-cooked egg seasoned with chopped chives

Per serving: 292 calories, 182 mg sodium

MEAL 2: LUNCH (1:00 P.M.)

Greek Chicken Salad (page 122)

Per serving: 286 calories, 266 mg sodium

Note: To make this salad kid-friendly, serve the main components (the chicken, edamame, and cucumber) separately, without the dressing.

MEAL 3: DINNER (5:30 P.M.)

Salmon with Pesto (page 210)

Per serving: 306 calories, 217 mg sodium

Note: Serve the pesto on the side and with a family-style salad.

MEAL 4: DESSERT (7:00 P.M.)

Oreo Delight (page 337)

Per serving: 295 calories, 69 mg sodium

ON-THE-RUN 1-WEEK MENU

Reminder: While the Cleanse meals (marked with an asterisk) are all single servings, most of the Salt Solution recipes yield more than one portion. This is perfect for days or weeks that you're on the run: You can cook once and enjoy leftovers for another meal. Also, you can easily make triple or quadruple portions of all the Mineral Boost Juices. Store extra servings in the fridge for up to 3 days. Shake before serving.

DAY
1

MINERAL BOOST JUICE (8:00 A.M.)

Berry-Mango Smoothie (page 40)

Per serving: 321 calories, 191 mg sodium

MEAL 1: LUNCH (12:00 P.M.)

One cup ready-made soup

(like Imagine Light in Sodium Organic Creamy Red Bliss Potato & Roasted Garlic Soup; or see page 63 for other options)

Served with a banana and 2 tablespoons unsalted almonds

Per serving: 293 calories, 221 mg sodium

MEAL 2: SNACK (4:00 P.M.)

White Bean Hummus* (page 44)

Per serving: 298 calories, 317 mg sodium

Note: This hummus can be made a day or two ahead and kept in the fridge. Make 2 servings of this hummus at once, store half in the fridge, and enjoy this snack on Day 3 as well.

MEAL 3: DINNER (7:00 P.M.)

Savory Pot Roast (page 146)

Per serving: 323 calories, 300 mg sodium

Note: A slow cooker makes this dinner a snap—do 15 minutes of prep in the morning, and dinner's waiting for you at the end of a long day. Enjoy leftovers for lunch on Day 5 of this week!

MEAL 4: DESSERT (9:00 P.M.)

Strawberry Yogurt Cup (page 327)

Per serving: 254 calories, 146 mg sodium

DAY
2

MEAL 1: BREAKFAST (7:00 A.M.)

Breakfast Burritos (page 81)

Per serving: 255 calories, 322 mg sodium

Note: These breakfast burritos can be made ahead of time, wrapped in foil, and stored in the fridge. Enjoy cold, or reheat in a toaster oven (leave foil wrap on) or microwave (remove foil, wrap in a paper towel) until warm. The recipe makes 4 wraps, so you can enjoy another one for breakfast on Day 5 of this week (and freeze 2 for next week).

MINERAL BOOST JUICE (11:30 A.M.)

Berry-Mango Smoothie (page 40)

Per serving: 321 calories, 191 mg sodium

MEAL 2: SNACK (3:30 P.M.)

Spicy Peanut Dipping Sauce
(page 289)

Served with 20 snow peas, 1 cup red bell pepper slices, and 1/2 avocado, sliced

Per serving: 301 calories, 244 mg sodium

Note: This sauce can be made ahead whenever you have a free 10 minutes. Refrigerate in a covered container up to 5 days.

MEAL 3: DINNER (6:30 P.M.)

Cinnamon Sweet Potato* (page 47)

Per serving: 307 calories, 289 mg sodium

Note: Bake a few sweet potatoes when you have time and store in the fridge. You can reheat a potato quickly in the oven or microwave for this quick meal.

MEAL 4: DESSERT (8:30 P.M.)

Peanut Butter Pudding (page 333)

Per serving: 258 calories, 195 mg sodium

Note: This pudding can be thrown together in only minutes and then just needs time in the fridge to chill. Make it the night before you want to enjoy it—and since the recipe makes 6 servings, you can share with family or friends, and save 1 pudding to enjoy on Day 4 of this week.

DAY
3

MEAL 1: BREAKFAST (8:30 A.M.)

Ready-made bar

(like Clif Crunchy Peanut Butter bar;
or see page 66 for other bar options)

Served with 1 medium apple

Per serving: 322 calories, 231 mg sodium

MEAL 2: LUNCH (12:30 A.M.)

Lentil Soup with Spinach and
Butternut Squash (page 104)

Per serving: 293 calories, 284 mg sodium

Note: Soup is a wonderful make-ahead meal.
Refrigerate or freeze individual portions, and you'll
always have a delicious and healthy meal on hand.

MINERAL BOOST JUICE (3:00 P.M.)

Berry-Mango Smoothie (page 40)

Per serving: 321 calories, 191 mg sodium

MEAL 3: SNACK (5:00 P.M.)

White Bean Hummus* (page 44)

Per serving: 298 calories, 317 mg sodium

MEAL 4: DINNER (8:00 P.M.)

Moroccan Chicken and Couscous
Salad (page 118)

Per serving: 292 calories, 215 mg sodium

Note: This salad cooks in 5 minutes and only takes
15 minutes of prep work. Even better, it keeps
fantastically. Make ahead, and refrigerate individual
portions. When you're ready to eat, you can heat a
portion in the microwave, let it warm to room
temperature, or enjoy right out of the fridge.

DAY
4

MINERAL BOOST JUICE (6:30 A.M.)

Mango-Avocado Smoothie (page 40)

Per serving: 304 calories, 145 mg sodium

MEAL 1: BREAKFAST (9:30 A.M.)

Three-Grain Ricotta Pancakes
(page 83)

Per serving: 292 calories, 277 mg sodium

Note: These pancakes freeze well, so make a batch whenever you have a bit of free time. Wrap individual servings in plastic wrap; then, during busy weeks, you can just thaw a serving and reheat in a toaster oven.

MEAL 2: LUNCH (12:30 P.M.)

Pita Pizzas (page 292)

Served with a salad made from 2 cups arugula, $\frac{1}{4}$ cup cubed avocado, 1 tablespoon pine nuts, 1 teaspoon olive oil, and 1 teaspoon fresh lemon juice

Per serving: 280 calories, 283 mg sodium

Note: You can make these pizzas ahead of time, wrap in foil, and reheat when you're ready for lunch. At work without an oven? Reheat in a toaster oven or the microwave. Assemble the salad at home and carry the dressing in a small container or plastic bag to pour on just before serving.

MEAL 3: DINNER (6:00 P.M.)

Ready-made frozen entrée
(like Amy's Light in Sodium Black Bean Enchilada; or see page 67 for other options)

Per serving: 320 calories, 380 mg sodium

MEAL 4: DESSERT (8:00 P.M.)

Peanut Butter Pudding (page 333)

Per serving: 258 calories, 195 mg sodium

DAY 5

MEAL 1: BREAKFAST (8:00 A.M.)

Breakfast Burrito (page 81)

Per serving: 255 calories, 322 mg sodium

MINERAL BOOST JUICE (6:30 A.M.)

Peanut Butter Smoothie (page 41)

Per serving: 325 calories, 210 mg sodium

MEAL 2: LUNCH (2:00 P.M.)

Savory Pot Roast (leftover from Day 1 of menu; see page 146 for recipe)

Per serving: 323 calories, 300 mg sodium

MEAL 3: DINNER (6:00 P.M.)

Mini Pizza* (page 43)

Per serving: 286 calories, 228 mg sodium

MEAL 4: DESSERT (8:30 P.M.)

Orange-Yogurt Pops* (page 48)

Served with 25 almonds

Per serving: 293 calories, 97 mg sodium

Note: Make the pops ahead of time, and they'll be ready in the freezer whenever you need a creamy treat.

DAY 6

MEAL 1: BREAKFAST (10:00 A.M.)

Fruit and Nut Breakfast Bars (page 93)

Served with 1 banana and ½ cup fat-free milk

Per serving: 283 calories, 80 mg sodium

Note: These bars can be made ahead, when you have a bit of time, and frozen. During busy weeks, you'll be thrilled that you can just grab one from the freezer for a delicious, quick breakfast.

MINERAL BOOST JUICE (10:30 A.M.)

Orange-Banana Cream Smoothie (page 41)

Per serving: 293 calories, 65 mg sodium

MEAL 2: SNACK (1:00 P.M.)

PB&J Graham* (page 42)

Per serving: 283 calories, 195 mg sodium

MEAL 3: DINNER (5:00 P.M.)

Salmon and White Bean Stuffed Pitas (page 137)

Per serving: 270 calories, 284 mg sodium

Note: To save time before dinner, make the filling ahead of time and stuff the pitas when you're ready to eat.

MEAL 4: DESSERT (8:00 P.M.)

Oreo Delight (page 337)

Per serving: 295 calories, 69 mg sodium

DAY 7

MEAL 1: BREAKFAST (7:00 A.M.)

Waffle Sandwich with Banana
and Strawberries (page 86)

Per serving: 270 calories, 260 mg sodium

MINERAL BOOST JUICE (10:30 A.M.)

Mango-Avocado Smoothie (page 40)

Per serving: 304 calories, 145 mg sodium

MEAL 2: LUNCH (1:30 P.M.)

Ready-made frozen entrée

(like Celentano Vegetarian Penne with Roasted
Vegetables; or see page 67 for other options)

Per serving: 300 calories, 290 mg sodium

MEAL 3: SNACK (4:00 P.M.)

Ready-made bar

(like Kind Walnut & Date bar; or see page 66 for
other options)

Served with 1 banana

Per serving: 240 calories, 41 mg sodium

MEAL 4: DINNER (7:30 P.M.)

Spinach, Chicken, and Mandarin
Orange Salad (page 129)

Per serving: 284 calories, 269 mg sodium

*Note: This Asian-inspired salad can be assembled in
a flash—make the dressing and cook the chicken
ahead of time. Then you just have to slice some
veggies, open a few cans, and you're ready to go!*

EASY ENTERTAINING 1-WEEK MENU

The Salt Solution recipes are perfect for easy entertaining—because they make multiple servings, each one can provide your friends and family with a delicious, healthy meal.

DAY

1

MINERAL BOOST JUICE (8:00 A.M.)

Peanut Butter Smoothie (page 41)

Per serving: 325 calories, 210 mg sodium

MEAL 1: BRUNCH (11:00 A.M.)

Eggs Benedict (page 74)

Per serving: 253 calories, 300 mg sodium

Note: Eggs Benedict is perfect for a brunch party. And you don't have to spend all of the party in the kitchen—you can make the sauce a day ahead of time and reheat it in the microwave when you're ready to serve.

MEAL 2: LUNCH (2:00 P.M.)

Mushroom and Zucchini Pizzas (page 141)

Per serving: 294 calories, 321 mg sodium

Note: Pizza is always a crowd pleaser. You can offer guests an array of toppings so they can pick their favorites.

MEAL 3: DINNER (6:00 P.M.)

Quinoa and Chicken Salad (page 119)

Per serving: 318 calories, 270 mg sodium

MEAL 4: DESSERT (9:00 P.M.)

Light Orange Cupcakes with Orange Yogurt Glaze (page 306)

Served with 1 cup fat-free milk

Per serving: 291 calories, 300 mg sodium

DAY 2

MEAL 1: BREAKFAST (7:00 A.M.)

Bacon-Mushroom Breakfast
Sandwich (page 101)

Per serving: 258 calories, 263 mg sodium

MINERAL BOOST JUICE (10:30 A.M.)

Almond, Blueberry, and Banana
Smoothie (page 40)

Per serving: 323 calories, 300 mg sodium

MEAL 2: LUNCH (2:00 P.M.)

White Bean and Escarole Soup
(page 106)

Per serving: 270 calories, 271 mg sodium

MEAL 3: DINNER (6:00 P.M.)

Greek-Seasoned Filet of Beef
with Cucumber Tzatziki, Broccoli,
and Pita (page 149)

Per serving: 278 calories, 321 mg sodium

*Note: This simple dish takes less than 30 minutes to
prepare, but it'll wow your company.*

MEAL 4: DESSERT (8:30 P.M.)

Bananas Canadienne (page 323)

Per serving: 298 calories, 5 mg sodium

*Note: An elegant dessert that takes just 20 minutes
total to prepare so you can spend more time with
your guests.*

DAY 3

MINERAL BOOST JUICE (7:00 A.M.)

Mango-Avocado Smoothie (page 40)

Per serving: 304 calories, 145 mg sodium

MEAL 1: BREAKFAST (9:30 A.M.)

Banana-Bran Muffins (page 99)

Served with 1 cup fat-free milk

Per serving: 258 calories, 309 mg sodium

MEAL 2: LUNCH (1:00 P.M.)

Chicken Summer Rolls (page 140)

Per serving: 267 calories, 245 mg sodium

*Note: These summer rolls are a great casual
lunchtime party dish. Diners can assemble their
own rolls with their favorite ingredients. Serve with
citrus fruit salad.*

MEAL 3: DINNER (5:30 P.M.)

Eggplant Parmesan* (page 42)

Per serving: 290 calories, 104 mg sodium

MEAL 4: DESSERT (8:30 P.M.)

Chocolate Fondue* (page 45)

Per serving: 295 calories, 36 mg sodium

DAY 4

MEAL 1: BREAKFAST (8:00 A.M.)

Baked Apples with Cranberries
and Yogurt (page 98)

Per serving: 282 calories, 24 mg sodium

MEAL 2: LUNCH (11:30 A.M.)

Cajun Rice and Beans (page 253)

Served with ¾ cup grapes

Per serving: 318 calories, 192 mg sodium

MINERAL BOOST JUICE (2:00 P.M.)

Berry-Mango Smoothie (page 40)

Per serving: 321 calories, 191 mg sodium

MEAL 3: SNACK (5:00 P.M.)

Herbed Cheese Spread (page 285)

Served with ½ cup cucumber slices, 1 cup
sliced red bell pepper, and 2 tablespoons
unsalted almonds

Per serving: 282 calories, 281 mg sodium

*Note: This cheese spread is a fantastic recipe for a
cocktail party.*

MEAL 4: DINNER (8:00 P.M.)

Salmon with Pesto (page 210)

Per serving: 306 calories, 217 mg sodium

DAY 5

MEAL 1: BREAKFAST (8:30 A.M.)

Oatmeal with Apricots, Almonds,
and Brown Sugar (page 90)

Per serving: 311 calories, 184 mg sodium

MEAL 2: LUNCH (12:00 P.M.)

Chicken Burgers with Spinach
and Quinoa (page 200)

Per serving: 295 calories, 364 mg sodium

MINERAL BOOST JUICE (3:30 P.M.)

Orange-Banana Cream Smoothie
(page 41)

Per serving: 293 calories, 65 mg sodium

MEAL 3: DINNER (6:30 P.M.)

Halibut Curry with Brown
Basmati Rice (page 217)

Per serving: 302 calories, 221 mg sodium

*Note: This exotic curry dish is ideal for a dinner
party. Serve with Indian naan bread and tropical fruit.*

MEAL 4: DESSERT (8:00 P.M.)

Arborio Rice Pudding with Soymilk
and Toasted Coconut (page 332)

Per serving: 303 calories, 180 mg sodium

*Note: Rice pudding pairs perfectly with the halibut.
Prepare it the day before, and all you have to do is
sprinkle it with toasted coconut and serve.*

DAY 6

MEAL 1: BREAKFAST (7:00 A.M.)

Hot Couscous Bowl* (page 47)

Per serving: 304 calories, 276 mg sodium

MEAL 2: SNACK (10:00 A.M.)

Dried Fruit Bites (page 322)

Served with 3 ounces 0% plain Greek yogurt

Per serving: 301 calories, 118 mg sodium

MEAL 3: LUNCH (1:30 P.M.)

Salad Niçoise with Basil Vinaigrette (page 123)

Per serving: 314 calories, 288 mg sodium

Note: This French-inspired salad is an elegant, simple dish to serve at a lunchtime party. Pair with some crusty bread and fresh fruit.

MINERAL BOOST JUICE (4:00 P.M.)

Mango-Avocado Smoothie (page 40)

Per serving: 304 calories, 145 mg sodium

MEAL 4: DINNER (8:00 P.M.)

Meatloaf with Mushroom Gravy (page 152)

Served with a salad made from 2 cups spinach, 1 teaspoon olive oil, and 1 teaspoon fresh lemon juice

Per serving: 294 calories, 333 mg sodium

DAY 7

MINERAL BOOST JUICE (7:00 A.M.)

Orange-Banana Cream Smoothie (page 41)

Per serving: 293 calories, 65 mg sodium

MEAL 1: BREAKFAST (10:00 A.M.)

French Toast with Raspberries and Almonds (page 85)

Per serving: 282 calories, 307 mg sodium

MEAL 2: LUNCH (2:00 P.M.)

Indian Lentil Stew (page 238)

Per serving: 305 calories, 260 mg sodium

MEAL 3: DINNER (6:00 P.M.)

Broiled Lamb Chops with Spinach and White Bean Sauté (page 157)

Per serving: 273 calories, 313 mg sodium

Note: Lamb chops are a delicious, healthy, and elegant dinner party dish. Serve with a big green salad and crusty bread.

MEAL 4: DESSERT (8:30 P.M.)

Raspberry-Swirl Cheesecake (page 304)

Topped with 1 tablespoon chopped unsalted almonds

Per serving: 301 calories, 303 mg sodium

Note: Everyone loves cheesecake—this dessert is the perfect end to any dinner party.

Endnotes

Introduction

1   Kuller, L. H., Margolis, K. L., Gaussoin, S. A., Bryan, N. R., Kerwin, D., Limacher, M., Wassertheil-Smoller, S., Williamson, J., and J. G. Robinson. 2010. Relationship of hypertension, blood pressure, and blood pressure control with white matter abnormalities in the Women's Health Initiative Memory Study (WHIMS)—MRI Trial. *J Clin Hypertens* 12: 203–12.

2   He, F. J. and G. A. MacGregor. 2010. Reducing population salt intake worldwide: From evidence to implementation. *Progress in Cardiovascular Diseases* 52 (5): 363–82.

3   http://americanheart.org/presenter.jhtml?identifier=3071860

4   Karppanen, H., et al. Why and how to implement sodium, potassium, calcium, and magnesium changes in food items and diets? *J Hum Hypertens.* 2005;19: S10–S19.

Chapter 1

1   www.americanheart.org/presenter.jhtml?identifier=4708

2   Centers for Disease Control and Prevention. Obesity and overweight. www.cdc.gov/nchs/fastats/overwt.htm.

3   Morris, M. J., Na, E. S., and A. K. Johnson. 2008. Salt craving: the psychobiology of pathogenic sodium intake. *Physiol Behav* 94 (5): 709–21.

4   Centers for Disease Control and Prevention. Application of lower sodium intake recommendations to adults—United States, 1999–2006. *MMWR Weekly.* 2009;58:281–3.

5   www.ncbi.nlm.nih.gov/pubmed/18070765?dopt=Abstract

6   He, F. J., Markandu, N. D., Sagnella, G. A., and G. A. MacGregor. 2001. *Hypertension* 38: 317–20.

7   *BMJ* 2009; 339:b4567

8   Diez Roux, A. V., Chambless, L., Merkin, S. S., Arnett, D., Eigenbrodt, M., Nieto, F. J., Szklo, M., and P. Sorlie. 2002. *Circulation* 106: 703–10.

9   www.nhlbi.nih.gov/hbp/hbp/effect/arteries.htm

10 He, F. J. and G. A. MacGregor. 2009. A comprehensive review on salt and health and current experience of worldwide salt reduction programmes. *J Hum Hypertens.* 23 (6): 363–84.

11 Ibid.

12 www.telegraph.co.uk/news/uknews/2262760/High-blood-pressure-increases-dementia-risk-six-fold.html

13 http://hyper.ahajournals.org/cgi/content/full/44/1/20

14 Hu, G., et al. Urinary sodium and potassium excretion and the risk of type 2 diabetes: a prospective study in Finland. *Diabetologia.* 2005;48(8):1477–83.

15 www.ncbi.nlm.nih.gov/pubmed/17273153

16 He, F. J. and G. A. MacGregor. 2010. Reducing population salt intake worldwide: From evidence to implementation. *Progress in Cardiovascular Diseases* 52 (5): 363–82.

17 Yu, H. C., Burrell, L. M., Black, M. J., et al. Salt induces myocardial and renal fibrosis in normotensive and hypertensive rats. *Circulation* 1998; 98:2621–28.

18 Klanke, B., et al. http://ndt.oxfordjournals.org/cgi/content/abstract/23/11/3456

19 http://kidney.niddk.nih.gov/kudiseases/pubs/kustats/index.htm

20 Heaney, R. P. Role of dietary sodium in osteoporosis. *J Am Coll Nutr.* 2006;25:271S-276S.

21 Weinberger, M. H., Fineberg, N. S., Fineberg, S. E., and M. Weinberger. Salt sensitivity, pulse pressure, and death in normal and hypertensive humans. *Hypertension* 2001, vol. 37, pp. 429-32.

Chapter 2

1 Asaria, 2007

2 Bibbins-Domingo, 2010

3 www.nal.usda.gov/afsic/pubs/ofp/ofp.shtml

4 www.heart.org/HEARTORG/Conditions/Cholesterol/PreventionTreatmentofHighCholesterol/Know-Your-Fats_UCM_305628_Article.jsp

5 Ibid.

6 Karppanen, H., et al. Why and how to implement sodium, potassium, calcium, and magnesium changes in food items and diets? *J Hum Hypertens.* 2005;19:S10-S19.

7 Dole 5 A Day Reference Center. "Phytochemicals." Available at: http://216.255.136.121/ReferenceCenter/NutritionCenter/Phytochemicals/pdf/index.jsp?topmenu=1.

8 www.foodnews.org/walletguide.php

9 Zemel, M. B., Richards, J., Russel, J., Milstead, A., Gehardt, L., and E. Silva. Dairy augmentation of total and central fat loss in obese subjects. *International Journal of Obesity* 2005; 29(4):341-47.

10 Zemel, M. B., Thompson, W., Milstead, A., et al. Calcium and dairy acceleration of weight and fat loss during energy restriction in obese adults. *Obesity Res.* 2004;12(4):582-90.

11 MayoClinic.com. "Whole grains: Hearty options for a healthy diet." Available at: www.mayoclinic.com/health/whole-grains/NU00204.

12 Harvard School of Public Health. "Health gains from whole grains." Available at: www.hsph.harvard.edu/nutritionsource/what-should-you-eat/health-gains-from-whole-grains/index.html.

13 Liu, S., Willett, W. C., Manson, J. E., Hu, F. B., Rosner, B., and G. Colditz. Relation between changes in intakes of dietary fiber and grain products and changes in weight and development of obesity among middle-aged women. *Am J Clin Nutr.* 2003;78:920-27.

Chapter 4

1 www.nyc.gov/html/doh/html/pr2010/pr002-10.shtml

2 www.huffingtonpost.com/2010/04/26/salt-reduction-coming-for_n_552929.html

3 www.iom.edu/Reports/2010/Strategies-to-Reduce-Sodium-Intake-in-the-United-States/Report-Brief-Strategies-to-Reduce-Sodium-Intake-in-the-United-States.aspx

Index

Underscored page references indicate boxed text. **Boldfaced** page references indicate photographs

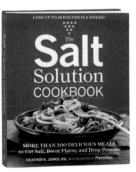